BAUDELAIRE: A SELF-PORTF

BAUDELAIRE:
A SELF-PORTRAIT

SELECTED LETTERS
TRANSLATED AND EDITED WITH
A RUNNING COMMENTARY

by

LOIS BOE HYSLOP

and

FRANCIS E. HYSLOP, JR.

GREENWOOD PRESS, PUBLISHERS
WESTPORT, CONNECTICUT

Library of Congress Cataloging in Publication Data

Baudelaire, Charles Pierre, 1821-1867.
  Baudelaire, a self-portrait.

  Reprint of the ed. published by the Oxford
University Press, London, New York.
  Bibliography: p.
  Includes index.
  1. Baudelaire, Charles Pierre, 1821-1867--
Correspondence. 2. Poets, French--19th century--
Correspondence.
PQ2191.Z5A28 1978   841'.8 [B]   78-16875
ISBN 0-313-20568-X

Reprinted in 1979 by Greenwood Press, Inc.
51 Riverside Avenue, Westport, CT 06880

Printed in the United States of America

10 9 8 7 6 5 4 3 2 1

TO THE MEMORY OF

THE REVEREND NILS BOE

AND

FRANCIS E. HYSLOP, SR.

FOREWORD

'I AM one whom men love not,—and yet regret,' Baudelaire wrote to Sainte-Beuve in 1865. Actually he was quoting from a poem by Shelley that he had found especially moving and beautiful. In effect he was writing his own epitaph. Since that day much has been written about the author of *Les Fleurs du Mal*, and each year new critical observations and new findings are being added to the vast store of information that has already been accumulated. Yet, despite recent attempts to interpret his work and personality, Baudelaire remains a baffling and enigmatic figure.

In an effort to better understand the man, critics have turned to his letters as an important source of first-hand information. Porché and others have seen Freudian overtones in the correspondence. Feuillerat has emphasized Baudelaire's exploitation of his mother. Sartre has interpreted the poet in terms of Existentialist psychoanalysis, not without a distortion of the facts, as Georges Blin has so well pointed out in *Le Sadisme de Baudelaire*. Although Sartre's thesis—that Baudelaire chose the miserable life that he led—is partly true, the reader is left with the impression that the author of *La Nausée* is unwilling to forgive Baudelaire for not having been an Existentialist saint. Still other critics, like Enid Starkie, have simply seen the poet grappling with his destiny and struggling to conquer the weaknesses in his complex and contradictory nature.

Enlightening and provocative as many of these explanations are, it would seem only reasonable and fair to give Baudelaire the opportunity to speak for himself. It is true that he was often baffled by his own singularity: 'I have so strange a heart that I myself am perplexed.' But it is also true that the reader who is acquainted with his letters will have a more just understanding of him than those who know only the excerpts quoted by critics in order to demonstrate a particular theory. Moreover, those quotations, when seen in their full context, often vitiate the very theory that they were intended to prove.

For the careful reader who seeks either to discriminate among the conflicting claims made by critics or to find his own key to the personality of the poet, the correspondence is an indispensable aid. It presents the most authentic portrait of a man who was astonishingly frank and yet a consummate actor. It gives an additional dimension to his work by adding to its richness and meaning. It dispels the legend which for so many years has falsified our conception of Baudelaire.

To read the poignant letters which show him at grips with his fate is to understand him better and as a result to pity and even admire him. The 'hypocritical reader' may find the letters exasperating and insincere. Others, like Asselineau, will only feel sorry for those who have been deceived by the ironic reserve with which he hid his pride and sensitivity.

From more than a thousand letters we have chosen about a hundred. We are deeply indebted to the late Jacques Crépet who, assisted in his last years by Claude Pichois, published a magnificent six-volume edition of the correspondence between 1947 and 1953. In general we have used complete or nearly complete letters. Significant passages from other letters have been included in the commentary. Inevitably there will be some differences of opinion about the choices, but we feel that the majority of the letters would have been included in any one-volume selection.

The commentary has been designed to bind the letters together in a continuous narrative and to help orient the uninitiated reader. Those who feel sufficiently acquainted with Baudelaire may wish to read only the letters.

We wish to thank Professor W. T. Bandy for the friendly interest which he has taken in our project and to make the following acknowledgments for translations of poems which have been included:

The Harvill Press, Ltd., and Pantheon Books, Inc., for the following translations by Roy Campbell included in *Poems of Baudelaire*, copyright 1952: lines from the poem about the 'frightful Jewess'; *To a Colonial Lady*; *The Living Torch*; untitled poem beginning 'What can you say, poor lonely soul of mine'; *Hymn*; and *Verses for Honoré Daumier's Portrait*.

The University of California Press for the translation by C. F. MacIntyre of several lines from *The Voyage* included in *One Hundred Poems from Les Fleurs du Mal*, copyright 1947.

Academy Library Guild for the prose translation by William Aggeler of *To One Who is Too Gay* included in *The Flowers of Evil*, copyright 1954.

Sir John Squire for the translation of *The Spiritual Dawn*, included in *The Flowers of Evil* (New Directions) edited by Marthiel and Jackson Mathews, copyright 1955.

1956.

CONTENTS

ERRATA

Page 3, line 4. In recent years a number of new letters have been discovered, among them the *Lettres inédites aux siens,* published by Philippe Auserve in 1966. As a result, this letter has become the sixteenth in the 1973 Pléiade edition of Baudelaire's correspondence.

Page 12, line 19. It has been irrefutably proved by Charles Hérisson that Baudelaire did not travel further than the islands of Reunion and Mauritius.

Page 18, line 3. In his preface to *Les Fleurs du mal,* Gautier maintains that Baudelaire "came only rarely and as a simple observer" to the meetings of the club.

Page 45, lines 29-35. It is now known that Deroy died in 1846, that Baudelaire evidently met Marie in 1845 or 1846, that she was perhaps his mistress in 1854-1855, that she left to tour Italy in 1855 and did not return to Paris until 1859. Marie appeared in *La Belle aux cheveux d'or* in 1847.

Page 46, line 26. In the 1973 Pléiade edition of Baudelaire's correspondence (Volume 7, page 804) Claude Pichois maintains that *Le Chat* was written for Jeanne. He argues that the letter was written for someone other than Marie Daubrun and that it perhaps dates from 1852.

Page 51, line 3. The 1973 Pléiade edition of Baudelaire's correspondence contains four letters and six notes written in 1864.

Page 52, line 12. It has recently been discovered that *La Tribune Nationale* was much less conservative than was formerly believed.

Page 74, lines 2-3. Musset and Dumas père were not among those who attended Madame Sabatier's dinners. Other frequent guests were the artists Meissonier and Gustave Richard and the composer Ernest Reyer.

Page 212, line 10. Actually, Baudelaire published several prose poems in 1864 and re-published a number of others, in addition to the six condemned poems in verse which appeared in the *Parnasse satyrique du dix-neuvième siècle.* In 1866, the six condemned poems, together with a number of others, were published by Poulet-Malassis under the title of *Les Epaves.*

Page 225, line 31. Until Léon Cellier (*Baudelaire et Hugo,* Corti, 1970) proved that Hugo was not in Brussels at this time, it was thought that the famous man was Victor Hugo. The identity of the person has not been established. In the French text Baudelaire simply uses the adjective "célèbre," followed by a blank.

PART ONE
Early Years

My youth was but a sombre storm
Pierced here and there by brilliant suns . . .

Early Years

WRITING from the Collège Royal at Lyons, where he was then a boarder, and signing his name 'Carlos' with a burst of romantic enthusiasm inspired perhaps by reading Hugo's *Hernani*, Charles Baudelaire makes his first appearance in his correspondence as a schoolboy twelve years of age. There is little here to suggest the Baudelaire of *Les Fleurs du Mal*. There is, to be sure, a concern for stylistic effect, a touch of irony, but there is also a sparkling vivacity, a vigorous, apparently carefree joy in living that is rarely found in his many letters. Were his high spirits the reflection of a momentary mood, or was Baudelaire attempting to mask his innermost feelings with a bit of bravado? The excessive pride which distinguished him all his life may well have encouraged him to conceal his loneliness from a half-brother to whom he was never entirely sympathetic and with whom he was later to break completely.

Years later in his autobiographical notes Baudelaire himself admits that his life at the Collège Royal was far from happy: 'After 1830, school at Lyons, blows, quarrels with my teachers and schoolmates, periods of deep melancholy.' And in that part of his intimate journals known as *Mon Cœur mis à nu*, Baudelaire refers to the loneliness and solitude which were to be the 'constant companions' of his life: 'A sense of *solitude* from the time of my childhood. In spite of my family—and especially in the midst of my companions—a sense of an eternally lonely destiny. Nevertheless, a very keen taste for life and pleasure.' Elsewhere in *Mon Cœur mis à nu* Baudelaire analyses with introspective awareness the contradictory qualities that marked him both as a child and as a man: 'Even as a child I felt in my heart two opposite emotions: the horror of life and the ecstasy of life.'

The precocious, sensitive child whose life was to be made tragic partly through this very contradiction, was born on April 9, 1821, to Joseph-François Baudelaire, aged sixty-two, and to his charming young wife of twenty-eight, Caroline Archimbaut-Dufays. Caroline had been born an exile in England and, after the death of her parents, had been brought up in Paris in the family of an old friend of her father. Penniless, but attractive, she married at the age of twenty-six a courtly, white-haired widower who had inherited a comfortable fortune after the death of his first wife. François Baudelaire, an intelligent, cultured man, had served as a tutor to the family of the Duc de Choiseul-Praslin.

3

During the Revolution he had courageously befriended his former master and in return was rewarded with a post in the Senate when the Choiseul-Praslins regained their position and influence.

With his elegant, eighteenth-century manners and his exquisite courtesy François left an indelible impression on his small son. Though he was only six when his father died, Charles never forgot the affectionate attentions he had known, nor the long walks in the Luxembourg Gardens where the distinguished old gentleman, a mediocre amateur artist, had pointed out to his son the beauties of art and architecture.

After his father's death Charles was drawn to his beloved mother in even closer intimacy. Her decision a year later to marry Captain Aupick, a brilliant career soldier, who was to become a general, an ambassador, and finally a senator, must have been a severe blow to the small child of seven who adored his mother and demanded all her love and affection for himself.[1] Captain Aupick was a man of scrupulous integrity who did everything in his power to develop in Charles the strength of character which he himself possessed. The bitter antipathy which Baudelaire was later to show his stepfather does not appear in his early letters where Charles carefully refers to him as 'my friend'. There is no doubt, however, that under his anxiety to please his father and beneath an exterior too proud to show his true feeling there must have lurked a festering resentment toward this man who had suddenly put an end to the idyllic happiness that marked the first seven years of his life.

In November 1831 Lieutenant-Colonel Aupick was ordered to Lyons where he became chief-of-staff of the General Headquarters. Charles was then ten years old and his stepfather, in the hope of forming his character, enrolled him as a boarder in the Collège Royal. At school his life was almost that of the barracks—rising at five-thirty, washing in icy water, breakfasting at seven-thirty after studying two hours in the cold morning air, marching to and from class to the sound of the drum. It was under such circumstances that the once pampered child wrote to his half brother, Claude, son of François Baudelaire by a previous marriage, with a note of gaiety that gave no hint of the loneliness he felt.

To M. Baudelaire, Deputy Judge
Lyons, November 22, 1833

Have a great many things to tell you, but *first of all* my excuses. My negligence has been partly a matter of self-pride; since you didn't answer, I thought it a question of honour not to write twice in succession. But I finally realized that was ridiculous; besides, as my elder I respect you, as my brother I love you. I promised at the beginning of my letter to tell you many things; very well, I am going to carry out my promise. I have just sprained my ankle, hence sticking plaster on top of sticking plaster (or plastre), and I detest sticking plaster as well as doctors.

They are building a suspension bridge made entirely of iron wire over the Saône at Lyons. All the shops are going to be lit with gass [*sic*]; all the streets are being dug up. The Rhone, that swift river with its unexpected floods, has just overflown its banks. For it is raining a great deal these days in Lyons. You know the glass factory which is located on a peninsula quite near the city (we students used to take walks over there); well, the Rhone kept encroaching on the istmus [*sic*], it gnawed, it ate. Last night it finally swept away the isthmus. This sort of thing often happens in the Rhone. An irregularity leads to a break; the tongue of land becomes an island; for the river is very swift.

My letter is vilely scribbled, since my pen is very poor, but after all I don't worry much about that. I am anxious to apologize for my negligence by a long letter. Just imagine what a cruel blow, I am kept from dancing by this little sprain, I who never miss a single quadrille.

And then! during my vacation, guess what, I acted in a comedy, and now I am going to act in a short play.

Perhaps there is a lot of nonsense in my letter; the ideas may seem as erratic as my handwriting. Our correspondence had been interrupted for so long that, thank heavens, it wasn't difficult to find material for this epistolary conversation. Besides, it's better to chatter in a friendly way than to talk a lot of rubbish and jargen [*sic*].

What! Théodore has won prizes! and . . . Charles hasn't earned any. By Jove! I shall win a few too. Tell Théodore that he will be the reason for my receiving a prize. One honourable mention in my class (the 4th) and one in translation from French into Latin (the 5th)! It is really pathetic: but I want to win some and I shall. Nevertheless, my congratulations to Théodore, and as for me, shame, shame! Tell him he is making a fool of me.

And how is my sister? Has she recovered? Mother asks to be remembered. I embrace you too. Tell me, or rather write me, all about your family and yourself.

Carlos

In 1836, when Charles was fifteen years old, M. Aupick was given a further promotion and was called back to Paris where Charles was sent to the famous Lycée Louis-le-Grand. Colonel Aupick, confident and proud of his stepson's intelligence, introduced him somewhat pompously to the principal: 'Sir, I am bringing you a gift; here is a student who will do honour to your school.' [2]

During the first year Charles justified the prediction of his stepfather by making a record that was sound, if not brilliant. In the meantime he was reading with avid interest the English and French Romantic poets, especially Sainte-Beuve, and writing a great deal of poetry. But a change seemed to have come over Charles. A schoolmate who had known him in Lyons found him 'altered, saddened, embittered'.[3] His polite insolence to his professors, his increasing insubordination became more noticeable, and suddenly, as a result of some trifling incident, Charles was dismissed from the school.

Since he had not yet obtained his *baccalauréat*, his parents sent him as a boarder to a M. Lasègue who was to prepare him for his examinations. It was while he was with M. Lasègue and his own mother, kindly middle-class people, that Charles wrote to his mother in a manner which suggests the Baudelaire we know—self-critical, yet incapable of self-discipline, sensitive, and most of all suffering from loneliness and need for his mother's understanding and undivided love.

To Madame Aupick
Tuesday, July 16, 1839

My dear mother, my kind mama, I don't know what to say to you, and I have all kinds of things to tell you. First I feel a great need to see you. How different it is to be with strangers—and it isn't exactly your affection and our laughter that I miss, it is a certain something which makes our mother always seem the best of all women and makes her good qualities suit us better than the good qualities of other women; there is such understanding between a mother and her son; they live so well side by side—that, my word, since I have been with M. Lassègue [*sic*], I have felt a little unhappy. I don't want you to feel that my pride has been hurt, because M. Lassègue has constantly disciplined me and because Mme. Lassègue has also had a hand in it. As for that, I thank him with all my heart; it is only proof of his kindness; it helps to form my character, I am glad of it; moreover, that's not what bothers me. The fact is I miss what I like most, a mind formed to my own taste, like that of my mother or that of my friend. Most assuredly, M. Lassègue and his mother are endowed with all kinds of fine qualities. But all of them—wisdom, love, common sense—have assumed a form I don't like. They have a certain triviality about them which repels me somewhat; I prefer such qualities to be displayed impulsively and more warmly, as with you and with my friend. In this house there is a perpetual gaiety that gets on my nerves.

They are certainly happier than we. At home I have seen tears, my father irritated and you on the verge of hysteria. But all the same, I *prefer us* that way.

And when I feel something within which stirs me,—how shall I express it?—a violent desire to embrace everything, a fear of being unable to secure an education, a dread of life, or quite simply the sight of a beautiful sunset seen from my window, to whom can I tell it? You are not here, and neither is my dear friend.

And so what has happened? I am worse than I was in school. At school I didn't do much work, but at least I did something—when I was expelled I was pretty well shaken up and I did a little more work at home—now *nothing, nothing,* and it is not a pleasant, poetic indolence, not at all; it is a depressing and stupid indolence. I didn't dare admit all this to my friend, nor reveal myself to him at my worst; for he would have found me too changed—he had seen me at my best. In school I worked occasionally, I read, I wept, I got angry at times; but at least I was living—now it's just the contrary—I'm as spiritless as one can be—with faults in abundance, and they are not admirable faults either. If only this painful life would induce me to change drastically—but no, of that energy which used to drive me sometimes towards good, sometimes towards evil, nothing remains, nothing but apathy, sullenness and boredom.

I have disappointed M. Lassègue—I have come down a notch in my own opinion—if I were alone, I should have worked badly perhaps, but I should have made an effort—with you or with a close friend I should have been all right—in strange surroundings I have been completely changed, disorganized, disconcerted. It seems, doesn't it, that I am using big words and clever subtleties to veil very ordinary faults. All these vexations are further complicated by the *baccalauréat.* I intend to have done with it at once and to pass my examination as soon as possible. I am going, and I have already begun, to do my utmost to review all the material within two weeks and to be ready for the beginning of August. To do this I have to study twenty-four questions a day—as for the competitive examination, I am going only as a substitute, that is to say I shall be called on to compose if someone is absent. Nevertheless, they have asked for my birth certificate in case of need.

After all, it is perhaps a good thing that I have seen some strangers, I shall love my mother all the more. It is perhaps a good thing to have been denuded and depoetized, I understand all the better what I lacked —it may be what is called a period of transition. During all this time your letters have hurt me and made me feel even more distressed.— Write me anyway; I love your letters. When I am lonely, I am glad to feel my mother's love envelop me; that's so much to the good. When you answer me, write me at length about my father. I beg you not to say a word of all this to M. Lassègue; he is so good that it would hurt him.

[No signature]

In August 1839 Charles passed his *baccalauréat* and wrote to M. Aupick to report the good news. At the same time he took the opportunity to congratulate his stepfather on his recent promotion to the rank of major-general. M. Aupick had gone with his wife to take the waters at Bourbonne-les-Bains in an effort to ease the pain caused by an old leg wound which had never properly healed.

If Charles at the age of eighteen felt any rancour at the necessity of asking his stepfather's permission to change lodging, if his pride was hurt by the fact that he had no news from his parents to report to those who questioned him, or that he had to ask for money to make a trifling purchase, his letter gives no indication of that fact. Its friendly, respectful tone seems an effort on his part to win back the good opinion which he feared he must have lost.

To Monsieur Aupick

August 13, 1839

I have just seen some good news and I have some to tell you as well. I have read in *Le Moniteur* this morning about your promotion, and I have been a *bachelier* since four o'clock yesterday. I did rather poorly in my examinations, except for Latin and Greek—in which I did very well—which is what saved me.

I am very happy about your promotion—from son to father these are not trite congratulations like all those you will receive. I am happy because I have seen you often enough to know how much you deserved it; it seems I am pretending to be a man and to be congratulating you as if I were your equal or your superior.—And so, to speak simply, be assured I am very happy.

I haven't written you for several days because of my examinations. I had first postponed them until August 20th, then I hurried to get them out of the way; and it was a good thing; that's why I was quite busy for a few days.

Now what should I do? I am in a rather embarrassing situation. I can't do anything, not even change my lodging, without your permission and you don't write me anything.   M. Charles Lasègue is going to leave the day after tomorrow—with him no longer here and with his parents constantly away, I think it would be rather indiscreet to remain, and M. Lasègue has given me to understand that he would not even dare to ask it of his parents. He wishes as prompt an answer as possible from you. Am I to return to the hotel, and in case I return there, am I to eat at my pension? I have already paid for two months there—from June 5th to August 5th.—If I leave it, I shall have to pay the difference. In short, I should like very much to have a letter from you. People ask me about you and I don't know what to say. Please answer me; you promised me a letter for a letter; so now you owe me one.

I am going to tell Madame Olivier about your promotion—much love to mama.[4] Fanchette would like to have permission to buy an apron. She doesn't have any more. Will you speak to my mother and, if possible, send me her permission to make the purchase?

Goodbye.

Charles

P.S.—Tell me about your leg and give me some news for everyone who will ask me about you.

Recently I saw in the office of the concierge a number of calling cards which are waiting your return, among others one from M. Lamartine [the poet] and another gentleman who was coming to say goodbye and who is leaving for Bourbonne. He is very pleasant.

Now that Charles had become a *bachelier*, his parents had high hopes that he would have a brilliant career in the diplomatic service. With his many influential connections M. Aupick could have been of invaluable assistance to his handsome son. But Charles was of another mind. To the horror of his parents he announced that he intended to becom~ a writer, and no amount of persuasion could make him think otherwise. From that moment Charles was in open revolt against his stepfather.

Sometime during the years 1839–41, as a result of a quarrel with M. Aupick, Charles was sent away to a pension in Creil, probably under the surveillance of the colonel who is mentioned in the letter. It seems very possible even that Charles may have been in Creil while his parents were convening the family council at which it was decided to send the recalcitrant young man on a long sea voyage.

From Creil Charles wrote to his mother in an effort, it would seem, to reinstate himself in her favour and to effect a reconciliation with M. Aupick. Consciously or unconsciously, he revealed his feeling of animosity toward his stepfather by referring to him as 'your husband', rather than 'my friend', the term he had used in his earlier letters.

It is only a coincidence that Charles refers to the poems he intends to send his mother as 'flowers'. There is here no connection with his publication of 1857, since the title 'Flowers of Evil' was not conceived until many years later and was actually the suggestion of Baudelaire's friend, Hippolyte Babou.

To Madame Aupick

[Creil, no date]

It's now nine or ten days that I have been here, my dear mama, and I'm beginning to get thoroughly bored. I am very sorry that you thought I had so great an aversion to my brother's home; Fontaine-bleau is less provincial than Creil. I am here among retired innkeepers, rich masons, and women who look like concierges. Nevertheless, I have found among the colonel's acquaintances a woman whose hands are white and who speaks French. I sneak in to see her as often as I can. The rest of the time I take refuge in the fields and I warm myself in the bright sunshine. Here everyone loves money; they quarrel over cards and gossip frightfully.

There is a person here whom I ought to love, for she is so good to me; sometimes she bores me with it! It is Madame Nemfray. She is the one who arranged my room before I arrived, who had curtains put in it, a wastepaper basket, a clock, and even covered a screen herself. One day I mentioned that tea was a good thing and the next day there was tea in the house all day long; another day I spoke of onion soup and we had onion soup at dinner, of chopped-bacon omelette and the next thing we were having chopped-bacon omelette for lunch. You see she is more fussy and more motherly than a mother; so if you write her, tell her how grateful I am to her. She told me that you hadn't been well. I hope and I believed that it was only from fatigue and from the excitement caused by the disturbance that I made at home.

You will get well, won't you, you will eat well, if only from a sense of pride, so that your husband will not reproach your son for having made you ill? Persuade him, if you can, that I am not a great scoundrel, but a decent fellow.

I embrace you and in my next letter I shall send you some flowers which will seem strange to you.

Charles

To keep peace at home Charles agreed, or pretended to agree, to prepare for the entrance examinations for the École des Chartes. He was placed in a well-known student lodging house, the Pension Bailly, whose boarders were chiefly the sons of wealthy provincial bourgeois. Here, lacking any real supervision, he plunged into the Bohemian life of the Latin Quarter.

At the Pension Bailly he became a member of the 'Norman School' founded by his good friend Le Vavasseur and made up of a number of amateur poets who were enormously influenced by the Romantic writers, and by Sainte-Beuve and Gautier in particular.

It was while he was living at the Pension Bailly that Baudelaire contracted the disease which was to undermine his health and to hasten his death. Like most of his friends of the Latin Quarter, Charles had chosen a mistress. But to the great surprise of his friends, the elegant, impeccably dressed dandy had singled out a small, ugly prostitute by the name of Sarah whom he called Louchette because of her squint-eyes. In verses written early in his youth and published eight years after his death Baudelaire describes the revolting ugliness of his mistress with a strange mixture of brutal realism and compassion. It was also to this same Sarah that Baudelaire refers in his sonnet of *Les Fleurs du Mal* which begins:

> One night when, near a fearful Jewess lying,
> As one corpse by another corpse, I sprawled—[5]

That Baudelaire was disturbed by what happened to him is apparent in the mocking, sardonic epitaph which he wrote for himself about this time—an epitaph which, as the critic Porché has pointed out, recalls the spirit of François Villon:

> Here lies one who, having too much loved a filthy broad,
> Still young was laid away beneath the sod.[6]

In the meantime Baudelaire's parents were becoming more and more disturbed by their son's conduct. His failure to present himself for his examinations, his mounting debts, his Bohemian friends, his shocking conversation, his insolent behaviour towards his father's friends, all led them to feel that drastic measures should be taken to bring him to his senses.

Whatever may have been the immediate cause of their determination, a family council was called and it was decided to take five thousand francs from Charles's inheritance with which to send him on a voyage to India. It was hoped that a break with his old associates might be beneficial and encourage him to change his ideas. At first Charles resisted strenuously, but later he ceased to raise objections and on June 9, 1841, he sailed from Bordeaux on a ship called *The Southern Skies*.

Nine months later, in February, Charles returned to France. According to some accounts, he entertained his friends with highly imaginative tales of his adventures; others maintain that he had very little to say about his journey. Likewise, there is some difference of opinion as to whether Baudelaire reached India or went only as far as Mauritius and the Ile de Bourbon.[7] From a scrupulous account kept by Captain Saliz we learn that Baudelaire was homesick to the point of being ill. We learn also of a strange blend of arrogance and studied courtesy in his manners, of his efforts to shock the bourgeois passengers, of the growing melancholy which finally alarmed the good Captain, and of his quiet courage during the five-day storm that battered the ship until it was badly damaged. Finally we learn how Captain Saliz left Charles at Bourbon with the understanding that he was to return to France on board the *Alcide*.[8]

But though Charles may never have reached India, the trip was to leave its unmistakable stamp on his poetry. It developed his sensibility and his imagination and gave him a store of images on which to draw.[9]

It was at the island of Mauritius where he stayed from September 1st to September 19th that Charles became acquainted with M. Autard and his wife in whose company he sought to escape the dull minds of his travelling companions.

At the Ile de Bourbon where the next stop was made Baudelaire refused to leave the ship (that, at least, was what he confided to Leconte de Lisle), and while the boat lay at anchor he wrote the charming, though somewhat conventional sonnet, *A une Créole*, which he enclosed in a letter to M. Autard. In his letter the reader sees at first hand that elegant, old-fashioned courtesy which Baudelaire had learned from his father and which was to characterize him throughout his whole life.

To M. Ad. Autard de Bragard

[Ile de Bourbon] October 20, 1841

My good M. Autard,

When I was at Mauritius you asked me for some verses for your wife, and I haven't forgotten you. As it is only right, proper, and fitting that verses addressed to a lady by a young man should pass through the hands of her husband before reaching her, I am sending them to you to show her, if you so choose.

Since I left you, I have often thought of you and of your excellent friends. I shall certainly not forget the happy mornings I spent with you, Madame Autard, and M.B. . . .

If I didn't love Paris and miss it so much, I would remain as long as possible with you and I would make you like me and find me less odd than I appear to be.

It is not very probable that I shall return to Mauritius, unless the boat (the *Alcide*) on which I am leaving for Bordeaux should go there to call for passengers.

Here is my sonnet:

> In scented countries by the sun caressed
> I've known, beneath a tent of purple boughs,
> And palmtrees shedding slumber as they drowse,
> A creole lady with a charm unguessed.
>
> She's pale, and warm, and duskily beguiling;
> Nobility is moulded in her neck;
> Slender and tall she holds herself in check,
> An huntress born, sure-eyed, and quiet-smiling.
>
> Should you go, Madame, to the land of glory
> Along the Seine or Loire, where you would merit
> To ornament some mansion famed in story
>
> Your eyes would burn in those deep-shaded parts,
> And breed a thousand rhymes in poets' hearts,
> Tamed like the negro slaves that you inherit.[10]

I shall await your arrival in France.

My respectful regards to Madame Autard.

C. Baudelaire

PART TWO

Apprenticeship

*It was partly through leisure that I grew. To my
great detriment, since leisure without fortune increases
debts. But to my great profit so far as sensibility,
meditation and the possibility of dandyism and
dilettantism were concerned.*

Apprenticeship

AFTER his return to Paris in 1842 Charles continued to live with his parents for a short time, although he remained adamant in his decision to devote his life to literature. M. Aupick had had to accept the decision, but he could not approve of the manner in which his stepson was spending his time with a group of profligate friends whose ideas and morals were so foreign to his own.

In April 1842 Charles reached his majority and came into possession of the fortune which had been left him in his father's will. Now that he was financially independent, he determined to leave his mother's house and to escape the presence of the man whose disapproval he had incurred. In that same month Charles left without warning, leaving only a note to explain his sudden departure to his distressed mother. His affection for her seems not to have lessened, as his many notes and letters testify, although at times it is submerged in thoughtless and often querulous demands for attention and financial assistance.

With the intention of subordinating his life to his work and confident of gaining literary success, Baudelaire moved to a modest one-room apartment on the Quai de Béthune. In this quiet and secluded corner of the Ile Saint-Louis he hoped to find the peace and solitude which he needed.

His taste for luxury and his natural inclination to pleasure made it more difficult than he had imagined to settle down to hard work. He was a brilliant conversationalist and would spend hours entertaining his listeners with his knowledge of art and literature, his paradoxical ideas, and his habitual mystifications. He gradually came to see less of his old friends from the Pension Bailly and to form a closer relationship with Louis Ménard and Théodore de Banville. Ménard was to become the distinguished Greek scholar of the Parnassian movement and Banville, though two years younger than Baudelaire, had already established a reputation for himself with his book of poems, *Les Cariatides*.

No later than the autumn of 1843 Baudelaire moved to 17 Quai d'Anjou into an apartment of the famous Hôtel Pimodan, a beautiful home built by a rich nobleman of the seventeenth century. In the Hôtel Pimodan lived the famous Roger de Beauvoir, known throughout Paris for his charm, his wealth, and his talent. His magnificent apartment, hung with velvet and filled with priceless antique furniture, could well have encouraged Baudelaire's own taste for the beautiful and the luxurious. In the Hôtel Pimodan there also lived a young painter, Boissard, in whose rooms Baudelaire smoked opium and hashish with other members of the Club des Haschischins.

It was in these surroundings that Baudelaire lived the life of a dandy and built up the legend that was to follow him throughout his career. In order to furnish his apartment with appropriate elegance he bought extravagantly from an unscrupulous antique dealer named Arondel who had a shop on the ground floor of the Hôtel Pimodan. Encouraged by Arondel, he not only bought furnishings and paintings (some of them forgeries) at exorbitant prices, but also borrowed large sums of money for which he signed promissory notes. It was in this way that Baudelaire piled up the debts which he was still struggling to pay at the time of his death in 1867.

In order further to play the rôle of dandy Baudelaire lavished care and money on his personal appearance as well. He would wear one striking costume after another—now a black velvet tunic held with a gold belt, now a bright blue suit with metal buttons, or black broadcloth trousers worn with a narrow-tailed coat and a fine linen shirt whose wide turned-back cuffs and open collar, fastened with a scarlet tie, gave him an air of aristocratic distinction. The picture painted at this time by his friend, Emile Deroy, reveals Baudelaire as a handsome, elegant dandy with none of the tragic bitterness that marks many of his later portraits and photographs.

In the meantime Baudelaire's prodigality had alarmed his parents to such an extent that they felt it necessary to intervene. Much to Charles's distress, there was already talk of establishing a legal guardianship. Before resorting to such extreme measures, however, it had been decided that Mme. Aupick should administer the estate and that Charles should receive a monthly income from M. Ancelle, who was soon to be made his guardian. In an undated letter written in 1843 we see the first reference made by Baudelaire to his new apartment and an expression of his willingness to hold to the terms set by his mother.

To Madame Aupick

[No date]

I shall send someone today to inform you about the living quarters that I have chosen.—I shall manage perfectly on the conditions that you have established for me. You yourself are to come and explain them to the owner of the house. Only there can be no question of *guardianship*. Should I find that you had made such an arrangement without my knowledge, I should leave at once and this time you wouldn't see me again, for I would go and live with Jeanne.—Since I don't want to go back to M. Leroy's, I am sending you the list of all the things I left there which will have to be brought by someone who can't give my address.

[No signature]

In his reference to the legal guardianship with which he was being threatened Baudelaire mentions for the first time the name of Jeanne, a name he will often repeat in later letters and in *Mon Cœur mis à nu*, first with gratitude and love, then with anger and disgust, and finally with remorseful pity and compassion. No other woman, not excluding his mother, can be said to have exerted greater influence upon him. *Les Fleurs du Mal* was to be filled with references to her dark beauty, to the perfume of her blue-black hair and to the sinuous grace of her rhythmic movements.

In spite of the prominent part she played in Baudelaire's life, Jeanne Lemer remains a somewhat mysterious figure. Known also as Jeanne Duval, Jeanne Prosper, and perhaps even Caroline Dardart, names she adopted in an effort to escape her creditors, she seems to have come into Baudelaire's life in the second half of 1842 and to have quietly disappeared again after his death in 1867.[11]

Nothing is known of her birthplace; friends all gave different accounts, varying from Santo Domingo to Capetown. Descriptions of her appearance are equally varied. Nadar, who knew her best, speaks of her on one occasion as a 'real Negress', on another as 'at least an undoubted mulatto', and on still another as a 'quadroon'. Banville calls her the 'beautiful black girl' and Prarond describes her as a mulatto with 'yellow, lustreless skin'. Discrepancies almost as marked are found in the descriptions of Jeanne's figure and of her hair. There are some who lead us to believe that she was extraordinarily tall and others who call her only fairly tall. Some describe her hair as extremely kinky and others as thick and wavy.

Baudelaire's own sketches of Jeanne show her to be tall with a tiny waist that emphasizes her young, rounded bosom and her broad full hips. Her face with its small nose and thick lips is made memorable by enormous, dark eyes—eyes 'like saucers', as Nadar once described them—and by luxuriant blue-black hair.

At the time he met her, Jeanne was probably a third-rate actress in a cheap theatre of the Latin Quarter. After he made her his mistress, Baudelaire installed her in a little apartment of her own on the Ile Saint-Louis where Eastern rugs and hangings provided a proper foil for the voluptuous beauty which he was to celebrate in poems such as *Les Bijoux* and *La Chevelure*.

By 1843 things were going less well for Baudelaire. His ever-increasing debts, his lack of success in publishing the little he had completed were, he realized, only an indication of failure in the eyes of his mother and his stepfather. More and more he came to dread his visits to his mother and to feel conscious of the critical eyes of her husband, her friends, and even of the servants. At the same time he was becoming aware of the measures to which his family might resort in an effort to prevent him from squandering his entire inheritance.

To Madame Aupick

March 3, 1844

I offer you my most sincere excuses for not having gone to see you. —The month had twenty-nine days, which upset my calculations, and the note didn't arrive until the 29th.

—Moreover, I am busy recasting my entire article.[12] The trip is so long that when I leave home, I don't feel equal to returning, and the day is wasted; when I stay home, I really have to work.

Besides,—and you are not going to like this reaction very well—I couldn't possibly describe to you the sad and violent effect produced on me by that vast, cold and empty house where I know no one but my mother.—I always steal furtively in and out; it has become unbearable to me. Do excuse me and leave me in my solitude until I succeed in producing a book.

I need my 425 francs.—Then I believe that, according to the conditions you set for me, you are to send me money for my expenses in March.

It seems to me it was poor taste on your part to send a friend or a servant in disguise to instruct a restaurant not to extend me any long term credit. Spare me that surveillance, since you have allowed me the small vanity of paying for things myself. And besides what's the use, since I don't care to go out often and I don't want to cause myself any new worries.

If I have any luck, I shall tell you immediately.

C. B.

Send me *all my papers*.

In spite of Baudelaire's promises to reform, Mme. Aupick decided to call a family council in an effort to determine what could be done to protect her son's financial interests. When it was discovered that in the course of two years he had already squandered half of his inheritance, it was agreed to appoint a legal guardian who would have complete control over the remaining capital and pay Charles the interest in monthly instalments.

Though Mme. Aupick tried to convince her son that the arrangement was intended only to safeguard his future, Charles was almost beside himself with rage and despair at the thought of the humiliation that faced him. In a final desperate attempt to avoid legal action he sent a pleading letter to his mother in which he presented all the arguments that seemed to him most persuasive. The M. Ancelle to whom he refers was a conscientious middle-class lawyer who was expected to serve as his guardian and who, in fact, had already co-operated with Mme. Aupick in the temporary arrangement she had made with Charles.

To Madame Aupick

[No date]

I beg you to read this most attentively, because it is very serious and because it is a final appeal to your good sense and to the deep love which you say you have for me.—First let me explain that I am sending you this letter in the strictest confidence, and I beg you not to show it to anyone.

Next I earnestly beseech you not to see in it any attempt to be pathetic or to move you other than by my reasoning. The strange habit which our discussions have taken of turning into rancour, which I myself do not usually feel, my agitated state, your decision not to listen to me any more, have forced me to resort to a letter in which I hope to convince you how wrong you are in spite of all your love.

I am writing all this very calmly, and when I think how ill I have been for the past several days as a result of anger and amazement, I wonder how I can possibly endure the accomplished fact!—In order to get me to swallow the pill you keep repeating that it is all quite natural and in no way degrading. That's possible, and I believe it; but really what does it matter that it is all right for most people, if it is *just the contrary* for me.—You have told me that you consider my anger and my distress as merely temporary; you assume that you are causing me a childish hurt that is only for my own good. But you must realize something of which you do not seem aware; the truth is that, unfortunately for me, I am not like other men.—What you consider a necessity and a momentary grief I cannot, I simply cannot endure.—

That is very easily explained. When we are alone you may treat me the way you like—but I emphatically reject everything that threatens my freedom.—Isn't it incredibly cruel to subject me to the jurisdiction of men who will be bored by the whole affair and who do not know me? —Between us, who can boast of knowing me, of knowing where I want to go, what I want to do, and of the amount of patience of which I am capable? I sincerely believe that you are making a grave mistake. —I tell you this calmly, because I consider myself condemned by you, and I am sure that you will not listen to me: but first of all please note that knowingly and voluntarily you are causing me infinite pain without realizing all the heartbreak it means.

You have failed to keep your word in two ways.—When you were kind enough to lend me eight thousand francs, it was agreed between us that at the end of a certain period of time you would have a right to take a certain percent on all the works that I might produce. —I have incurred some new debts and when I told you that they were very small, you promised to wait a little longer. In fact, a few trifling advances added to the money I earned could have quickly wiped them out. But now you have made up your mind so impetuously; you have acted so quickly that I no longer know what to do—and I am forced to give up my plan. I had imagined that my first work, which was quite scholarly, would come to the attention of various people and would bring you a number of compliments, and that, when you saw that I was making some money, you wouldn't refuse me new advances, and that in this way at the end of a few months I should have been cleared of my debts, that is I should have been at the point where I was after you lent me the eight thousand francs.[13]—But not at all; you refused to wait—to wait even two weeks.

Just consider your fallacious reasoning and your illogical conduct.— You are causing me infinite pain and taking steps quite insulting to me just when my success is perhaps beginning, on the very eve of the day I have promised you for so long.—That is precisely the time you choose to dumbfound me,—for as I have told you, I refuse to accept the *guardianship* as something harmless and inoffensive.—Already I feel the effect,—and in this matter you have made an even more serious mistake in believing that it will act as a stimulant.—You can have no idea what I felt yesterday, you can never imagine the complete discouragement that came over me when I saw that things were getting serious—a sudden impulse, as it were, to let everything go, not to bother about anything, not even to go and get my letter from M. Ed. Blanc, to merely say quietly to myself: what's the use, I don't need it any more—there is nothing left for me but to be satisfied to squander in idiotic fashion anything she will give me.

It is proof of a grave error on your part that M. Ancelle should have said to me in Neuilly: 'I told your mother that, if letting you squander everything would lead you to work and to choose a profession, I would advise her to let you have your way; but that would never be the case.' I don't think it's possible to say anything more insolent and more stupid.—I have never dared to go that far and to tell myself calmly that I would squander everything. I am quite sure that you are not as indulgent as he, and as for me, I am too fond of my liberty to act so foolishly.—Now, although I am only your son, you ought to have enough respect for my person not to subject me to the jurisdiction of strangers, when you realize the full extent of the pain it will cause me.—And consider the difficulties of what I have undertaken. Most certainly, and I assure you, dear mother, that this is not a threat designed to make you yield, but the expression of what I feel—the result will be just the contrary of what you expect—that is, complete prostration.

Now I'm coming to something which doubtless will have more importance for you than all sorts of promises and than all my hopes.

You have been led, you told me, by an anxious and enduring love. You want to save what capital I have in spite of myself. I have no objection to that, I have never had the least intention of consuming it completely—I am ready to yield to you every possible means of safeguarding it for me.—There is one exception, however; the one you have chosen.—Of what importance to you is the means, provided you obtain the desired result? Why do you insist on using the only one that causes me such frightful pain?—The one that is most odiously distasteful to my nature—arbiters, judges, strangers.—Of what use are they?

Lastly, not knowing anything about the law, I talked vaguely to you of a gift devised in such a way that it would revert to me in case of death. I don't know whether that is possible; but you will not be able to persuade me that, among all the tricks of the legal profession, there are not other ways to satisfy you than that which you wish to use.—And why?—Come—can anyone be more honest and more sincere than I—can I give you more striking proof of my good faith and of the agreement of my will with yours?—I prefer to be without money, and to give myself over to you completely rather than to undergo a court ruling—the one is at least a free act, the other is an attack on my liberty.

To conclude, I most humbly beg you to spare yourself great grief and to spare me a frightful humiliation.—But for heaven's sake, no arbiters, no strangers—no secrets, I want everything postponed until I have had a long talk with you and M. Ancelle.—I am going to see him this evening; I am hoping to bring him to you. But I am certain, absolutely certain that after a first success, it will be easy for me, provided you help me a little, to achieve a successful position *quickly*.

I earnestly beg you again—I am sure you are mistaken—after that —if I haven't satisfactorily explained how much more pleasant and reasonable it would be to arrive at an amicable understanding, do what you wish, and let come what may.

M. Edmond Blanc has given me a very good letter with which I'm going to try to extricate myself at the office of the *Revue [de Paris]* this morning.—A last time, think over carefully the fact that I'm asking nothing more than a change of methods.

Charles

Baudelaire's impassioned appeal to his mother proved futile, and on September 21, 1844, the legal guardianship was established by the civil court at her request. At the time the guardianship became effective, Charles possessed a capital of 35,000 francs, the income from which he continued to receive until his death. It is true that, thanks to the precautionary measures taken by his family, he was never completely destitute, yet burdened as he was by the debts of his youth, the full extent of which he may not have dared admit, he was forced to borrow constantly during the next twenty-three years of his life in order to pay his creditors. Ancelle with a tenacious concern for the material welfare of his irascible ward conscientiously, though often shortsightedly, resisted his too frequent demands for loans or advances. Infuriated by his guardian's reluctance to accede to his requests as well as by his well-intentioned and often bungling admonitions, Charles turned again and again to his mother in the hope of obtaining the financial assistance of which he was ever in need.

*   *   *

In his brief autobiographical notes Baudelaire lists the name of Sainte-Beuve as one of the writers with whom he came into contact after his return to Paris in 1842. It was probably not until 1844, however, the same year in which the legal guardianship was established, that Baudelaire came to be personally acquainted with the eminent French critic. In a letter which he apparently wrote that very year, and which could well have initiated their friendship, the younger poet enclosed a long and rather laboured poem which may have been composed several years earlier. Although it is not one of his best poems, it does throw an interesting light on his early youth and adolescence. Nowhere else has the author of *Les Fleurs du Mal* revealed the extent to which he was influenced by the unhealthy romanticism of Sainte-Beuve's only novel *Volupté* and of his *Poésies de Joseph Delorme*. He had absorbed everything, as he tells us, 'the miasmas, the perfumes, the soft whispering of dead memories'. Even more he had found in Amaury, the morbid, neurotic hero of *Volupté*, those very qualities which were to wreck his own life and were to offer him excuses for his inaction and his constant self-analysis.

There seems little doubt that Baudelaire was entirely sincere in his praise of Sainte-Beuve. Throughout his life he never ceased to admire and respect the author of *Les Causeries du Lundi*. In 1851, in an article on Pierre Dupont he was to go so far as to maintain the superiority of Sainte-Beuve's verse over that of Victor Hugo. And in 1859, in his critical study of the poetry of Théophile Gautier he was to credit Sainte-Beuve, Hugo and de Vigny with having given 'new life to French poetry, dead since the time of Corneille'.

It is not too strange that Baudelaire felt so strong an affinity with the older writer and critic. Both attempted to conquer new domains in poetry, to seek new sensations and to analyse those sensations; both were led towards the same blasphemies and the same satanism. But where Sainte-Beuve had voiced his sentiments in a manner that was lustreless and undistinguished, Baudelaire succeeded with far greater genius in giving magnificent poetic expression to conceptions that were often quite similar.

The signature Baudelaire-Dufays which appears at the end of the letter was inspired by his mother's maiden name, Caroline Dufays. This same signature or variants thereof appear frequently in Baudelaire's correspondence from the end of 1844 into 1848.

There is no record of any letter that Sainte-Beuve may have written in reply.

To Sainte-Beuve

[No date]

Sir,

Somewhere Stendhal has said this, or something like this: *I am writing for a dozen souls whom I shall perhaps never see, but whom I love without having seen.*

Do you not find these words an excellent excuse for the importunate, and is it not clear that every writer is responsible for the liking that he inspires?

These verses were written for you, and so ingenuously that, when they were finished, I wondered if they did not seem impertinent and if *the person praised* did not have the right to be offended at the eulogy. —I hope that you will be kind enough to give me your opinion.

> Young and beardless then, seated on old oak benches
> more polished and shining than the links of a chain
> which each day are made more smooth by the touch of
> man's skin, sadly we dragged out our boresome hours,
> crouching and stooped beneath that square of lonely
> sky where children, at ten, drink the bitter milk of
> learning. It was in those old days, memorable and
> never to be forgotten, when our professors, forced
> to enlarge the classic yoke and still hostile to your
> verses, gave way before our wild skirmishes and al-
> lowed the schoolboy, triumphant and unruly, to have
> Triboulet [14] freely bellowed in Latin. In those days
> of pale adolescence, who did not feel the torpor of
> cloistered weariness—our eyes lost in the dull blue
> of a summer sky or in the dazzling whiteness of the
> snow—who did not strain with sharp and eager ear
> and, alert like a pack of hounds, catch the distant
> echo of a book or the cry of a rioting mob?
>
> It was especially in the summer when the lead roofs
> melted that those great blackened walls were filled
> with sadness, when the dog days or the smoky autumn
> flooded the skies with their monotonous fire and
> made the shrill falcons, terror of the white pigeons,
> go to sleep in the graceful turrets; season of rev-
> erie, when for a whole day the Muse clung to the clap-
> per of a bell; when Melancholy, at noon while all
> was asleep, chin in hand at the end of the corridor,
> —with eyes darker and more blue than the Nun whose

sad and obscene story is known to all—dragged its
foot weighed down by precocious grief, its forehead
still damp from the languor of its nights.[15]

—And then came the unhealthy evenings, the feverish
nights which make young girls become enamoured of
their bodies and cause them to contemplate before
their mirrors—sterile pleasure—the ripe fruits
of their nubility,—and then the softly insouciant
Italian evenings—which reveal knowledge of deceitful pleasures,—when sombre Venus pours out from
dark balconies floods of musk from her fragrant cen-
sers.

. . . .

It was amid the rival charms of these enticing attractions, matured by your sonnets and prepared by your
verses, that one evening, having sensed the nature of
your book, I carried away over my heart the story of
Amaury. Every mystic abyss lies close to doubt.—I
who at fifteen, drawn toward the abyss, had readily
understood the sighs of René and who felt a strange
thirst for the unknown—I felt penetrating into even
my smallest vein the draught which filtered slowly
drop by drop within me.[16]—I absorbed all of it,
the miasmas, the perfumes, the sweet whispering of
dead memories, the slow interweaving of symbolic
phrases,—murmuring rosaries of mystic madrigals;—a
voluptuous book, if ever there was one.—And ever
since, whether in the depths of wooded asylums or beneath the suns of different zones, the eternal lul-
ling of the intoxicating waves and the recurring
sight of endless horizons carries my heart back to
the divine dream,—whether in the oppressive leisure
of an August day, or in the shivering idleness of
winter,—under the clouds of smoke that mask the
ceiling, I have everywhere sought the profound
mystery of this book so dear to those numbed souls
whom destiny has marked with like maladies, and
before the mirror I have perfected the cruel art

with which a demon endowed me at birth, of scratch-
ing my wound and making it bleed in order to create
from sorrow a voluptuous pleasure.

Poet, is this insult or praise? For with respect
to you I am like a lover in the presence of a phan-
tom, with an enticing gesture, whose hand and eye
have, to draw one's strength, unknown charms.—All
those we love are vessels of gall drunk with closed
eyes, and the heart which grief attracts dies each
day, blessing the arrow that transfixes it.[17]

Baudelaire-Dufays

17, Quai d'Anjou

It soon becomes apparent to even the most cursory reader of *Les
Fleurs du Mal* that many of its poems were inspired by Baudelaire's
love of the plastic arts. This enthusiasm was not, as might be supposed,
the outgrowth of his literary activity, but rather dated back to his
early childhood, perhaps to the days when he had strolled with his
father in the Luxembourg Gardens and listened to his descriptions and
explanations of the many statues that line its walks. 'To glorify the
cult of images (my great, my only, my first passion),' Baudelaire wrote
in *Mon Cœur mis à nu*, a statement confirmed in an autobiographical
note where he alludes to a 'lasting taste since childhood for all plastic
representations'.

Baudelaire's fondness for the arts became even more marked as he
grew older and more mature. While living at the Pension Bailly, he
would pay almost daily visits to the Louvre and, as his friend Prarond
has recalled, was passionately fond of Michelangelo, Titian, and
Delacroix. After moving to the Hôtel Pimodan, he cultivated the
acquaintance of the painters Boissard and Deroy and frequented
studios, museums, and cafés where artistic questions were discussed.
On the red and black papered walls of his apartment the young dandy
hung Delacroix's Hamlet lithographs, a head of *La Douleur* by
Delacroix, and a copy by Deroy of Delacroix's *Femmes d'Alger*. In
fact it was in Delacroix, whose genius he was one of the first to
recognize, that the youthful writer found his greatest stimulus.

It is not surprising then that Baudelaire's first important publication
should have been in the field of art criticism and that it should have
served in part as a glorification of the painter Delacroix. The *Salon*

28

de 1845, as it was called, adhered to the traditional pattern established nearly a hundred years earlier and reflected its author's enthusiasm for the critical works of both Stendhal and Diderot.[18] Of special interest is Baudelaire's appeal to the artists of the day for greater originality and for an expression of 'the heroism of modern life'.

Although the *Salon* attracted considerable attention, it did not open the way to success as Baudelaire had anticipated. His hope of obtaining a favourable offer or of signing a lucrative contract proved futile and he found himself more and more harassed by growing debts and by the financial restrictions imposed by the guardianship. During the three years that he had been separated from his family he had written some of the more brilliant poems that were to appear in *Les Fleurs du Mal*, yet he had succeeded in placing only one.[19]

As the months passed and Baudelaire came to realize the difficulty of earning a living with his pen, he sank deeper and deeper into a state of depression. Haunted by a sense of failure which was no doubt magnified by the critical attitude of his parents, he resorted to desperate measures that must have deeply shocked even the imperturbable and worthy Ancelle.

To Ancelle

June 30, 1845

When Mademoiselle Jeanne Lemer brings you this letter, I shall be dead. She does not know that. You know my will. Except for the portion set aside for my mother, Mademoiselle *Lemer* is to inherit all that I shall leave after you have paid certain debts, a list of which accompanies this letter.

I am dying tormented by anxiety. Remember our conversation yesterday. I desire, I wish my last instructions to be strictly followed. Two persons can challenge my will, my mother and my brother—and they can challenge it only on the pretext of insanity. My suicide joined to the various disorders of my life can be of service to them in depriving Mademoiselle Lemer of what I wish to leave her. I must therefore explain my *suicide* and my conduct with regard to Mademoiselle *Lemer*, —in such a way that this letter addressed to you, to be read by you to her, can serve in her defence in case my will is challenged by the persons named above.

I am *killing* myself—without *sorrow*.—I feel none of those perturbations which men call *sorrow*.—My debts have never been a cause of *sorrow*. Nothing is easier than to dominate such things. I am killing myself because I can no longer live, because the weariness of going to sleep and the weariness of waking are unbearable for me. I am killing myself because I am useless to others—*and dangerous to myself*. I am killing myself because I believe I am immortal and because *I hope*.—While I am writing these lines, I am so completely lucid that I am still editing some notes for *M. Théodore de Banville*, and I have all the strength necessary to busy myself with my manuscripts.

I give and I bequeath all I possess to Mademoiselle Lemer, even the little furniture I have and my portrait—because she is the only being in whom I have found any peace. Can anyone blame me for wanting to pay for the few pleasures I have found on this hideous earth?

I *scarcely* know my brother—he has neither lived *in me nor with me*—he has no need of me.

Nor is this money needed by my mother, who so often and always unintentionally has embittered my life. She has her *husband*, she possesses a *human being*, an affection, *a friendship*. I have only *Jeanne Lemer*. I have found peace only in her, and I do not wish and I cannot bear the thought that anyone should want to dispossess her of what I give her under the pretext that I am not sane. You have heard me talk to you these last days.—Was I mad?

If I knew that by asking my mother herself and by revealing to her the profound humiliation I feel within me, I could persuade her not to disturb my last wishes, I would do so at once—so sure am I that being a woman she would understand me better than anyone else—perhaps she will be able by herself to dissuade my brother from UNINTELLIGENT opposition.

Jeanne Lemer is the only woman I have loved,—she has nothing. And it is to you, M. Ancelle, one of the few men I have found endowed with a kind and noble mind that I entrust my final instructions regarding her.

Read this to her; let her know the reasons for this legacy and her defence, in case my final dispositions should be opposed. As a prudent man try to make her understand the value of even a small sum of money. Try to think of some reasonable idea which can be profitable to her and which will make my dying wishes useful to her. Guide her, counsel her; shall I dare to say: love her—for my sake at least. Point out to her my terrible example—and show her how disorder of mind and life leads to sombre despair or to complete destruction.—*Reason and practicality! I beg you!*

Do you really think this will can be contested, and that the right to do a truly good and reasonable act before I die can be taken from me?

You can surely see now that this will is not merely a piece of braggadocio nor an attempt to defy the ideas of family and of society, but simply the expression of what remains human in me,—love, and the sincere desire to serve a creature who was once my joy and my repose. Goodbye!

Read this to her.—*I believe in your loyalty and I know that you will not destroy it.*

Give her some money *at once*. She knows nothing of my *dying* wishes,—and is expecting to have me help her out of her difficulties.

Even should his last wishes be disputed, a dead man certainly has the right to do something generous.

The other letter, which she will bring you and which is intended only for you, contains the list of what must be paid to keep my name clear.

C. Baudelaire

Several scholars have expressed the view that Baudelaire's attempt at suicide was only a dramatic effort on his part to effect a reconciliation with his parents in the interest of having his debts paid. The fact that he inflicted only a slight knife wound on himself and that he afterwards joked about the matter with his friends has been cited as proof that he was perpetrating a hoax. It must be remembered, however, that this was not the only occasion on which Baudelaire contemplated suicide. Moreover, throughout his life he did his utmost to conceal his innermost feelings from all his friends. Even to his mother he could not always unburden his heart: 'how can you know me so little that you don't realize I naturally feel the need to hide all my thoughts? *Call it DANDYISM? an absurd love of DIGNITY,*—anything you wish . . .' [20] Perhaps to conceal his unhappiness and his insecurity from the probing eyes of others, or simply to attract attention, he would shock and deceive people by inventing the most monstrous lies about himself. It was only to be expected then that Baudelaire would jest about a situation in which he might otherwise have appeared slightly ridiculous.

Even if his attempted suicide was merely a hoax, his urgent plea to M. Ancelle makes it clear that Baudelaire was deeply attached to Jeanne. Moreover, it would seem that his attachment was partly based, whether consciously or unconsciously, on a feeling of being rejected by his mother: 'She has her *husband*, she possesses a *human being*, an affection, a *friendship*. I have only *Jeanne Lemer.*' In his self-conscious, almost theatrical letter these lines seem to explain, more than anything else, the motives that prompted his action and that found their source in his bitterness and loneliness. Ever since the establishment of the legal guardianship, Baudelaire's feeling of rejection had been intensified by the realization that his mother had obviously yielded to the influence of M. Aupick. To have sided with her husband against her own son was in the eyes of Baudelaire tantamount to a betrayal.

The attempted suicide had as a result the temporary reconciliation of Charles with his parents. Charles was taken home, where he was invited to remain, and a few of his most pressing debts were paid for him. Only a few months later, however, he felt impelled to leave and go his own way once more. It is typical that he should have explained his sudden departure to Louis Ménard by saying: 'They drink only Bordeaux wines at home and I like nothing but Burgundy.' [21] Far more sincere and plausible is the explanation found in the note that he left for his mother.

To Madame Aupick

[1845?]

I am leaving and I shall not return until I am in a better financial and mental condition. I am leaving for several reasons. First I have fallen into a frightful mood of depression and apathy and I need a long period of solitude in which to recover and regain my strength.—In the second place it is impossible for me to make myself what your husband would like me to be; consequently, it would be robbing him to live any longer under his roof; and finally I do not think it *decent* to be treated by him as he apparently wishes to treat me.—I shall probably have to live a very hard life, but I shall be better off that way.—Today or tomorrow I shall send you a letter to tell you which of my effects I need, and where you are to send them. My decision is firm, irrevocable and the result of careful thought; so you must not find fault, but try to understand.

B. D.

Having turned his back on his family for the second time, Baudelaire took a room at the Hôtel de Dunkerque, 32 rue Lafitte, where he set about renewing his literary activities. On the 24th of November, 1845, he published anonymously in the *Corsaire-Satan* a satiric article, *Comment on paie ses dettes quand on a du génie*, in which he lampooned Balzac's use of ghost writers in order to increase the earnings from his literary output.

The fact that Baudelaire attacked a writer for whom he always showed the most sincere admiration may have stemmed, as Eugène

Crépet has suggested, from indignation at Balzac's willingness to debase his genius.[22] What seems even more plausible is that it represented a form of rationalization on the part of its author. That Balzac with his great genius had been obliged to prostitute his art in an effort to pay his debts may have served as an excuse in Baudelaire's mind for his own lack of financial success as a writer.

Baudelaire did not succeed in publishing anything further until February 1846 when his long short story, *Le Jeune Enchanteur*, appeared in *L'Esprit public*. In his letters to his mother the young author rather surprisingly fails either to mention the story by name or to make any comment other than a casual reference to his latest publication. His strange reticence has assumed new significance in the light of a recent discovery. For many years *Le Jeune Enchanteur* puzzled critical readers who felt that it was neither compatible with other works of its author nor worthy of his name. It was not until 1950 that the distinguished scholar, Professor W. T. Bandy, found the solution to the problem.[23] Quite by accident he came across a story, *The Young Enchanter*, published anonymously in 1836 in an English keepsake volume. Careful investigation proved the author to be the Reverend George Croly, an English divine, who had preferred to hide his secular, literary activities in anonymity. Baudelaire, who had learned some English from his mother and had studied it at school, simply translated Croly's story.

That Baudelaire should have stooped to outright plagiarism is somewhat disappointing to his admirers, but that he should have done so only a few months after attacking Balzac for a similar defection is ironic to say the least. In his desperate need for money and in his eagerness to impress his family he apparently found that the easiest way out was the very expedient he had condemned in another. Perhaps the realization of this fact prompted him to add a final conciliatory paragraph when, on August 23, 1846, he signed and republished the Balzac article in a small newspaper known as *L'Echo*. As a sort of afterthought he concludes: 'Should anyone maliciously take this for the *scoffing* of a small newspaper or for an attack on the glory of the greatest man of our century, he would be shamefully mistaken; I have tried to show that the great poet could find a solution for a bill of exchange as easily as for the most mysterious and complicated novel.'

To Madame Claude Baudelaire
[About March 3, 1846]

Madame,
You will perhaps be curious to know how Baudelaire-Dufays treats

a subject as difficult and at the same time as natural as Love: I am sending you this booklet which I have just penned; I cannot chose a better
judge than you, I place myself under your jurisdiction with complete
confidence.

If my brother could only see me pleading my cause, or rather that
of the human race, before the Court of Love, as I call it in the pamphlet
that I am sending you, he would be able to appreciate the vocation
which draws me to the Muses, just as I am able to understand the
enthusiasm with which he devotes himself to the difficult and tedious
tasks of Themis. To each his lot in this world; to me falls that of instructing my fellow men on how to conduct themselves so as to find
happiness: thus, very shortly, I shall have the honour of sending you,
Madame, my *Catéchisme de la femme aimée*, with the hope that you will
read it and give me your comments. You will see how I define instinc-
tive attraction. My entrance into the profession reveals a partisan of
love in the manner of *Antony*; but you may judge whether it is a love
to be disdained.[24]

What will you say about the rules of conduct and advice that I give
to that deceitful sex which can do no more than feign love? I want
the lover who is really in love to be constant, and you have proof of it
in this sentence alone. 'But *love well*, *vigorously*, *gallantly*, *orientally*,
ferociously the one whom you love, so that your love may not torment
another's love.'

This short passage will doubtless make you wish to read the whole
article and the *Catéchisme* which is about to appear.

Be kind enough, Madame, to be my providence in the career that
is opening up for me through the *medium of love*—I almost said
through the influence of women.

Please accept my respectful greetings proffered with the eagerness
and enthusiasm of a poet who wishes to follow in the steps of a
Petrarch or a Parny.

Your very humble servant,
Baudelaire-Dufays

It is to *Choix de maximes consolantes sur l'amour* that Baudelaire
refers with such obvious pride in his stilted letter to Félicité Baudelaire, wife of his half-brother Claude. Published in the *Corsaire-Satan*
on March 3, 1846, less than a month after the appearance of *Le Jeune
Enchanteur*, it gave new confidence to its young author and offered him
an excuse to impress Claude and his wife with his literary ability.

34

Though Baudelaire wrote comparatively few letters in 1846, the *Maximes* are perhaps as revealing as any letters he might have written. Beneath their deceptively impersonal humour one can sense much of Baudelaire's own experience and perceive something of the nature of his relationship with Jeanne and perhaps even with the Louchette of his days at the Pension Bailly. Surely the author must have been thinking of his squint-eyed mistress when he describes a thin woman as a 'well of mysterious pleasures' and when he professes to believe that ugliness has indisputable merits. In the eyes of her lover the ugliness of a once beautiful woman has the exquisite poignancy of a strain played by Paganini. Her very unattractiveness has the power to evoke 'memories of lost hopes', if only through 'an association of ideas', and thus to constitute an essential part of her lover's happiness.

For the curious and the blasé, Baudelaire continues, ugliness has a more mysterious appeal. Its enjoyment stems from the 'thirst for the unknown' and from 'the taste for the horrible' which is to be found, if only in its incipient form, in men and women alike. This thirst for the unknown was to haunt Baudelaire all his life. In his poem *Le Voyage* it finally leads him to welcome death itself as a means of finding the *new*:

> Pour us your poison that it may renew
> our strength. Fire burns our brains. Now let us leap—
> Heaven or Hell, what matter?—into the deep,
> at the bottom of the Unknown to find the *new*.[25]

References to Jeanne seem even more obvious than those to Louchette. The young lover is cautioned not to teach spelling to his mistress 'unless to become her lover you must be her teacher of French'. In offering his flippant advice Baudelaire was no doubt speaking from first-hand experience. Did he not bitterly complain to his mother in 1852 that he himself had offered to teach Jeanne, but that she 'refused to learn anything'? In 1846, however, Baudelaire was able to persuade himself, or at least to assure others, that stupidity had its advantages. Surely he must have been thinking of Jeanne's magnificent dark eyes when he affirms: 'Stupidity is often the ornament of beauty; it gives to the eyes the dull limpidity of blackish pools and the oily calm of tropical seas.'

If the *Maximes* suggest Baudelaire's awareness of Jeanne's stupidity, they also seem to indicate his consciousness of her infidelity. What should be done, he asks, by the man 'caught between an hereditary and paternal taste for morality and an overpowering desire for a woman worthy of scorn? Numerous base infidelities, an habitual liking for low places, shameful secrets accidentally discovered inspire horror for one's idol . . . Virtue and pride cry out: Flee. Nature whispers: Where can you flee?'

The solution that Baudelaire offers is one that he himself seems to have chosen, though perhaps for different reasons: 'Tell yourself boldly with the candour of a philosopher: less vicious, my ideal would have been less complete. I contemplate it and I submit. . . .' Baudelaire's philosophic candour seems to have been mere whistling in the dark, a form of rationalization that could comfort his wounded pride and explain his continued attachment to Jeanne. Letters written later in life will show that he was unable to accept this somewhat theoretical conception of the 'ideal'.

Baudelaire concludes his *Maximes* by cautioning the young lover not to imitate the cheap antics of a Don Juan, who far from being the romantic idler glorified by Musset and Gautier, was merely an 'old dandy worn out from his many travels and acting like an utter fool in the presence of an honourable woman in love with her husband'. Perhaps nowhere else in his article is Baudelaire writing with more sincerity than in his condemnation of the Don Juan type. His advice is entirely consistent with the respect and courtesy he showed to women throughout his life. It is the same respect that marked his youthful letter to Mme. Bragard and that endeared him to his charming old friend, Mme. Meurice.

Les Maximes consolantes sur l'amour were followed a month later by another essay, in many respects no less autobiographical in nature. Published in *L'Esprit public* on April 15, *Conseils aux jeunes littérateurs* reveals Baudelaire's ideas as a young man of twenty-five concerning the man of letters and his art. Most of these ideas he carried with him throughout his life, some he later contradicted or reversed, taught by the bitterness of his own experience. To the Baudelaire of 1846, still young and full of hope, *guignon* (bad luck) was merely an empty word. 'Those who say: I have no luck, are those who have not yet had enough success. . . .' To the Baudelaire of 1852, embittered by poverty and failure, *guignon* had become something very real. Men like Poe, Hoffman, and presumably Baudelaire himself were 'destinies doomed by fate' who bore 'the words *bad luck* written in mysterious characters in the sinuous folds of their foreheads'.[26]

If Baudelaire changed his mind about the matter of bad luck, he remained ever convinced of the high seriousness of his calling. Both in the *Conseils* and elsewhere he consistently maintained that poetry is the 'most honoured of all the arts', since it 'satisfies the most imperious need . . . every healthy man can do without food for two days, but without poetry—never!' Moreover, he attributed the same importance to careful workmanship that he did in his later writing. His belief that 'inspiration is decidedly the sister of daily work' was one which he reiterated on many occasions, though he himself to his great dismay seemed constitutionally unable to put the precept into practice.[27]

Amusingly enough, Baudelaire's own personal experience becomes the source of his concluding advice to his fellow writers. Perhaps none of his readers suspected the real sincerity that lay behind these words of caution: 'Never have any creditors; if you insist, pretend to have them. . . .'' As for a mistress, the man of letters should restrict himself to one of two types: the prostitute or the stupid woman. Baudelaire could have been deliberately trying to shock his more serious readers or he could have been attempting to rationalize his own experience. After all, according to his own admission, Jeanne belonged to both categories.

The most important of Baudelaire's publications in 1846 was the *Salon de 1846*, which appeared in May, a month after the *Conseils aux jeunes littérateurs*.[28] With its astute criticism, its freshness and enthusiasm, its abundance of ideas about art, it helped to establish Baudelaire's reputation among his contemporaries as a notable art critic. The author's easy familiarity with painting, whether that of Delacroix or the more obscure American painter, George Catlin, reveals the breadth of knowledge which he had gained from his frequent visits to the Louvre in the company of his friend, the artist Deroy.

Toward the end of 1846 Baudelaire was further encouraged by the publication of two of his poems which were later to be included in *Les Fleurs du Mal: L'Impénitente* and *A une Indienne*.[29]

1846 had proved to be one of the most productive years in Baudelaire's literary career. 1847 was to begin auspiciously with the long-delayed publication of *La Fanfarlo* which, like the *Maximes*, is as revealing as much of his correspondence. As early as 1843 Baudelaire in writing to his mother had referred to its imminent publication, and in a short note in 1844 he had again mentioned working on his 'interminable novel'. It was only on January 1, 1847, however, that his novelette or long short story finally appeared in the *Bulletin de la Societé des gens de lettres*.

The chief interest of *La Fanfarlo* lies in its penetrating analysis and self-portrait of the author. Everything—from the physical description of Samuel Cramer with his 'pure and noble brow, his eyes shining like drops of coffee . . . and his hair pretentiously arranged in a Raphael-esque manner' to the subtle psychological motives that explain his conduct as a writer and a social being—seems to be modelled on

Baudelaire himself and finds direct or implicit corroboration in his life and in his writings.

Samuel, we are told, was afflicted by the same lethargy of which Baudelaire accused himself throughout his life, a lethargy which devoured 'that half of his genius with which heaven had endowed him' and which resulted at times in a 'powerlessness so colossal and so enormous as to be epic'. His was a 'sombre nature streaked with brilliant flashes of light—lazy and enterprising at the same time,—fecund in difficult projects and in ludicrous failures'.

Like Baudelaire, Samuel showed an eclectic taste in reading and would be carried away by enthusiasm now for one writer, now for another. In the dim candlelight of his room could be glimpsed a volume of Swedenborg as well as 'one of those shameful books whose reading is profitable only to minds possessed by an immoderate taste for the truth'.

Perhaps Baudelaire was thinking of certain passages in his *Salons* when he spoke of Samuel's tendency to appropriate rather freely from others and of his failure to differentiate between what seemed beautiful enough to be his and what was really his. Certainly no better analysis of Baudelaire's debt to other writers could be found than that in which he exonerates his young hero: 'He was at the same time all the artists that he had studied and all the books that he had read, and yet in spite of this imitative faculty, he remained profoundly original.'

Samuel's explanation for his morbid verses, for the 'mystic incense' which he reserved for the 'sultaness of low places' is one which throws an interesting light on Baudelaire's own experience. 'It is hate for everyone and for ourselves that has led us towards these lies. It is from despair at not being noble and handsome by natural means that we have so strangely painted our faces. We have so much subjected our hearts to sophistries and we have so abused the microscope in order to study the hideous excrescences and the shameful warts with which it is covered . . . that it is impossible for us to speak the language of other men.' The same despair that Samuel felt seems to be reflected in many of the poems of *Les Fleurs du Mal* and could explain certain aspects of Baudelaire's personal behaviour.

The parallel between Samuel and Baudelaire is just as obvious in their manner of living. Samuel has the same epicurean tastes in food and drink as his creator, he shows the same tendency to go to extremes, the same love for mimeticism and for dramatizing to himself his moods of joy and despair, the same generosity to his friends and acquaintances. But it is especially in Samuel's ideas of love that we recognize the author of *Les Fleurs du Mal*. The sensual satisfaction that he derives from all feminine adornments—rustling fabrics, perfumes, jewellery, make-up—all the *mundus muliebris*, as it is called in *Les Paradis artificiels*, is apparent in almost everything Baudelaire wrote and was one of the important sources of his poetic expression. Yet, paradoxically enough, love for Samuel was 'less an affair of the senses than of the reason. It was essentially admiration and desire for the beautiful. ... He loved a human body as a material harmony, as a beautiful piece of architecture, plus movement; and this absolute materialism was not far from the purest idealism.' The pure idealism or aesthetic pleasure felt by Samuel seems to characterize only certain aspects of Baudelaire's love for Jeanne, but it does anticipate in striking fashion the love which he is soon to express for both Marie Daubrun and for Mme. Sabatier.

After the appearance of *La Fanfarlo* Baudelaire seems to have sunk into one of those periods of lethargy which were to occur so frequently in his life and which made him appear, like Samuel Cramer, a veritable 'god of impotence'. In the entire course of the year he succeeded in publishing only one short poem—a sonnet, *Les Chats*, which his friend Champfleury reproduced in the *Corsaire-Satan* for December 14.

Meanwhile his relationship with his mother was becoming more strained, although a note written by him on March 13, thanking her for a loan, indicates they were still on somewhat friendly terms. Perhaps it was late in the year 1847 that Baudelaire had the bad taste to write to Mme. Aupick demanding that she pay him a visit in Jeanne's apartment where he was confined as a result of some illness.

To Madame Aupick

[No date]

When I tried to get dressed to go and see you, I found the doors were double-locked. It seems the doctor doesn't want me to move.

So I can't go and see you; when I write you, it is M. Ancelle who answers me and who forbids me to visit you. Besides, I have been locked in.

Do you take my illness as a joke and do you have the heart to deprive me of your presence?—I tell you I need you, I must see you and talk to you. Do come, do come *at once*—don't be prudish. I am staying with a woman, but I am ill and I can't leave.

If you can't do what I ask, you must at least tell me what can be done. I am put in solitary confinement, I am locked in, you don't answer me when I write you, I am told that I can't see you. What's the meaning of all this? I beg you, do come and see me, immediately, immediately—and no protests.

Charles

Madame Duval, rue de la Femme-sans-Tête, 6.

P.S.—I assure you that if you don't come, it will only cause further mishaps.

I *want* you to come alone.

Baudelaire's peremptory request seems only to have antagonized Mme. Aupick and to have resulted in a temporary estrangement. The unhappy writer could not long do without his mother's help, however. In December, looking back on the wasted year, Baudelaire wrote her a desperate appeal in which he humbled his pride and confessed all the misery of his existence. The plans which he hopefully outlined were never to be realized. Although he wrote several articles about caricaturists, he never produced the history of caricature mentioned in his letter and announced on the cover of the *Salon de 1845*. Nor did he succeed in writing either the history of sculpture or the novels to which he alludes.

As usual, Mme. Aupick was moved by her son's appeal and lent him money to alleviate his plight.

To Madame Aupick
Saturday, December 4, 1847

In spite of the cruel letter with which you answered my last request, I thought I could turn to you once more, although I realize perfectly what annoyance it will cause you and what difficulty I shall have in making you understand the legitimacy of this request, but I feel so convinced that it can be infinitely and definitively useful that I hope to make you share my conviction. Notice that I say *once more*, which I sincerely think means: the last time. Without doubt I am indebted to you for providing me with some of the things indispensable to a life more adequate than that which I have been leading for some time, that is to say a few pieces of furniture. But now that the furniture has been bought, I am left without a cent and without certain indispensable objects which can readily be guessed, a lamp, a water-filter, etc. . . . Suffice it to say that I have been obliged to hold a long discussion with M. Ancelle in order to obtain wood and coal. If you knew what an effort I had to make to take my pen in hand and apply to you again, since I despair of making you understand—you whose life is always so comfortable and well-ordered—how I could find myself in such straits! Imagine a perpetual idleness, caused by perpetually straitened circumstances, combined with a profound hatred of that idleness and the absolute impossibility of ever extricating myself because of a perpetual lack of money. Certainly in such a case it is better (however humiliating it may be to me) to turn to you again, rather than to indifferent people who would not show me the same sympathy. This is what has just happened to me. Very happy to have lodging and furniture, but in need of money, I had been trying for two or three days to obtain some when, last Monday evening, exhausted by fatigue, boredom, and hunger, I entered the first hotel I came across. I have been staying there ever since, *and for a good reason.* I had given the address of this hotel to a friend to whom I had lent money four years ago in the days when I had some, but he has failed to keep his word. Moreover, I have spent very little, thirty or thirty-five francs in one week, but that is not my whole problem. Even supposing you were kind enough to help me out of my foolish predicament with a benevolence that is unfortunately always insufficient, what shall I do TOMORROW? For idleness is killing me, devouring me, consuming me. I don't really know how I have enough strength to overcome the disastrous effect of this idleness and to still retain an absolute clarity of mind as well as a constant hope of fortune, happiness, and peace. Now this is what I beg of you *on bended knee,* so much do I feel that I have reached the limit of my own patience as well as that of others. Send me, *even if it costs you a great deal of trouble and even if you are not convinced of the real need of this last favour, not only the amount of money in question, but enough for me to live on for about twenty days.* You may arrange it in whatever way you wish. I have such complete confidence in the use I shall make of my time and in my will power that *I am absolutely certain my mind would be saved,* if I could lead a regular life for two or three weeks. It is one last attempt, *it is a gamble.* Risk the unknown, my dear mother, I beg you. The explanation of these last six years, so strangely and disastrously spent,—had I not enjoyed a health of mind and body that nothing could destroy—is very simple;—it may be summed up in this way: thoughtlessness, putting off the most obviously rational plans until the morrow, consequently poverty and more poverty. If you want an example—it has happened that I have had to stay in bed three days because I had no clean linen or because I had no wood. Frankly, laudanum and wine are poor remedies for unhappiness. They make time pass, but they do not remake life. And it takes money even to stupefy oneself. The last time you had the kindness to give me fifteen francs I hadn't eaten for two days—forty-eight hours.—I was forever going back and forth to Neuilly, I didn't dare confess my mistake to M. A. and I kept myself going only with the brandy which I had been given, I who detest liqueurs and am made ill by them. May such admissions—for your sake and mine—never be known by other men and by posterity! For I still think that posterity is my concern. It would seem incredible that a rational being with a good and sensitive mother should have fallen into such a plight. So this letter, addressed only to you—the first person to whom I have confided in this way—must not get out of your hands. You must find in your heart sufficient reasons to understand why such complaints can be addressed only to you and must remain unmentioned. Moreover, before writing you, I thought of everything, and *I resolved never again to see M. A.,*—if you should make the mistake of considering this last attempt as routine and similar to the others and show him this letter or tell him about it. I have just re-read these two pages and they seem strange to me. I have never dared to complain so much. I hope that you will be kind enough to attribute this excitation to the *suffering unknown to you* which I am experiencing. The apparent idleness of my life, which is in contrast to the ceaseless activity of my mind, throws me into incredible rages. I am angry with myself for my faults and I am angry with you for not believing in the sincerity of my intentions. The fact is that for several months I have been living in an abnormal state. Now—to come back to the main point of the proof which I wanted to give you—my absurd existence can be more or less explained in this way: foolish expenditure of the money assigned to my work. Time flies, necessities remain. *One last time,* wishing to put an end to this situation and believing in my will power, I am begging you to make an effort, a last gamble, as I said before,—*once more*—even if it should seem exorbitant to you and should cause you some inconvenience. I can *guess* and understand very well how intolerable and troublesome any irregular expenditures must be to a housewife, especially to you with whom I have lived; but I am in an extraordinary mental state; I wanted to see once again if my mother's money could be of any help—and I am thoroughly convinced of it; I suffer too much not to wish to put an end to my situation *once and for all.* This phrase has already occurred several times, I believe.

And indeed in spite of the terrible grief that I should feel in leaving Paris and in saying goodbye to so many beautiful dreams, I have made the sincere and firm resolution to do so, if I cannot succeed in living and doing my work for a considerable period of time with the money which I am asking of you. It would be a matter of going far away. Some people whom I met on the Ile Bourbon have been kind enough to remember me; there I shall find a position very easy to fill, a fine salary for a country where life is easy when one is once established, *and the boredom, the horrible boredom and intellectual debility of warm and blue lands.* But I shall do it as a punishment and as an expiation for my pride, if I fail to carry out my final resolutions. Don't try to determine what kind of official post it might be. For it could almost be considered domestic. It is a matter of teaching *everything,* except chemistry, physics and mathematics, to the children of a friend. But let's not speak any further of this, for the possible necessity of this solution makes me shiver. I only add that in case I should find it proper *to punish myself for having failed in all my dreams,* I should insist, since an easy and sure life would await me there, *that all debts left behind me be paid.* The very thought of this debasement and of this renunciation of my capacities makes me shudder. So I beg you not even to show this letter in confidence to M. A., so shameful do I find it for a man to doubt his own success. I have until the month of February to accept or refuse, and I intend to give you proof on New Year's Day that your money has been well spent.

Now this is my plan: it is extremely simple. About eight months ago I was asked to write two important articles which are still unfinished, one a *history of caricature,* the other a *history of sculpture.* This will mean six hundred francs and will take care of only my pressing needs. Now these articles would be mere child's play for me.

After New Year's Day I am starting a new kind of writing,—that is to say the creation of purely imaginative works—the Novel. It is needless for me to point out to you the gravity, the beauty and the infinite possibilities of that art. Since we are concerned with material questions, suffice it to say that whether *good* or *bad,* everything *sells;* it is only a matter of assiduousness.

Now I have decided that most of my creditors are so sick and tired of pressing claims which they consider unredeemable and so aware of having shamefully robbed me that I could perhaps reduce the total sum of my debt to six or eight thousand francs at the most. With care and persistence that sum is easy enough to obtain, judging from the experience I have had in all the confused activity of newspaper offices and publishing houses. Whom shall I entrust with the painful task of conferring with them—myself, M. A. or someone else? I still don't know. But when this first step has been taken and when, moreover, I have allowed a few months to elapse to prove that not only can I pay my debts, but that I can also desist from making others, I shall ask your promise to help me with your testimony and your efforts to have the free disposition of my fortune restored to me. Then too you will return those cruel letters which you mentioned and which you judge so severely. If you only knew the complication of great and small troubles that cause my perennial difficulties! At least I have tried this time to write a respectful letter which can show you the absolute clarity of my mind in my good moments; but the unfortunate thing is that I need you and that I can't approach you on any matter without appearing to be selfish.

I am very tired. I feel as if a wheel were spinning in my head.—A last time, my dear mother, I beg you in the name of my welfare.—It is the first time I have confided to you at such length so many plans that are dear and important to me. May this convince you that from time to time I consent to humble my pride before my mother!

Don't mention my age to me any more. All educations, as you know, are not the same, and that fact must be taken into consideration. The longer the time that has elapsed from the day of birth to the moment marked for success, the more quickly one must act and profit by the time that remains.

But once again, I feel that my intentions are so good that it would be truly unfortunate if I have not made myself understood. Time is flying and a few more days of idleness can ruin me. As I told you, I have so abused my strength that I have come to the uttermost limits of my own patience and I am incapable of a last great effort unless I am given a little help.

If by any chance you should think of asking M. A. for money, don't tell him why, and since it is to you I have turned *let me have the pleasure of receiving this favour from you alone.* Reply immediately; *for three days I have been getting up my courage to write you and have not dared.* You can trust the messenger.—Something else. For a long time now you have been trying to exclude me completely from your presence. I suppose you hope that this exclusion will hasten the end of my difficulties. Whatever my mistakes may have been, it is not a crime to want to see you, and do you think my spirit is strong enough to endure perpetual solitude? I am *pledging my word not to come and see you until I have good news to bring you.* But from that time on I beg to see you and to be well received and in such a way that your manner, your expression and your words will protect me in your house against everyone.

Goodbye. I am happy I have written you.

Charles

To Madame Aupick
Sunday, December 5, 1847

I thank you with all my heart. Never did help come more opportunely. You may be certain that I realize full well the value of the money. Your letter did not cause me less pain, I am sure, than mine must have caused you. I know all that and I have guessed everything.

But I hope one day to return *everything* to you; don't think that *by that* I am referring especially and brutally to money; *I want to return to you more than your money.*—If you are kind enough to write me, as you let me understand you would, my address, which you may not know, is 36 rue de Babylone.—What you have sent me will suffice—*of necessity.* I understand the value of this sum and I shall have to make sure that I use it to the best advantage.

Charles Baudelaire Defayis

Do not give my address to anyone.

The passionate love that Baudelaire had once felt for Jeanne Duval seems to have subsided by 1845 as letters to his mother and stepfather will confirm. In the need that he felt for feminine companionship the poet turned to a young actress, Marie Daubrun, best known for her rôle in *La Belle aux cheveux d'or* (1853), a title borrowed by the author of *Les Fleurs du Mal* for the poem he later called *L'Irréparable.*

Baudelaire apparently met Marie about 1847 in the studio of Emile Deroy where the lovely green-eyed actress was posing for a picture. From 1850 to 1860 she was to play an important rôle in his life and for a time (perhaps in 1854 and again somewhere between 1855 and 1859) she seems to have become his mistress. Meanwhile, Baudelaire did everything in his power to help Marie advance in her career, even soliciting the support of George Sand whose ideas and works he despised.[30]

45

When Banville replaced Baudelaire in the affections of Marie, the rift produced in the friendship of the two poets was neither very serious nor of long duration. Marie finally chose between the two in 1859 when she accompanied Banville, ill and almost dying, to Nice. The critic Feuillerat believes that the grief and indignation occasioned by Marie's decision inspired Baudelaire to write the enigmatic *A une Madonne* in which 'irresistible infatuation' mingles strangely with 'exasperated revolt'.[31]

Baudelaire's feeling for Jeanne, as revealed in his poetry, had been passionate and deeply sensual. With a love that was sometimes ecstatic and tender, but more frequently bitter and despairing, he had adored the 'strange deity dark as night', whose 'black poison' raced in his veins. To her lover, Jeanne more often than not represented all that was evil. She was 'a pitiless demon', a 'monster of indolent mien', a 'queen of sins', an 'accursed being', a 'vile animal'.

For Marie, Baudelaire seems to have felt a more 'pure emotion', as he describes it in the only letter to her that is extant. Though his poems show occasional notes of sensual passion when thoughts of the actress 'torment and arouse obscure desires', the feeling is usually one of tenderness and quiet affection. Marie is addressed as 'madonna', 'sister', and 'child' and is even enjoined to play the rôle of comforter and mother.

Whatever the nature of Baudelaire's feeling, however, there is little doubt that Marie inspired a number of important poems to be found in *Les Fleurs du Mal: L'Irréparable, Chant d'automne, Causerie, A une Madonne, Le Beau navire, Le Chat,* (Dans ma cervelle . . .), *Le Poison, L'Invitation au voyage, Ciel brouillé,* and perhaps even *A Celle qui est trop gaie,* usually attributed to Mme. Sabatier.

To Madame Marie Daubrun

[No date]

Madame,

Is it really possible that I am not to see you again? That is the vital question for me, for I have reached the point where your absence has already become an enormous deprivation for my heart.

When I learned that you were giving up sitting and that I, unwittingly, was the cause, I felt a strange sadness.

I wanted to write you, although I do not set much store by letters; one almost always regrets them. But I am risking nothing, since I have made up my mind to give myself up to you forever.

Do you realize that our long conversation on Thursday was most extraordinary? That very conversation left me in a new state of mind and is the occasion for this letter.

A man said: 'I love you,' and pleaded, and a woman answered: 'Love you? Never! One alone has my love and anyone who came after him would be most ill-fated; he would gain only my indifference and my contempt.' And that same man, merely to have the pleasure of looking longer into your eyes, allowed you to speak to him about another, speak only about him, become passionately excited talking and thinking of him. All those confidences of yours had a very strange effect on me, for now you are no longer a woman to be desired, but a woman to be loved for her frankness, for her passion, for her freshness, for her youth and for her impulsiveness.

I have lost a great deal through these explanations, since you were so positive that I had to yield at once. But you, Madame, you have gained a great deal: you have inspired in me profound respect and esteem. Remain that way always and guard carefully that passion which makes you so beautiful and so happy.

Come back again, I implore you, and I shall become gentle and humble in my desires. I deserved your contempt when I answered you that I would be content with crumbs. I was lying. Oh! if you knew how beautiful you were that evening! I do not dare pay you compliments, that would be so commonplace . . . But your eyes, your lips, your whole being, vibrant with life, now come before my closed eyes,—and I know only too well that this is final.

Come back, I beg you on my knees; I do not say that you will find me without love, but yet you will be unable to keep my thoughts from straying to your arms, to your beautiful hands, to your eyes that reflect your whole life, to your whole adorable sensual being; no, I know that you will not be able to do that; but have no fear, you are for me an object of worship and it is impossible for me to defile you; I shall always see you as radiant as before. Your whole being is so good, so beautiful, and so sweet to breathe! You are for me life and movement, not so much because of your vivacity and your impassioned nature, as because of your eyes which can inspire only immortal love in a poet. How can I ever tell you how much I love your eyes and how much I appreciate your beauty? It holds two contradictory charms which in you are not contradictory—the charm of a child and that of a woman. Oh! believe me when I tell you from my innermost heart: you are an adorable creature, and I love you very deeply. I am bound to you forever by a pure emotion. In spite of your wish, you will henceforth be my talisman and my strength. I love you, Marie, that is undeniable; but the love which I feel for you is that of a Christian for his God; never give an earthly and often shameful name to this incorporeal and mysterious worship, to this sweet and chaste attraction which unites my soul to yours against your will. That would be a sacrilege.—I was dead, you gave me life again. Oh! you do not know all I owe you! I have drawn unknown joys from the depths of your tender glance; your eyes have initiated me into the happiness of the soul in all its most perfect and most delicate form. You are henceforth my only queen, my passion, and my beauty; you are that part of my being which a spiritual essence has formed.

Through you, Marie, I shall be strong and great. Like Petrarch, I shall immortalize my Laura. Be my guardian Angel, my Muse, and my Madonna, and lead me along the path of the Beautiful.

Please answer me, if only a single word, I implore you, only a single word. In everyone's life there are days of uncertainty and of decision when an expression of friendship, a glance, a few scribbled lines impel one to some stupid action or to some splendid folly! I swear to you that I have reached that point. A word from you will be a blessed object to be contemplated and committed to memory. If you knew how much you are loved! See, I am kneeling at your feet; one word, say but one word . . . No, you will not say it.

He is indeed happy, a thousand times happy, the man whom you have chosen among all, you so full of wisdom and beauty, you, so desirable in talent, mind, and heart! What woman could ever take your place? I do not dare ask you for a visit, you would refuse. I prefer to wait.

I shall wait for years, and, when you see that you are loved stubbornly, but with respect, and with complete unselfishness, you will remember then that you began by ill-treating me and you will admit that you were unkind.

In a word, I am not free to refuse the blows which my idol is pleased to inflict on me. It was your pleasure to send me away, it is my pleasure to adore you. That question is settled.

Ch. Baudelaire
15, cité d'Orléans

PART THREE

An Interlude

My intoxication in 1848.

An Interlude

OUR knowledge of Baudelaire's activities in 1848 depends mainly on the testimony of his friends and associates. Only one long letter and four notes are known to have been written by him, and none of these throws any real light on the minor rôle he played in the Revolution. Some years later, in an effort to analyse his state of mind in 1848, Baudelaire himself jotted down a few revealing notes in his *Journaux intimes*: 'My intoxication in 1848. What was the nature of that intoxication? Taste for vengeance; *natural* pleasure in destruction.—Literary intoxication; recollection of things read.'

The taste for vengeance to which Baudelaire refers was presumably motivated by his intense dislike for his stepfather, who personified in his mind the society that had rejected him and failed to recognize his genius. The fact that General Aupick was constantly winning honours while he himself had yet to achieve any real success only added to his resentment. Baudelaire's letter to his mother in December of 1847 had plainly revealed his feeling of ignominious failure. Ironically enough, it was in that very month that General Aupick was named commandant of the Ecole Polytechnique. All the pent-up hatred in his heart must have been loosed, when in February during the first few days of the Revolution, he went marching through the streets, brandishing a new rifle and shouting, 'We must go and shoot General Aupick!' [32]

The '*natural* pleasure in destruction' which Baudelaire admits led him to take part in the Revolution was apparently related to his idea of sin and evil and to his belief that man's pleasure in doing evil derives from the conscious knowledge of his wrongdoing. A note in *Pauvre Belgique* seems to further explain the 'pleasure' to which he refers and to relate it, incidentally, to his ideas regarding the pleasures of love: '*In my case*, when I consent to be a republican, *I am doing evil, in the full knowledge of the fact.* . . . I say: *Long live the Revolution!* as I would say: *Long live Destruction! long live Expiation, long live Punishment! long live Death!*' [33]

As for the 'literary intoxication' to which he alludes, Baudelaire may have been referring to the revolutionary articles which he had read in socialist newspapers, such as *La Démocratie pacifique*. He may likewise have been referring to the influence of his literary friends and associates, such as Thoré, Proudhon, and Pierre Dupont. In February Baudelaire even joined with Champfleury and Toubin in the publication of a revolutionary newspaper, *Le Salut public*, hastily composed at the Café Turlot.[34] However, the paper abruptly ceased publication after two issues (February 27 and March 1 or 2), mainly for want of financial support.

During the early 'June days' Baudelaire was once again seized by revolutionary enthusiasm and succeeded in alarming his more prudent friends by shouting revolutionary sentiments with reckless abandon in the streets.

But though Baudelaire was carried away from time to time by his revolutionary intoxication, he was never completely consistent in his views. In fact, from April to June he was associated with the conservative newspaper, *La Tribune Nationale*, and in October he even enjoyed a brief career as editor-in-chief of a conservative provincial newspaper in Châteauroux, known as *Le Représentant de l'Indre*.[35] Perhaps it was an effort to explain or rationalize this inconsistency that prompted him to affirm in the same passage of *Pauvre Belgique* the desirability of being both 'victim and executioner . . . in order to feel the Revolution in two ways!' and of deserting one cause in order to experience what it meant to serve another. It was only after Napoleon's *coup d'état* on December 2, 1851, that Baudelaire irrevocably relinquished democratic ideas and movements.[36]

When it came to Baudelaire's attention that his trip to Indre had been made possible through his stepfather's generosity, he wrote a letter of acknowledgement which could only have further annoyed the general. For several months M. Aupick and his wife had been living in Constantinople where the general was serving as envoy extraordinary and minister plenipotentiary. Either before they left Paris or in the months following, Charles seems to have quarrelled with his mother. The fact that he wrote no letters to her in Constantinople and that he failed even to mention her name to his stepfather would indicate that there had been a complete estrangement. The eminent Baudelaire scholar, Jacques Crépet, believes that Mme. Aupick's instructions to Ancelle date from this period: 'I refuse to make up our differences. I cannot and I will not excuse so quickly the harsh words that he has dared to address to me, his mother. I shall grant him my affection only when he is worthy of it. Let him refrain hereafter from writing to me.'

To M. Aupick [36a]

Paris, December 8, 1848

The day before yesterday, M. Ancelle told me that my trip to Indre, which I made some time ago, had been paid by you without my knowledge, and it was not to his kindness, as I had believed, but to you that

I owed the money. M. Ancelle was wrong to say nothing and to hide this gift from me in the first place; for, to begin with, I would not have blushed in the least to receive this money from you, and, in the second place, if he had said to me: 'I received a sum of five hundred francs for you,' instead of squandering it little by little on a fruitless trip, I could have spent it more usefully in a lump sum while remaining in Paris.

I confess that I was as greatly astonished by M. Ancelle's admission regarding the gift, as I was by his care to conceal it at first. I was, I admit, very greatly surprised that you deigned to think of me once more and to concern yourself with my everlasting financial worries, especially after the harsh manner with which you received me a few days before your departure.

With that excitable obstinacy, that violence which is peculiar to you, you maltreated me merely because of a poor woman whom *I have loved for a long time only from a sense of duty, that's all.* It is strange that you, who so often have talked to me at such great length about spiritual feelings and about duty, have not understood this strange liaison, in which I have nothing to gain and in which atonement and the wish to repay devotion play the leading rôle. However numerous the infidelities of a woman may be, however hard her character, when she has shown flashes of good will and devotion, that is enough to make an unselfish man, a poet especially, feel obliged to recompense her. I ask your pardon for insisting on this point, but I have felt deeply hurt that you didn't understand from the very first the quite simple meaning of my request. If I have written nothing since that time regarding this matter, it was owing first to my fear of afflicting you without a sufficiently developed preliminary explanation and second, to the necessity of postponing projects which require, in order to be accomplished, a state of stability and tranquillity greater than that which I have at present. But nevertheless I come back to this and I feel obliged to give you these explanations: today at the age of twenty-eight years less four months, possessed with an immense poetic ambition, separated forever from *respectable people* by my tastes and by my principles, what difference does it make if, while building my literary dreams, I also accomplish a *duty*, or what I consider a duty, at the expense of vulgar ideas of honour, money, and fortune? Please observe that I am by no means begging for assent; it is only the admission that I could well be right; and, in the second place, that if the matter were left entirely to my will and if some unforeseen event or reflection should happen to thwart it, I could well compromise with myself and drop my projects.

Now I must have the courage to tell you bluntly that *if I myself have never thought of asking you for money*—since you were the one to take the initiative, which made me realize you were still thinking of me—I have imagined that you might still be able to come to my aid. New Year's Day will soon be here; that is the time when I must change my lodging. With what I am to get from M. Ancelle and what I shall receive elsewhere, if you were able between now and then to add 250 francs, or, if that is absolutely impossible, to authorize him to lend them to me for you, I should carry out several projects which I have had on my mind for a long time, among others to rescue my poor dear manuscripts which are everlastingly being held; provided they are still intact.

That is the cruel thing which I had to tell you.

The remaining 23 days will give you time to reply. I should be happy if you would be kind enough to write me a few lines yourself and not have M. Ancelle transmit to me either your decision or the thoughts which you may want to write me.

The only thing that interests me as far as you are concerned is to know how your crossing was, if you are well, and if your health is better than it was here.

As for me, despite the fact that literature is less popular than ever, I am still the same, that is to say I am convinced that my debts will be paid and that my destiny will be gloriously fulfilled.

Another reason which would make me happy if you were able to comply with my request is that I very much fear a revolutionary uprising, and that nothing is more deplorable than to be absolutely without money at such a time.

Goodbye. I presume you will not be angry with me because of my letter. You will doubtless be where you are for a long time. I am sure you will not be recalled by a new government ... Perhaps if I am richer, I shall go to Constantinople in a year; for my passion for travel never leaves me.

Charles

The year 1849 was to be strangely blank in Baudelaire's literary career. Nothing was to come from his pen until June 1850 when he published two poems in *Le Magasin des Familles: Châtiment de l'Orgueil* and *Le Vin des honnêtes hommes*, later known as *l'Ame du Vin*.

Baudelaire's personal life in 1849 seems to have been no less mysterious. A fragment of a letter addressed to Ancelle indicates that he had gone to Dijon for some unknown reason—perhaps to escape his creditors, perhaps to find peace and quiet in which to work. In his biography of the poet, Asselineau mentions the fact that Baudelaire went to Dijon to edit a government newspaper. Since no evidence has ever been found to support his claim, it now seems fairly evident that Asselineau confused Baudelaire's literary activities in Dijon with his journalistic venture in Châteauroux.

The letter to Ancelle furnishes no information relating to Baudelaire's stay in Dijon, but it does reveal a complete reversal of the revolutionary ideas which he had held early in 1848.

To Ancelle

Dijon, December 1849

. . . Madier de Montjau, who was returning from some legal triumph, after winning some sort of political trial, passed through here; he came to see us.—You know he is considered a remarkably talented young man. He is one of the great minds of democracy. He was pitiable! He was playing the rôle of an ardent revolutionary. I talked to him about the socialism of the peasants,—an inevitable socialism, ferocious, stupid, bestial, a socialism of the torch or of the scythe. He got frightened; that cooled him off.—He recoiled at my logic. He is a perfect fool, or rather a very vulgar opportunist.

[No signature]

1850 found Baudelaire still in Dijon, whence in January he wrote a long letter of complaint to Ancelle. Everything had gone wrong for Baudelaire. He had been ill—perhaps a recurrence of the syphilis contracted many years before. He was dissatisfied with the copy of his poems made to his order by a calligrapher in Paris. He was exasperated by Ancelle's careless delay in sending him his monthly allowance. He was irritated by life in his dreary hotel room in Dijon and tormented by his inability to pay his creditors and make his escape to better quarters. Small wonder that even years later Baudelaire could not refer to Dijon without 'grinding his teeth', as Asselineau has recounted in his biography.

Much of Baudelaire's letter to Ancelle is so filled with financial details that it is of little interest to the reader. Its real importance lies in the expression of the author's attitude toward Ancelle. Though Baudelaire is almost brutal in his criticism of his guardian, it is nevertheless apparent that he feels a genuine affection for him. There seems little doubt that Baudelaire's break with his mother left him distraught and unhappy and that his need for her maternal love and protection brought him closer both to Jeanne and Ancelle.

To Ancelle
Dijon, Thursday, January 10, 1850
Read with care

I have been rather seriously ill as you know. My stomach has been somewhat upset by laudanum; but it's not the first time, and it is strong enough to recover.

Jeanne came yesterday morning and spoke quite at length of her conversation with you. I have had nothing but trouble now for a long time. I wasn't surprised then to hear things which prove that you understand nothing at all about my life; but more of that later.

. . . .

Jeanne, whom I've hounded at length about her talk with you, maintains you told her that if she wrote you and proved the need of an advance, you would doubtless make it. *That is strange and quite humiliating for me:* how do you expect one to throw away money in a small town where work is the sole remedy for boredom? I don't know what Jeanne will do, or whether the wish to leave this hotel will prompt her to do something which I consider improper, but I repeat that if you count two hundred francs *for January,* which I have not received, and two hundred for February, you are not making me an advance, you are not doing me any favour, you are not departing from our agreement. If you knew how tiring it is for me to constantly come back to these cursed questions of money! That will come to an end some day.

You told Jeanne a great many other things, but I no longer have the heart to reproach you. You are a great big child. Moreover, I have often enough rebuked you for your sentimentality and proved the needlessness of your pity for my mother. Leave all that aside forever and, if I am somewhat crackbrained in that respect, pity me and leave me in peace. The same holds true for Jeanne. There are many other things, but let's go on. If you should happen to see Mlle. Lemer again, please don't trifle with her any more, don't talk so much and be more serious. I have been accustomed to tell you plainly everything I think, so you mustn't hold that against me.

. . . .

Your position with regard to me is strange. It involves not only a legal relationship, but also one of sentiment, so to speak. You can't possibly be unaware of that. I, who am so little inclined to sentimentality, have not been able to escape that fact. The sombre solitude that I have created around myself and *which has only bound me more closely to Jeanne* has led me to consider you as something important in my life. I'm coming to the point. If your relationship with me is inevitably such, what is the meaning of your failure to understand my interests on many occasions? *What is the meaning of your partiality toward my mother whom you know to be guilty?* What is the meaning of so much drivel, of your egoistic maxims, of your incivilities, your impertinences? It's quite true that I have retaliated, but all this is not reasonable. Our relationship must improve. This long absence will not be bad from that standpoint. Moreover, *for every sin there should be forgiveness*, which you know I translate: there is nothing irreparable. . . .

[No signature]

Baudelaire must have returned to Paris early in 1850, for in May he wrote several notes to Gérard de Nerval arranging for theatre tickets for himself, his mistress and Poulet-Malassis. Too poor to afford separate establishments, he was evidently living with Jeanne, who had assumed the name of Caroline Dardard; at least he gave her name and address, 46 rue Pigalle, as his postal address. In January 1851, Mme. Aupick, apparently prompted by some report of her son's penury, sent a sum of money to Ancelle and asked that it be given to Charles. Indignant at his mother's refusal to communicate directly with him, Baudelaire wrote a letter in which he made no attempt to hide his bitterness and in which he addressed Mme. Aupick very formally with the pronoun *vous*.

To Madame Aupick
Thursday, [January] 9, 1851

Several months have passed since I decided to write to you. Several times I have tried, and several times I have been obliged to give up the attempt. My endless troubles and the solitude of my thought have made me somewhat hard and also, no doubt, very clumsy. I should like to be able to express myself more gently, but even if your pride should find it unseemly, I hope that your reason will understand my good intentions and the merit I have shown in taking this step, which formerly would have been so pleasant to me, but which, in the circumstances that you have created, must irrevocably be my last attempt.

That you should have deprived me of your affection and of all the relations that every man has the right to expect from his mother, concerns your conscience, and perhaps also that of your husband. That is something which I shall doubtless have to determine later on.

But there is a certain delicacy which warns us that we should not pretend to be obliging to persons whom we are insulting, or at least, who are doing us no harm. For that is a new insult. You can guess that I am referring to some money received by M. Ancelle. What! He receives money, without a letter for me, without a word stipulating or advising its use. Just remember that you have lost all right to *philanthropy where I am concerned*, for I cannot speak of maternal sentiment. It is to your interest obviously to show human sentiments to someone other than me. You have feelings of remorse. For my part, I do not wish to accept the expression of your repentance unless it takes another form, or to use plainer terms, *if you do not immediately become a mother again in every respect*, I shall be obliged to have a bailiff arrange, through M. Ancelle, that all acceptance of money coming from you be cut off, and I shall take measures to assure the strict observance of my wishes.

I don't believe it is necessary to emphasize the importance of this letter and of your reply which should be sent TO ME, TO ME, do you understand? My future conduct with regard to you and also my conduct with regard to myself depends on your reply or on your silence. In exactly three months I am going to be *30 years* of age. That arouses in me many reflections that are easy to guess. Thus *morally* a part of my future life is in your hands. May you write me what I hope!

If you deign to understand the importance of this letter, you will doubtless add in your answer very precise details about your health.

Since you have such a great influence over M. Ancelle, you should tell him when you write him to make life less difficult and more endurable for me.

I wish, I *insist* that he should have no part in the question that I am discussing with you today. I shall not accept any answer from his lips.

Charles Baudelaire

In June 1851 the Aupicks returned to Paris on their way to Madrid where General Aupick was to assume the post of ambassador. Through Ancelle Mme. Aupick had made arrangements to meet her son and to effect a reconciliation. Ancelle had promised Mme. Aupick that his ward would go to visit her, but Charles protested that his dignity forbade him to set foot in her house. At the same time he told Ancelle that respect for his mother prevented him from receiving her in the presence of one she hated, an obvious reference to Jeanne. He suggested that his mother come to Neuilly where he could be alone with her.

Mme. Aupick was deeply shocked and distressed to see her son after her absence of three years. Years later in a letter to Asselineau she recalled her surprise: 'When I came to Paris to spend two months between embassies in Constantinople and Madrid, in what a cruel position I found him! What destitution! And I, his mother, with so much love in my heart, so much good will for him, I could not rescue him.' [37]

The meeting between mother and son resulted in a reconciliation which did much to dispel Baudelaire's feeling of depression. Five days later in a calmer and happier mood he writes his mother again, addressing her with the familiar *tu*.

To Madame Aupick

Thursday, June 12, 1851

My dear mother, I should be happy to see you MONDAY the 16th. *Tomorrow, the day after tomorrow and Sunday, I am compelled to work.* I have nothing special to tell you; it is only for the pleasure of seeing you.

If you can come, try to arrange to spend a rather long time. *If you can't come*, let me know by letter, because otherwise I *would wait for you* indefinitely.

If in your unpacking you have found the *famous pipe and the tobacco*, do bring them.

Charles

In July Mme. Aupick left for Madrid to rejoin her husband who had preceded her there a few weeks earlier. By the end of August Baudelaire was already in financial difficulties and was obliged to write his mother for help. He had bought furniture for his new apartment on the money which he expected to earn from the publication of an article on caricature. The work was not immediately accepted and Baudelaire found himself with only twenty francs in his pocket.

As usual, his apologies are mingled with self-reproach and with the confession of his incapacity for concentrated effort, a confession which is confirmed by the reports of all those who knew him best.

To Madame Aupick
Saturday, August 30, 1851

Dear mother, I'm afraid I am going to cause you some annoyance. I had promised to write twice a month, and now I have been in my new quarters for six weeks and I still haven't written to you. That comes from my vanity in wanting to send you some good news in my first letter. Well, there is nothing, nothing, or almost nothing. Since I make a point of keeping you informed about everything I do, I am sending you a small brochure for which I was well paid and which you will read because I wrote it, for otherwise I do not attach any importance to it.[38]

. . . .

I am very disturbed and very sad. It must be admitted that man is a very feeble animal, since habit plays so large a rôle in virtue. *I have had all kinds of trouble in getting back to work*. I ought to erase the word BACK, for I believe I have never really started. What an extraordinary thing! A few days ago I had in my hands some of Balzac's early manuscripts. No one can possibly imagine how blundering, how foolish, how STUPID that great man was in his youth. And yet he came to have, to acquire, so to speak, not only grandiose conceptions, but enormous intellectual powers as well. But he worked CONSTANTLY. It is certainly very consoling to think that through work one obtains not only money, but also indisputable talent. But at the age of thirty Balzac had for some years gotten into the habit of working constantly, until now I have nothing in common with him except debts and projects.

I am really very sad. You will doubtless read with pleasure or rather with the vain eyes of a mother the voluminous work [apparently an article on caricature] which I shall send you *next month*; but after all, it doesn't amount to much. You will see some surprising pages no doubt, but the rest is only a mass of contradictions and divagations; as for any real erudition, it has only the appearance. And next? Next, what shall I show you? My book of poetry? I know that a few years ago it would have been sufficient to establish a man's reputation. It would have caused a devil of a stir. But today conditions, circumstances, everything has changed. And if my book falls flat, what next? the drama, the novel, perhaps even history. But you don't know what days of doubt are. Sometimes it seems to me I have become too rational and that I have read too much to conceive anything original and true. I am too learned and not hardworking enough. But perhaps in a week, I'll be full of confidence and imagination. As I write, I realize I wouldn't admit this to a friend for anything in the world.

But there is no going back. During the course of 1852 I must get rid of my incapacity and before *New Year's Day I must have paid some debts and published my verses.* I shall end by learning that sentence by heart.

Speaking of Balzac, I attended the première of *Mercadet le faiseur.* The same people who tormented that poor man so much are insulting him after his death. If you read the French papers, you must have imagined that it was something dreadful. It is, quite simply, an admirable work. I shall send it to you.

Reply IMMEDIATELY. Do whatever is necessary to keep your letter from being lost. Tell me how I should write you. Add some details about your journey and ESPECIALLY about your health. Don't forget to *date* your letters, as you always do. And now let me express the profound joy, reassuring to my conscience, which I continue to feel as a result of having renewed with my mother the natural relations which should never have been interrupted.

A warm embrace.

Charles

PART FOUR

Joseph de Maistre and Edgar Allan Poe

de Maistre and Edgar Poe taught me how to think.

Joseph de Maistre and
Edgar Allan Poe

EIGHTEEN-FIFTY-TWO was to be a momentous year in the life of
Baudelaire. It was in that year that his admiration for Edgar Allan
Poe, first felt in 1847, was renewed and intensified until it became a
dominating passion never again to leave him. At the same time, life
with Jeanne was becoming more intolerable than ever. So desperate had
Baudelaire become that he finally admits to his mother the full truth
of the situation in words which strikingly recall the prediction made
by Samuel Cramer five years earlier: 'an implacable and grave voice
whispers in our ear that passions are deceiving, that a beautiful face is
the result of our myopia and a lovely soul the product of our ignorance,
that there must come a day when the idol, to more clear-sighted eyes, is
an object, not of hate, but of surprise and scorn.' [39]

To Madame Aupick
Saturday, March 27, 1852
2 p.m.

It is two o'clock; if I want my letter to leave today, I can spend only
two and a half hours writing you, and I have a great many things to
tell you. I am writing you from a café opposite the General Post Office
in the midst of all the noise of billiards and other games in order to
have more peace and a chance to think. You will understand all this
shortly.

How does it happen that in nine months one can't find a single day
to write to one's mother, even to thank her? It is really incredible! And
every day to think of it and every day to say to oneself: I am going to
write. And the days all fly away filled with innumerable fruitless
errands or with composing sickly articles hastily written in order to
earn some money. You will find in this letter a few things which I am
sure will please you and will prove to you that even if I am still suffering a great deal as a result of certain faults, my mind is growing rather
than going to seed; you will find other things which will grieve you.
But haven't you encouraged me to tell you everything, and, after all,

to whom would you have me complain? There are days when solitude exasperates me beyond measure.

My letter will be very confused. That is the inevitable consequence of my state of mind and of the little time that I have at my disposal. I shall divide it into sections as it were, as I remember some of the most important things which I have to tell you and which I have been turning over in my mind for a long time.

I am enclosing in this letter some articles of mine which I have clipped out of a periodical so as not to make my letter overweight. I shouldn't mind having you read them when you have time. I seriously doubt that you will understand them entirely; I don't mean to be rude in saying this. But they are very *particularly Parisian*, and I doubt that they can be understood outside of the *milieux* for which and about which they were written. *Les drames et les romans honnêtes*, marked with pencil: 0, 2, 3, 4, 5, 6. *L'école païenne:* 6 [*sic*]. *Les deux crépuscules:* 7, 8.

I have done something else which you will like better and with which I am quite satisfied. Since I can't enclose books in a letter, you will have to be good enough to rent or buy, I don't know which, from M. Monnier (reading room or bookshop?), who is the correspondent for the *Revue de Paris* in Madrid, the issue which appeared in Paris March 1st and the one which will appear in Paris March 31st and which will probably arrive in Madrid April 5th or 6th. I have discovered an American author [Poe] to whom I feel incredibly drawn, and I have written two articles on his life and his works. They are written with enthusiasm; but you will doubtless find in them some indications of a very extraordinary excitement. That is the result of the painful and mad life which I am leading; moreover, it was written at night; sometimes working from *ten o'clock to ten o'clock*. I am forced to work at night in order to have peace and to avoid the insufferable annoyances inflicted on me by the woman [Jeanne] with whom I'm living. Sometimes I leave home in order to be able to write, and I go to the library or to a reading room, or to a wineshop or to a café, as I have done today. As a result I'm in a state of perpetual irritation. It certainly isn't possible to do long works in this way.—I had forgotten much of my English which made the task even more difficult. *But now I know it very well*. I think that I have finally completed it *satisfactorily*.

Don't take it into your head to give yourself the small maternal pleasure of reading all this before answering me. *Answer me first*, if

only three lines; and put off until the next day, or the day after, the
advice or the ideas which my letter will suggest to you.

This letter leaves this evening, the 27th
— 28th
the 29th it will be in Bayonne.

I suppose
that it will arrive in Madrid the 1st, which is hard to believe, and that
you will answer me April 2nd.

I can have your answer the 7th.

I understood nothing of what you told me in one of your letters
about *the mail.*—Those *four* poor letters and three odd volumes of
Racine are all the treasures that I have kept which belonged to you,
you who have sacrificed yourself so often and have let nothing turn you
against your son.—I went to the post office and they told me that the
embassy mail doesn't arrive until the 10th. And so it is impossible for
me to make use of it and the same is true for you; you must therefore
send me your reply in care of Mme. Olivier,—*I shall pay the postage*—and
not in care of M. Ancelle; he would be apt to wait two days, or even
longer, before informing me. I am not asking you to write to me *at my
home address. In addition to the fact that Jeanne knows your handwriting*
—I don't have a single drawer which can be locked!—will I ever know
what fancy may strike me or where I shall sleep? It has happened that
I have fled from my home for two weeks at a time in order to refresh
my mind. At the post office they couldn't give me any exact information about the time required for mail service between Bayonne and
Madrid and they told me I couldn't prepay my letter, although at the
same time they said that the embassy had the right to refuse it as lacking postage. I don't understand anything about it. Also, to be sure that
it reaches you I am writing on the envelope: *personal and confidential*
with my initials C. B. If M. Aupick should guess, he can't consider it
impertinent.—To get back to my business.—I am going to explain
myself very quickly, but I shall do it in such a way that these few words
will contain many ideas for you who know me.

Jeanne has become an obstacle not only to my happiness—that
would be a trifling matter, for I too can sacrifice my pleasures and I
have proved it—but also to the perfecting of my mind. The nine months
which have just elapsed have been a decisive test. The important duties
which I have to accomplish—payment of my debts, winning my titles
to fortune, gaining fame, making amends for all the griefs I have caused

67

you—all these can never be accomplished under such conditions. *Formerly she had some good qualities,* but she has *lost* them; and I have gained in clear-sightedness. Is it at all possible TO LIVE WITH A PERSON who has no gratitude for your efforts, who hinders them through her clumsiness or her constant malice, who considers you only as her servant and her property, with whom it is impossible to exchange a word on politics or literature, a creature *who refuses to learn anything,* although you had offered to teach her yourself, a creature WHO DOESN'T ADMIRE ME and who isn't even interested in my studies, who would throw my manuscripts in the fire if that would bring her more money than having them published, who sends away my cat which was my only diversion at home and brings in dogs *because* the sight of dogs makes me ill, who doesn't know or want to understand *that to be penurious for only ONE month* would allow me to finish a long book, thanks to this momentary respite? Is that possible? I have tears of shame and rage in my eyes while I am writing you this; and really I am very glad that there are no weapons at home; I am thinking of the times when it is impossible for me to be reasonable and of the terrible night when I cut her head open with a table. That is what I have found, where ten months ago I thought I would find comfort and peace. To sum up all my thoughts in one and to give you an idea of all my reflections, I believe *once and for all* that the woman who has suffered and given birth to a child is the only one who is the equal of man. To beget children is the only thing which gives moral intelligence to the female. As for young women without status and without children, they show nothing but coquetry, implacability, and elegant debauchery.—I had to come to a decision, however. For four months I have been thinking about it. But what was I to do? A frightful pride outweighed even my suffering: not to leave this woman without giving her a fairly substantial sum of money. But where was I to obtain it, since the money that I was earning and that I should have saved was disappearing day by day and since my mother, to whom I no longer dared write without having some good news to report, couldn't offer me so large an amount, not having it herself. You see I have thought it all out. And yet I must leave. *But I must leave* FOREVER.

This is what I have decided: I shall begin at the beginning; that is to say by going away. Since I can't offer her a large sum, I shall give her money a few more times which will be no trouble for me, since *I am earning rather easily* and since by working assiduously I can earn even more. BUT I SHALL NEVER SEE HER. She may do what she wants. Let her go to hell, if she wishes. I have wasted 10 years of my life in this struggle. All the illusions of my youth have disappeared. There is nothing left but a bitterness which may last forever.

And what is to become of me? I don't want to set up a small apartment, because even now it would involve too many dangers, in spite of the fact that I have really changed. A furnished room in a hotel 'repels me. While waiting for something better, I have decided to take refuge with a doctor who is a friend of mine and who has offered me for 150 francs, instead of the 240 which he asks of others, a beautiful room, a lovely garden, excellent food, a cold bath and two douches a day. It is a German treatment which is very helpful for an excited condition such as mine.

I want to take advantage of the end of the quarter and of the moving on April 7th—*our apartment has already been rented by our successors*—to take my leave. But I haven't a cent. *I have written several things which will be printed next month*, BUT AFTER THE 8*th*. Do you understand the catastrophic situation now? What shall I do? I have said to myself: M. Ancelle may not have received a cent from my mother. Perhaps too she has *absolutely nothing*, since on leaving Paris she warned me that she would have greater expenses than before. But at least she can *send me* a note which will authorize M. Ancelle to give me a rather large sum to effect all these changes in one day. Later on she will return it little by little, *if that is possible*.—Except for the deficit which you knew about before you left, I have adhered *to the precise and regular conditions* stipulated by M. Ancelle.—This, my dear mother, is what I dare ask of you in circumstances SO DECISIVE. *There are two back quarters in addition to all the bills that have to be settled on leaving a district, meat, wine, groceries, etc.*, amounting to 400. Now it would be advisable to arrive at my doctor's with 150 francs to pay for the first month in advance. Finally I should like to buy a few *books*—the lack of books is unbearable—and a few clothes. Despite my suffering I can't keep from laughing at the sermon you preached me in your last letter on the correlation between human dignity and dress, since it happens that the one suit you bought me nine months ago is all that covers the animal that is writing you.—Lastly, I should like to be able to placate *a very old creditor*, who can get me into *very serious* trouble. All this doubtless amounts to a great deal, but please notice, my dear mother, that some money, *no matter how little*, is most urgent. In a pinch, I would do what I have done so often, *I would deprive myself of all that is not immediately indispensable.*

It is now twenty minutes after four. I am in a hurry, I shall go to the home of Mad. Olivier on April 7th. I beg you, I implore you not to speak to M. Ancelle in confidence about the use of this money. *I confide to him only what I want to confide.* But you treat M. Ancelle like a brother or a father, which doesn't suit me at all. This letter is serious enough, I imagine, to give you a safe guarantee of the good use of this money. At the worst, a THOUSAND FRANCS would be sufficient. But with only four hundred I should still carry out my plan. However, I wouldn't even have five francs for my personal needs and I would have to wait for my small April earnings to apply as I go along to my purchases and to the clinic.

I shall write you again tomorrow, for I have enough ideas in my head to fill twenty pages. But don't wait for my second letter before answering me, and postpone, if you can't do otherwise, the ideas or advice that will come to you; think first of the letter that I should like to show M. Ancelle. Tomorrow, or the day after, I shall try to write you something more comforting and amusing. One word more: M. Ancelle told me about your *butterflies*; the good man didn't understand what that meant. But I understood. So take care of your eyes; get all the medical advice you can. Remember that some day I may be living with you and that the sight of a blind mother, while increasing my duties, which would be a small matter, would cause me constant grief.

Some other time I shall tell you about political events and about the shattering effect they have had on me.

Goodbye. Pity me in thinking of the intolerable punishment I have brought on myself.

Please ask at the bookstore for my two pieces on Edgar Allan Poe.

Charles

The article on Poe which Baudelaire urges his mother to read was the first of three sympathetic essays in which he passionately defends the American writer. It was through these essays and even more through his translation of Poe's stories that the latter came to enjoy tremendous popularity not only in France, but in other countries of the non-English-speaking world as well.

Baudelaire's enthusiasm for Poe had first been aroused in 1847 when he read in a socialist paper, *La Démocratie pacifique*, several stories translated by Isabelle Meunier, the English-born wife of the socialist leader, Victor Meunier. Baudelaire himself had published a translation of Poe's *Mesmeric Revelation* in July 1848. The intervening years apparently found him occupied with other matters and it was not until 1851 that the name of Poe appears in the published correspondence of the French poet. In October of that same year Baudelaire wrote an urgent request for the best editions of Poe available in London.

In 1852, with the publication of his forty-page study of Poe in the March and April issues of the *Revue de Paris*, Baudelaire renewed his ardent devotion to his American contemporary. From then until his death he made every effort to carry out his intention of making Poe 'a great man in France'. That he succeeded magnificently is acknowledged by critics almost without exception.

In a letter to Maxime du Camp, editor of the *Revue de Paris*, Baudelaire reveals a second important influence in his life, that of the authoritarian philosopher Joseph de Maistre whose political and theological doctrines had a decisive influence on the thought of the young poet. In fact, it was his reading of de Maistre and Poe that caused Baudelaire to break away from the republican ideas with which for a long time he had become infatuated.[40]

To Maxime du Camp

Sunday, May 9, 1852

I don't know how to thank you enough for the pleasure it [the story] gave me.[41] It is even more curious and beautiful than you had led me to believe. There is a passage more beautiful than the one in which the Arab messenger answers those who wish to stop him by saying: *I am bearing the words of one prophet to another prophet*,—it is the one in which the old Jacob kisses all the places on the body of the messenger that his son Joseph had touched,—and the one in which Joseph, his face covered by a veil, confers with his brother Benjamin. —Every time I read Moslem works I recall the great words of de Maistre: *properly understood, Islam is nothing but a reformed church—* or: *one of the phases of Protestantism*,—or something of that sort.— Please accept all my thanks.

Charles Baudelaire

A second letter to du Camp gives us our first glimpse of Baudelaire as a translator. *The Pit and the Pendulum*, which was to appear in the *Revue de Paris*, was the second story of Poe to be translated by his French admirer and was followed by a stream of translations that represent a very considerable portion of his literary production. It has been claimed that the five volumes of Poe translations would alone assure Baudelaire an important place in the history of French literature.

To Maxime du Camp

Thursday, September 16, 1852

Since I am sure that when you stop by the press this evening you will be angry or at least surprised by the absence of my manuscript, and *since I don't want you to be worried*, I am writing to inform you of the necessity of finding a certain M. Mann on whom depends the interpretation of a LACUNA and of PASSAGES which are literally UNTRANSLATABLE, because they have been *altered* (I believe). That prevented me from sending the manuscript of *The Pit and the Pendulum* to the printer yesterday morning, but it is ready and even if I should not be able to collate my British edition with M. Mann's original American edition *today*, I shall *positively* send my work *tomorrow*, and count on filling in the lacuna after the proofs have been printed.

. . . .

Charles Baudelaire

Baudelaire's mention of M. Mann has proved to be of greater significance than might first appear to the reader. It was, in fact, one of the clues that led Professor W. T. Bandy to make a startling discovery. M. Mann was not, as some critics had supposed, the famous pedagogue Horace Mann, but rather a Mr. William Wilberforce Mann, an American correspondent who came to Paris during the 1850's to gather a collection of journals relating to the Revolution of 1848. From Mr. Mann Baudelaire evidently obtained copies of the *Southern Literary Messenger* in which had appeared two obituary notices about Poe. From an article written by John M. Daniel and published in the *Messenger* for March 1850, Baudelaire had translated almost word for word approximately twenty-five pages of his forty-page essay on Poe. From another issue of the *Messenger* printed in November 1849, in which appeared an obituary notice on Poe by John R. Thompson, Baudelaire had also borrowed considerably, though far less extensively than from Daniel.

Perhaps the consciousness of his plagiarism was one reason for Baudelaire's dissatisfaction with his essay on Poe. At the time of its publication he had written somewhat enigmatically to his friend Poulet-Malassis: 'I have had a long article on a great American writer published in the *Revue de Paris*. But *I'm afraid the first time may be the last. My article stands out like a blemish.*'

Bandy's explanation of Baudelaire's plagiarism is both reasonable and convincing. 'Knowing the extreme originality and independence of Baudelaire in respect to literary and other criticism, there is only one conclusion that can be drawn from the facts. . . . It is that when Baudelaire wrote his brilliant essay on Poe's life and works he was almost as ignorant of the latter as he was of the former.' [42] Bandy has gone on to demonstrate that in 1852 Baudelaire had only the Wiley and Putnam edition (1845) of Poe and that he had not seen the Redfield edition and the Griswold *Memoir* at the time he wrote his essay.

Professor Bandy's discovery has even more far-reaching significance, for it helps to solve the problem of the extent of Poe's influence on the poems of *Les Fleurs du Mal*. As he points out, 'it would appear that virtually all the poems which were published in the first edition of 1857 were written before 1850. If, as late as 1852, Baudelaire had read, and probably not long before, only three or four of Poe's poems and none of his critical articles, it stands to reason that such critics as Lemonnier and Rhodes, who have minimized the possibility of such influence, are on very solid ground.' [43]

*   *   *

Separated from Jeanne and spurned by Marie, Baudelaire turned in December 1852 to the charming and warm-hearted Mme. Sabatier for the understanding and inspiration that he needed.

Born in 1822, Aglaé-Joséphine Sabatier was the illegitimate daughter of the Vicomte d'Abancourt and of Lea Marguerite Martin, a sewing maid, who before the birth of her daughter was persuaded by the Vicomte to marry a forty-three-year-old sergeant in the army, André Sabatier.

A woman of great charm and beauty, Mme. Sabatier is known to us today through the paintings of Meissonnier and Ricard, and through the sculpture of Jean Baptiste Clésinger. A bust of Mme. Sabatier by Clésinger still stands in the Louvre and a statue, *La Femme piquée par un Serpent*, caused a sensation when it was exhibited in the Salon of 1847 where gaping onlookers were scandalized by the orgiastic pose and expression of the model.

Judith Gautier, who was taken by her father to visit Apollonie, as she was called, describes her as 'rather tall, well proportioned with slender ankles and wrists and charming hands. Her silky hair of burnished chestnut seemed to fall in thick waves which reflected the light. Her skin was clear and smooth, her features regular with something gay and pert about them, her mouth small and smiling. An air of triumph spread about her an effect of light and happiness.' [44]

In her apartment on the rue Frochot where she had been established by her lover, Count Alfred Mosselmann, a wealthy Jewish banker, Mme. Sabatier entertained members of the literary and artistic world. Gautier, Flaubert, Clésinger, Feydeau, du Camp, Musset, Barbey d'Aurevilly and the elder Dumas were among those who attended her famous Sunday dinners. Though she was no prude and showed few scruples about deceiving her lovers, her sympathetic and generous nature, her kindness and thoughtfulness made her loved by everyone in her circle.

Although Baudelaire had known *la Présidente*, as Gautier liked to call her, from his days at the Pimodan, he did not attend her Sunday dinners until 1851 when he was brought there by the author of *Emaux et Camées*. It was in December 1852 that Baudelaire sent Mme. Sabatier his first letter in which he enclosed his famous poem, *A une Femme trop gaie*, later called *A celle qui est trop gaie*.[45]

The natural conclusion that Baudelaire wrote the poem for Mme. Sabatier has been questioned by Feuillerat who suggests that it was really written against Marie Daubrun and later offered to Apollonie as a revenge against the actress who had rebuffed him.

To Madame Sabatier

Thursday, December 9, 1852

The person for whom these verses have been written is most humbly *entreated* not to show them to *anyone*, whether they please or displease her, even if they should seem utterly ridiculous to her. Deep feelings have a reticence which ought never to be violated. And is not the absence of a signature an indication of this invincible reticence? He who wrote these lines, lost in thoughts of one who fills his dreams, has loved her dearly without ever telling her and will *always* cherish for her the most tender affection.

To One Who is Too Gay

Your head, your bearing, your gestures
Are fair as a fair countryside;
Laughter plays on your face
Like a cool wind in a clear sky.

The gloomy passer-by you meet
Is dazzled by the glow of health
Which radiates resplendently
From your arms and shoulders.

The touches of sonorous colour
That you scatter on your dresses
Cast into the minds of poets
The image of a flower dance.

Those crazy frocks are the emblem
Of your multi-coloured nature;
Mad woman whom I'm mad about,
I hate and love you equally!

At times in a lovely garden
Where I dragged my atony,
I have felt the sun tear my breast,
As though it were in mockery;

Both the springtime and its verdure
So mortified my heart
That I punished a flower
For the insolence of Nature.

Thus I should like, some night,
When the hour for pleasure sounds,
To creep softly, like a coward,
Toward the treasures of your body,

To whip your joyous flesh,
And bruise your pardoned breast,
To make in your astonished flank
A wide and gaping wound,

And, intoxicating sweetness!
Through those new lips,
More bright, more beautiful,
To infuse my venom, my sister! [46]

After Baudelaire left Jeanne in April 1852, he had hoped that before long he could write to his mother and tell her of his success in publishing his translations of Poe. Month after month good fortune seemed to elude him and he was still unable to send her any favourable news.

Finally a publisher, M. Lecou, came to his rescue and offered to print everything that he had written. When the project failed to materialize, Baudelaire wrote in desperation to his mother and told her of the harrowing situation in which he found himself. Tortured by anxiety, he pours out his whole heart and confesses all the troubles that haunted him even in his dreams.

To Madame Aupick

Saturday, March 26, 1853

I know I am going to cause you great distress, it would be impossible for you not to notice in my letter my unhappy frame of mind, not to mention the confessions I have to make to you. But there is nothing else for me to do. In spite of the many letters I have written you *in my imagination*—for I have planned for a whole year to write you each month—my letter will be short. I am in such a dilemma that I scarcely have an hour to write a letter which should be a pleasure for me and which is just the contrary.—I have made such a muddle of my life that for a long time I haven't even found time to work any more.

I am beginning with the hardest and most painful news.—I am writing you while burning my last two logs, and with my fingers frozen.—I am going to be sued for failure to make a payment that was due yesterday.—I shall be sued for another debt at the end of the month. This year, that is from last April until now, has been a real disaster for me, in spite of the fact that I had in my hands the means to make it otherwise. I have the utmost confidence in you; the wonderful indulgence you showed me on your way through Paris permits me to tell you everything, and I hope you'll not believe me completely mad, especially since I recognize my own folly. Besides, what's the use of pretending and of concocting a letter filled with false confidence and joy at a time when my mind is so tortured by anxiety that I either can't sleep at all, or I have frightful dreams and fever?

Why haven't I written before, you may say.—But you don't know what shame is,—and moreover what deterred me was the promise I had made myself never to write you unless I had good news to report.—And also my pledge never to ask you for a cent.—Today that is impossible.

After I received your money *a year ago*—as a result of a mistake which was in no way my fault I received more than you had intended—I immediately applied it as I had told you. I paid the year's deficit and I lived alone. Here my troubles began again.—I was living in a

76

house where the landlady made me so unhappy by her trickery, her nagging, her deceptions, and I was so miserable that I left, as I usually do, without saying a word. *I didn't owe her anything*, but I was foolish enough not to give her any notice after I had left,—hence the amount I owe her represents rent for a room that I did not use. I found out that this vile creature had had the audacity to write you.—Now, thinking I would soon be able to send for my things, I left *all my books, all my manuscripts, some completed, others begun, boxes full of papers, of* LETTERS,—DRAWINGS,—*in short* EVERYTHING,—*all my most valuable things: papers*.—About this time a publisher, a rich and obliging man [M. Lecou], became enthusiastic about me and asked me for a book.— Part of the necessary manuscripts were *there*;—I tried to make a fresh start, I bought other books and I obstinately refrained from writing you. On January 10th I had to deliver my book [the first volume of his Poe translations] in accordance with my contract, I received my money, and I turned over to the printer a manuscript so filled with mistakes that, after the first pages *had been set up in type*, I realized there would have to be so many *corrections and changes* that it would be better to break the *formes* and to *reset them again*. You may not understand this terminology; it means that the part that had been set up in type by the printers was worthless,—through my fault—and that I was honour bound to pay for the waste. The printer, not receiving the corrected proofs, got angry; the publisher thought I was crazy and became furious!—To think it was he who so distinctly had told me: *don't worry about anything, you have been looking for a publisher for several years; leave things to me and I will print everything you write.* The poor man! I made him lose his sales for the winter, and now for three months I haven't dared to write to him or see him. The book is still on my table, *unfinished.*—I have paid half the printing costs.—A copyright agreement is doubtless going to be arranged between France and the United States which will make the publication of our book impossible without additional expense.—Really, it's enough to make me lose my mind.—This book was the starting point of a new life.— It was to be followed by the publication of my poetry, by the reprinting of my *Salons* including my work on the *Caricaturistes*, left with that abominable creature of whom I was speaking, and for which I have received more than two hundred francs from the *Revue de Paris*, which keeps me from getting a cent more out of it.

This man who believed me *crazy*, who can't understand my delay, and whose kindness to me was the beginning of my literary reputation, must now take me for a *thief*. Can I ever effect a reconciliation with him?

That's not all.—The Opera,—the director of the Opera has asked me for a new type of libretto to be set to music by a new musician of high repute. I think that they were even considering having it done by *Meyerbeer*. It was a piece of good fortune and could have meant an income for life. There are people fifty years of age with established reputations who have never obtained such a favour.—But poverty and disorder create such apathy, such melancholy that I missed every appointment.

Luckily I didn't receive a cent.

That's not all.—The associate director of the Théâtre du Boulevard has asked me for a play.[47] It was to have been read this month—*it isn't done*. Because of my connections with this gentleman, the leader of a claque lent me 300 francs which were intended to avert another disaster last month. If the play were done, it would be nothing; I would have the debt paid through the associate director, or I would have it taken out of the future profits of the play or the sale of my tickets. But the play isn't done; there are scraps of it *being held by my former landlady*; the debt falls due in six days, at the end of the month; what is going to become of me?—What is going to happen to me?

There are times when I long to sleep forever; but I can't sleep any more, because I am always thinking.

I don't need to tell you that I have spent the winter without heat. But that is a mere trifle.

And so, to sum up matters, it has been *proved* to me this year that I could really earn money, a lot of money even, with proper application and perseverance.—But my previous troubles, my endless poverty, a new deficit to meet, the slackening of my energy through small vexations, and finally to admit everything, my inclination to reverie have nullified everything.

I have something else to tell you.—I know you to be so good and intelligent that I make it my duty to tell you everything.—All my torments have not yet been enumerated.

A year ago I separated from Jeanne, as I had written you,—I was hurt because you doubted it; why do you suppose I need or desire to hide anything from you? For some months I went to see her two or three times a month, to bring her a little money.

It happens that she is now seriously ill and in the most utter poverty. —I never speak of it to M. Ancelle; the wretch would only feel too happy about it.—It is obvious that a small part of what you will send me will go to her.—I am sorry now that I told you this, because in your gross maternal arrangements you are capable of sending her money through M. Ancelle without telling me.—That would be a grave impropriety. You don't want to hurt me again, do you? That idea is going to grow, to obsess me, and to torture me.—Finally, I am going to explain to you what I am suffering in regard to Jeanne; she has indeed made me suffer, hasn't she? How many times—and to you quite recently—a year ago—haven't I complained!—But in the face of such utter ruin, of a melancholy so profound, I feel my eyes filled with tears—and to tell you everything—my heart filled with reproaches.—Twice I have sold her jewels and her furniture, I have made her incur debts for me, sign notes, I have beaten her unmercifully, and finally, I have constantly set her an example of a debauched and misguided life. She suffers and says nothing.—Isn't that cause enough for remorse? And am I not guilty in this matter, as in all the others?

In your old age I ought to have given you the joy that my talent could lead you to expect,—I haven't done it.

I am guilty toward myself;—this disproportion between my will and my intellectual faculties is incomprehensible to me.—Why, having a true and clear idea of duty and of practicality, do I always do the opposite?

That idiotic Ancelle didn't tell me he had written you some time ago that I was in good health. That imbecile doesn't see anything and doesn't understand anything, regardless of the problem. I don't want to disturb you, there isn't any reason to do so. Besides, I have such robust health that it can withstand anything. But this abominable life and the brandy—which I'm going to stop—have upset my stomach for some months, and in addition I am unbearably nervous—just like a woman. Of course, it was inevitable.

Do you understand now why in the midst of the frightful solitude which surrounds me I have understood so well the genius of Edgar Poe and why I have written so well about his wretched life?

In this connection I shall tell you that that confounded book and the loss of confidence on the part of my publisher, and the delays and the mishaps which I am afraid of—for example, the international treaty I mentioned just now and finally the very fact that the agreement so definite three months ago is becoming more vague and *uncertain* each day—all this torments me for another reason. I had given myself the pleasure of preparing a very special surprise for you. I wanted to send M. Aupick a beautiful copy printed on fine paper and in a beautiful binding.—I am quite aware that any exchange of affection between him and me is impossible,—but he would have understood that the sending of a book, which will be on the whole a very curious one, was a proof of my esteem (if I can ever get it done) and a proof that I value his. You would have known that and you would have felt some satisfaction. That was my only goal. *I beg you not to mention a word of this.*

I don't know whether I should congratulate you on his recent nomination [to the Senate]—for perhaps you would have preferred to stay in Madrid.

Fearing my letter would find you no longer in Madrid, I have inquired about the time of your arrival from M. Ancelle, from Madame Olivier, and at the Foreign Office. They haven't been able to give me any information. In any case I am posting this letter and it is leaving tonight, the 26th; if you reply with your usual promptness, I can have your answer April 7th, just *one day before* a new crisis. From now until then *I have no idea* how I shall stave off the devilish blows I am expecting.—I shall try to progress gradually with my book like a man who hasn't a cent, who is at his wits' end.

I almost forgot to speak of the amount of money; but really it is so frightful that it makes me ill to write about it. I have managed to go a year without having recourse to your purse; needless to say, I am constantly making plans never to resort to it again, but most surely, if I do need your help again, it will not be for another year.

—Get back my books and manuscripts.

—Pay for the remaining printing costs.

—The two loans whose payment falls due, one today and the other (*the creditor in the theatre business*) at the end of the month.

—A pile of small debts, very small, but adding up to a substantial amount.

—My rent and a restaurant bill.

—Help that unfortunate Jeanne.

All this represents *exactly*, *exactly* a year's income, 2,400 francs.— Obviously, you haven't put that aside for me,—I believe that is impossible. Fortunately, the small debts can be put off, and I shall sacrifice the lesser to the most urgent.—*Perhaps, perhaps,* I shall be able to make some money between now and the 7th with the last fragments of E. A. Poe which I want to include in the book.

I still have millions of things to tell you;—but I am terribly pressed for time;—for example,—that you must not worry, as I know you do, about the old account with *M. Ancelle.* It is an insignificant matter for him; it is a debt which is too small not to be easily wiped out when I can decrease the other old ones.

—That I have a plan which I believe a good one and of which I have been thinking for almost two years—completely outside the field of literature—to earn an enormous amount.—It is to be postponed until after my reconciliation with my publisher and the publication of two or three volumes.—If by this means I don't succeed in making good the frightful arrears,—remember the interest is accruing—I shall be forced to make a desperate effort to succeed in the theatre.

—That I have had reason to complain very seriously about your friends,—about M. Olivier a year ago;—I actually thought he talked as if he were *in his dotage.* I had written you an account of that fantastic scene, but I have started several letters which were left with all my papers some months ago.

—About *M. Emon* [a retired army officer and a close friend of M. Aupick], who very rudely insulted me without any provocation on my part.—I wanted to put him in his place by physical force, but with him, as with M. Olivier, I restrained myself. As for M. Olivier, I had written him a letter, but I didn't send it; I restrained myself, as I said, only for your sake.

Etc., etc. . . . .

M. Ancelle tires me to death, and I see him as little as I can. Frankly, have you asked him to report to you about my feelings and my ideas? You know that such a thing would be enough to completely exasperate me, and moreover I abhor middle class morality.

A few days ago I was reading in a newspaper a news item from a Spanish paper saying that the poor of Madrid would miss you. I confess that my first thought was unkind, then I couldn't help laughing as I kept thinking about it. In short, I understood that you were seeking in every way to do honour to your husband, which is very natural.

Write directly to M. Charles Baudelaire, 60 rue Pigale, in PARIS, and don't worry about paying the postage. I don't think one can prepay a letter.

I am enclosing in this letter some portions of that poor interrupted book. One of the most remarkable has been published in the *October* number of the *Revue de Paris*, translated by me; in the same issue there was a poem of mine [*Le Reniement de Saint Pierre*], very dangerous and for which I was almost prosecuted.[48] If you haven't read those two pieces and if you have time, ask for them in the reading room. Isn't it at the place of someone named *Monier* in Madrid? It is called *The Pit and the Pendulum*, the October issue.

But I beg you, *answer me before reading all that.* You will doubtless see it later assembled in one volume.

Poor dear mother, there is very little room for love in this abominable letter. You wouldn't believe me, would you, if I told you that ten times I have planned to obtain money to go to Madrid only to clasp your hand?—You wouldn't believe me if I told you that, plunged in my frightful melancholy, I often talk with you very softly.—You would think that these are only fabrications of filial courtesy. I have so strange a heart that I myself am perplexed.

Doubtless then I shall see you soon; just as one dresses in his finest clothes for solemn occasions, so I shall try to adorn my poor mind to receive you properly.—I have often asked various people how you were,—they have always answered: *well*. Is that true?

One word more.—Send me the maximum amount of money, that is to say the most you can without causing yourself any inconvenience, for, all things considered, it is very just that I should suffer,—and if you don't have any money, authorize me to get some from M. Ancelle, even though you may not have sent him any since the month of April.

Don't blame me too much; once this painful crisis has passed, I shall get on my feet again.

I embrace you and clasp your hands.

Charles

6o, rue Pigale

Baudelaire's second letter to Mme. Sabatier, addressed to Apollonie, consists only of an unsigned poem which in *Les Fleurs du Mal* bears the title *Réversibilité*. The poem has none of the sensual character of *A Celle qui est trop gaie*. On the contrary, like all the other poems dedicated to her, it shows qualities which, for want of a better word, have been called spiritual. Mme. Sabatier has become an angel of gaiety, of goodness, of health, of beauty, of happiness, joy and light. It is interesting to note that almost from the beginning of their acquaintance

Mme. Sabatier is asked to play a completely platonic rôle, that what the poet asks of her is *only* her *prayers*.

To Madame Sabatier

Versailles, May 3, 1853

To A.

Angel of gaiety, have you tasted grief?
Shame and remorse and sobs and weary spite,
And the vague terrors of the fearful night
That crush the heart up like a crumpled leaf?
Angel of gaiety, have you tasted grief?

Angel of kindness, have you tasted hate?
With hands clenched in the shade and tears of gall,
When Vengeance beats her hellish battle-call,
And makes herself the captain of our fate,
Angel of kindness, have you tasted hate?

Angel of health, did ever you know pain,
Which like an exile trails his tired footfalls
The cold length of the white infirmary walls,
With lips compressed, seeking the sun in vain?
Angel of health, did ever you know pain?

Angel of beauty, do you wrinkles know?
Know you the fear of age, the torment vile
Of reading secret horror in the smile
Of eyes your eyes have loved since long ago?
Angel of beauty, do you wrinkles know?

Angel of happiness, and joy, and light,
Old David would have asked for youth afresh
From the pure touch of your enchanted flesh;
I but implore your prayers to aid my plight,
Angel of happiness, and joy, and light.[49]

Less than a week after sending Mme. Sabatier his poem *Réver-sibilité* Baudelaire wrote her a letter in which he enclosed a third poem, to be known in *Les Fleurs du Mal* as *Confession*. Saved from being completely trite by flashes of the poet's brilliant style, the poem reveals less of Baudelaire's temperament than does the accompanying letter. If Baudelaire feared ridicule in the poetic expression of his love, it is even more probable that he feared appearing ridiculous in assuming the rôle of a lover, especially since his feeling for Mme. Sabatier seems to have been inspired less by passion than by admiration.

To Madame Sabatier

Monday, May 9, 1853

Really, Madame, I ask your pardon a thousand times for this stupid, anonymous doggerel which smacks horribly of childishness; but what can I do about it? I am as egoistic as a child or as an invalid. I think of persons I love when I suffer. Usually I think of you in verse and when the verses are finished, I cannot resist the desire to have them read by the person who inspired them.—At the same time, I hide myself like someone who is terribly afraid of appearing ridiculous.—Isn't there something essentially comic in love?—especially for those who are not involved.

But I swear to you that this is really the last time I shall expose myself to ridicule; and if my ardent friendship for you lasts as long as it had lasted before I said a word to you about it, we shall both be old.

However absurd all this may seem to you, remember there is a heart which it would be cruelty to mock and in which your image is always alive.

> Once, only once, beloved and gentle lady,
>   Upon my arm you leaned your arm of snow,
> And on my spirit's background, dim and shady,
>   That memory flashes now.
>
> The hour was late, and like a medal gleaming
>   The full moon showed her face,
> And the night's splendour over Paris streaming
>   Filled every silent place.
>
> Along the houses, in the doorways hiding,
>   Cats passed with stealthy tread
> And listening ear, or followed, slowly gliding,
>   Like ghosts of dear ones dead.

Sudden, amid our frank and free relation,
  Born of that limpid light,
From you, rich instrument, whose sole vibration
  Was radiancy and light—

From you, joyous as bugle-call resounding
  Across the woods at morn,
With sharp and faltering accent strangely sounding,
  Escaped one note forlorn.

Like some misshapen infant, dark, neglected,
  Its kindred blush to own,
And long have hidden, by no eye detected,
  In some dim cave unknown.

Your clashing note cried clear, poor, prisoned spirit,
  That nothing in the world is sure or fast,
And that man's selfishness, though decked as merit,
  Betrays itself at last.

That hard the lot to be a queen of beauty,
  And all is fruitless, like the treadmill toil
Of some paid dancer, fainting at her duty,
  Still with her vacant smile.

That if one build on hearts, ill shall befall it,
  That all things crack, and love and beauty flee,
Until oblivion flings them in his wallet,
  Spoil of eternity.

Oft have I called to mind that night enchanted,
  The silence and the languor over all,
And that wild confidence, thus harshly chanted,
  At the heart's confessional.[50]

1853 had been a year of disappointment for Baudelaire. Though he had published several Poe stories serially in *Le Paris* (*The Telltale Heart* in February and *The Black Cat* and *Morella* in November), he had failed to find a publisher for his volume of *Histoires Extraordinaires*.

His only other publications for the year had been a translation of Poe's *The Raven* (*L'Artiste* for March) and a rather extraordinary essay, *Morale du Joujou* (*Le Monde littéraire* for April) in which the author shows an amazing understanding of child psychology and a sympathy for the poor that seems surprising coming from his pen.

As the year drew to a close Charles wrote a bitter, reproachful letter to his mother in which he relates his perennial financial difficulties which had recently been aggravated by the expense he assumed in arranging for the burial of Jeanne's mother.

To Madame Aupick

Monday, December 26, 1853

You will not hold it against me if I admit that your letter remained unopened on my table for two days; it arrived when I was so depressed that I was in a mood not to open letters for three months, for your handwriting is beginning to cause me the same terror as that of my enemies, the creditors, who exasperate me with their incessant demands.

. . . .

Among the strange things that you wrote me a fundamental goodness appears which impels me to keep you informed of my sad affairs and to ask for your help.—Besides, didn't you tell me, and it is the only thing that really struck me—*Don't hide anything from me.*

. . . .

As for your fears about my personal *degradation* in the midst of poverty, be assured that all my life, whether I was in rags or living decently, I have always spent two hours in grooming myself. Don't debase your letters with such nonsense.

With regard to your eternal, very just, but also rather unconsidered reproaches about my work: *Your book! when is your book going to appear? Your articles, when are your articles going to be published?* I have only one thing to say. Anyone who has lived as I have will understand. A month has just passed, that is *twice* the time necessary to finish the book. Well, I haven't had five days of peace in the month.

. . . .

If I had a considerable sum of money today—say a hundred francs —I would not buy shoes or shirts, I would not go to the tailor or to the pawn shop. Yesterday was the latest date allowed for carrying out what I regard as an obligatory duty, that is the exhumation and re-burial of a woman who gave me her last resources without murmuring, without complaining, *and especially without offering any advice. . . .*

86

THAT obligation comes before the shoes. Besides, I am so accustomed to physical discomforts, I know so well how to put two shirts under a torn coat and trousers, so threadbare that the wind cuts through them. I know so well how to put straw or even paper soles in worn out shoes that I hardly feel anything except moral suffering. Nevertheless, I must confess that I have reached the point of being afraid to make brusque movements or to walk very much for fear of tearing my clothes even more.

· · · · · · · · ·

Charles

In February 1854 Baudelaire sent another anonymous letter to Mme. Sabatier in which he enclosed the poem later known as *Le Flambeau Vivant*. The letter gives not the slightest hint of any emotion other than that of warm affection and 'gratitude for the good she has done'.

The poet's feeling of gratitude is not difficult to explain. Since his separation from Jeanne, he had been more lonely than ever. He may have ceased to love Jeanne, but while she was with him he at least felt that he belonged to someone, that he was not completely alone in the world.

Moreover, as Enid Starkie has so well pointed out: 'Temperamentally he was incapable of living without the society of women. He may have professed to despise them, but he could not do without them ... merely by their presence they inspired him and he held it his highest bliss to be permitted to live in the shadow of the woman he loved, asking nothing in return "comme aux pieds d'une reine un chat voluptueux".' [51]

In Mme. Sabatier Baudelaire found something which he had encountered in no other woman—kindness, thoughtfulness, and appreciative interest. It is not strange that he should have responded to the warmth and charm for which she was known and that he should have idealized the woman who helped to dispel his loneliness and make him less conscious of his inadequacies and failures.

Just as important as his dependence on feminine companionship was the poet's desperate need for some understanding and appreciation of his literary talent. Though he himself was convinced of his own poetic powers, he was still more or less unrecognized by the public, and what was even worse, he was considered a failure by his family and by Jeanne. Jeanne was too stupid and self-interested to appreciate the strange beauty of his verse, his mother too full of doubts, too much influenced by her son's lack of worldly success.

Bau.lelaire's 'innocent desire to show them [his verses]' to Mme. Sabatier must have been prompted in part by his very need for recognition and appreciation, however small, and by his anxiety to prove, if only to Apollonie, that he was not inferior to the more successful members of her circle.

The poem, like the letter, is devoid of any passionate or sensual overtones. If the sentiments or even the expressions have any similarity to those in Baudelaire's letter to Marie Daubrun, it is not necessary to believe that the poem was originally written for her. A woman's beauty arouses much the same emotional responses the world over and similarities of expression are often the result of paucity of imagination or lack of inspiration. Moreover, in almost everything he wrote Baudelaire shows a marked tendency to repeat a felicitous phrase or expression.[52]

To Madame Sabatier

Tuesday, February 7, 1854

I do not believe, Madame, that women in general know the full extent of their power, whether for good or for evil. Doubtless, it would not be wise to let them all know the truth. But with you one risks nothing; your soul is too full of kindness to leave room for *conceit* or for cruelty. Moreover, without any doubt you have been so surfeited and so satiated with flattery that only one thing can really flatter you any more and that is the knowledge that you are doing good —even without knowing it, even while asleep, merely by the fact that you are alive.

As for this *cowardly anonymity*, what shall I say, what excuse shall I offer except that my first mistake determines all the others and that the die is cast.—Suppose, if you will, that harassed at times by persistent grief I find comfort only in the pleasure of writing verses for you and that then I am obliged to balance the innocent desire of showing them to you with the horrible fear of displeasing you.—That is what explains my *cowardice*.

> Those lit eyes go before me, in full view,
> (Some cunning angel magnetized their light)—
> Heavenly twins, yet my own brothers too,
> Shaking their diamond blaze into my sight.
>
> My steps from every trap or sin to save,
> In the strait road of Beauty they conduct me.

They are my servants, and I am their slave,
Obedient in whatever they instruct me.

Delightful eyes, you burn with mystic rays
Like candles in broad day; red suns may blaze,
But cannot quench their still, fantastic light.

Those candles burn for death, but you for waking:
You sing the dawn that in my soul is breaking,
Stars which no sun could ever put to flight! [53]

Do you not agree with me that the most exquisite and perfect beauty, the woman most worthy of adoration, you yourself for example, could not desire a better compliment than the expression of gratitude for the good she has done?

No change of mood is apparent in the poem, known to us today as *L'Aube Spirituelle*, which Baudelaire sent to Mme. Sabatier in still another anonymous letter.

No explanation accompanies the poem. A single sentence written in *English* is the poet's only comment. Crépet and Blin suggest that the sentence was inspired by one which Griswold had used in writing of Poe: 'After a night of insanity and exposure . . .'

Twenty years later, Mme. Sabatier shows she had not forgotten Baudelaire's words when in writing a 'friend' she prefaced her letter with the familiar phrase 'Day of pleasure and desolation! . . .'

To Madame Sabatier

[No date]

After a night of pleasure and desolation, all my soul belongs to you.

When upon revellers the stained dawn breaks,
The fierce ideal comes with it; at that hour,
Stirred by some terrible avenging power,
An angel in the sated brute awakes.

Above the stricken, suffering man there glow
Far azure plains of unimagined bliss
Which draw his dreaming spirit like the abyss.
O pure, beloved Goddess, even so

89

Over smoked wrecks of stupid scenes of shame
Brighter and rosier thy sweet memory
Hovers before my wide eyes hauntingly.

The sun has dimmed and charred the candles' flame,
And thus, my glorious all-conquering one,
Thy shade is peer to the immortal Sun.[54]

Apparently Mme. Sabatier was often in the thoughts of Baudelaire during the month of February. On the 16th he sent her still another letter together with a poem singing her praises. Since the poem contains certain striking phrases similar to those in his letter to Marie, Crépet and Blin argue that the poem was originally written for the actress and that Baudelaire simply transferred the dedication to Mme. Sabatier. The possibility certainly exists, and there is no doubt that Baudelaire, like most other poets, would have felt no qualms in making the transfer. Yet it is also true that the author, lacking fresh inspiration, may simply be repeating expressions that he found most appropriate to the occasion. In either case, it is obvious that the nature of his emotion was not such as to awaken his highest poetic powers.

Whether written for Marie or Apollonie, the poem corroborates the fact that Mme. Sabatier had given the poet new hope, that she had helped dispel his loneliness and that his 'poor lonely soul' had responded to the 'sweetness of her authority'. Mme. Sabatier is neither sister, friend, nor mistress, but what the poet had once called Marie: 'guardian Angel, Muse, and Madonna'.

The accompanying letter only emphasizes the idealistic nature of the emotion expressed in the poem and leaves no further doubt about his feeling toward her, especially in its concluding lines.

To Madame Sabatier
Thursday, February 16, 1854

I do not know what women think of the adoration which they sometimes inspire. Some people claim that they must only laugh at it. They are credited with being merely vain or cynical. As for me, I think that a noble heart can only be proud and glad of its beneficent influence. I do not know if I shall ever be granted the supreme happiness of speaking personally to you of the power you have acquired over me and of the constant glow which your image creates in my mind. I am simply happy for the time being to swear to you once again that no love was ever more disinterested, more ideal, more imbued with respect than

that which I secretly cherish for you and which I shall always hide
with the care which this tender respect commands of me.

> What can you say, poor lonely soul of mine,
> Or you, poor heart, so long ago turned sour,
> To the best, dearest, loveliest, whose divine
> Regard has made you open like a flower?
>
> We'll set our pride to sing her highest praise:
> Naught to her sweet authority compares:
> Her psychic flesh is formed of fragrant airs.
> Her glances clothe us in a suit of rays.
>
> Be it in solitude at dead of night,
> Or in the crowded streets of glaring light,
> Her phantom like a torch before me streams.
>
> It speaks: 'I'm beautiful. These orders take.
> Love naught but Beauty, always, for my sake,
> Madonna, guardian Angel, Muse of dreams.' [55]

Another letter which Baudelaire sent Mme. Sabatier in May has
been described by Crépet and Blin as an example of 'diabolical decep-
tion or of disarming sincerity'. A third possibility need not be over-
looked. From the beginning of their friendship Baudelaire had made
every effort, both in his letters and in his verse, to prove to Apollonie
that his devotion was entirely platonic. His insistence on anonymity
seems only another pretext to keep their relationship on formal terms,
for by this time Mme. Sabatier could hardly have failed to know that
her correspondent was Baudelaire.

The poet's letter of May 8 almost seems a calculated effort to prevent
Apollonie from thinking of him as a lover. With what appears an
amazing psychological astuteness, he sets up certain barriers that only a
woman lacking in self-pride would attempt to tear down. He subtly
reminds her of her *duties* elsewhere, he praises her lover, he speaks of
the respect and high esteem in which she was held by him as well as by
others (as if in granting him her favours she would destroy that
respect). Above all he makes it clear that he himself considers anonymous devotion infinitely superior morally to pursuit; all those who
believe otherwise are in his opinion *boors*. As a final touch he assures
Mme. Sabatier that he is primarily an egoist who uses her mainly as a

source of poetic inspiration. Baudelaire could hardly have been more explicit in expressing his disapproval of a more intimate relationship.

The poem, a particularly beautiful one with its pure idealism and its lovely singing quality, is appropriately known today as *Hymne*. For some reason it was not included in *Les Fleurs du Mal*, but appeared several months later in *Le Présent*.

To Madame Sabatier

Monday, May 8, 1854

It is a long time, Madame, a very long time since these verses were written.—Always the same deplorable habit of indulging in reveries and anonymity.—Is it shame of this ridiculous anonymity, is it fear that these verses may be bad and that my ability was not equal to the depths of my feeling that made me so hesitant and so timid this time? —I have no idea.—I am so afraid of you that I have always hidden my name, believing that an anonymous devotion—which would evidently seem ridiculous to all the fashionable, materialistic boors who could be consulted on the matter—was after all quite innocent—could upset nothing, could disturb nothing, and was infinitely superior morally to a stupid, vain pursuit, to a direct attack on a woman who has her affections—and perhaps her duties—elsewhere. Are you not—and I say it with some pride—not only one of the most loved—but also the most greatly respected of all people?—I want to give you proof.—Laugh at it—laugh heartily if it amuses you—but say nothing about it.—Do you not think it perfectly natural, logical and human that a man deeply in love should hate the fortunate lover, the possessor?—That he should find him inferior and offensive?—Well, some time ago chance led me to encounter *that person*—how shall I express to you—without being ludicrous, without bringing a smile to your mischievous face that is always so filled with gaiety—how happy I was to find a gracious man, a man who could please you.—Heavens! do not so many subtleties bespeak a want of sense?—To make an end of it, to explain to you my silences and my ardour, an ardour that is almost religious, I will tell you that when my being is plunged in the blackness of its natural evil and folly, it dreams profoundly of you. From this stimulating and purifying reverie a happy accident is usually born.—You are for me not only the most attractive of women;—of all women, but even the dearest and most precious of superstitions.—I am an egoist, I make use of you.—Here are my wretched verses.—How happy I should be if I could be certain that these lofty conceptions of love have some

chance of being received in a secret corner of your cherished thoughts!
I shall never know.

> To the most lovely, the most dear,
> The Angel, and the deathless grail
> Who fill my heart with radiance clear—
> In immortality all hail!
>
> Into my life she flows translated
> As saline breezes fill the sky
> And pours into my soul unsated
> The taste of what can never die.
>
> Sachet, forever fresh, perfuming
> Some quiet nook of hid delight;
> A lone forgotten censer fuming
> In secrecy across the night.
>
> How, flawless love, with truth impart
> Your purity and keep it whole,
> O unseen grain of musk who art
> The core of my eternal soul?
>
> To the most lovely, the most dear,
> The Angel, and the deathless grail,
> Who fill my life with radiance clear—
> In immortality all hail! [56]

Forgive me, I ask no more of you.

Judging from the letter written to his mother in December, it is
obvious that 1854 had been no kinder to Baudelaire than the preceding
years. His financial distress was growing worse rather than better. His
only publication was a series of translations from Poe which *Le Pays*
began to print in installments in 1854 and continued with several interruptions until April 1855.

After taking refuge from his creditors for a few days in the Hôtel
d'York, Baudelaire had moved from his cheap room on the rue Pigalle
to another in the Hôtel du Maroc on the rue de Seine. There too he
found he could not escape his creditors. In a letter written to his mother
in July he told how he had been forced to hide in a dressing room while

his old creditor, Arondel, sat waiting to pounce upon his victim. It was only when the hotel proprietor succeeded in convincing Arondel that Baudelaire had been called to the press office that the unscrupulous moneylender finally took his departure.

That Baudelaire's lonely life was becoming more than he could bear is revealed by his statement to his mother that he intended to return to concubinage. 'The other one' to whom he refers is thought to have been Marie Daubrun who, according to Feuillerat, had undertaken a few months before to 'console' the poet. Whether or not Feuillerat is correct in his assumption, it is true that Baudelaire's letters are filled with references to the charming actress. On the 14th of August he had written his mother: 'Today is Marie's birthday.—The person whom I've mentioned to you spends her nights caring for her dying parents, after having played her stupid five acts. I'm not rich enough to buy her any gifts, but a few flowers sent this evening would be sufficient proof of my feeling.'

On October 14th Baudelaire had written to Paul de Saint-Victor asking him to put in a good word for Marie in the hope that she might obtain a rôle in a revival of Dumas' *Mousquetaires*. He concludes: 'Mlle. Daubrun is one of those people who are now good, now bad, depending on circumstances, nerves, encouragement, or discouragement.'

And a few days later Baudelaire wrote a second letter to Saint-Victor in which he thanked the drama critic for the favourable remarks he had made about Marie's performance in *Oiseaux de proie*.

There is certainly no doubt that if Marie was not the other woman of the letter, she was often in the poet's thoughts during the course of the year.

To Madame Aupick

Monday, December 4, [1854]

My dear mother, doubtless you'll not be surprised to find that I have waited so long before thanking you for the sudden, quite unexpected assistance that you have given me. You know my strange life, and you know that every day brings its share of exasperations, quarrels, embarrassments, errands and work, so it is not very surprising that I postpone for two weeks letters that I consider duties. Today, on my own initiative, I am writing to ask for your aid. I certainly need it, for if, thanks to the bizarre life that has been imposed upon me, asking for my own MONEY always gives me the painful sense of being a *beggar*, you can imagine the effect produced on me by the necessity of imploring a favour. Those wretched one hundred francs of yours touched me; they enabled me to keep going, and nothing more; if I had used them for one of the important things that I have in mind, I should have had nothing left. They paid the five or six small debts which constantly harass us in this quarter of the city. What was most disagreeable for me about that wretched one hundred franc note, which you believed was an enormous aid, was the thought that it was a privation for you.

Today my needs are exactly the same as for the month just past. YES or NO, can I get some clothes? I will not say: can I walk down the street without attracting attention—I don't give a hang about that— but should I resign myself to going to bed and staying there for lack of clothes?

．　　．　　．　　．　　．　　．　　．

I am going back to concubinage and if I am not living with Mlle. Lemer by January 9, I shall be with the *other one*. At all costs I have to have a *family*; it is the only way to work and spend less.

．　　．　　．　　．　　．　　．　　．

I am beset by a thousand torments; I am waiting for proofs as if they were the *Messiah*. The editor of *Le Pays* has asked for me several times.—They are afraid to start publishing my series of translations again for fear I'll leave them in the lurch. How could they fail to trust the promptness of a man who leads as deplorable a life as I do?

Friends are making me realize that if I don't hurry with my projected plays, which are being considered favourably, I might experience one of those misfortunes which have so often afflicted me and which leave behind them a persistent regret.

Finally, I have also been behind for a long time with the *Revue de Paris.*

I'm worried to death.

I happen to recall something that struck me in our last conversation —it has to do with a certain anxiety which you expressed relative to steps you thought I might take in the civil court [concerning the guardianship]. Indeed I am capable of taking such steps, but not stupid enough to do so without having *some chance* of success. And unfortunately, I am obliged to admit that in the present circumstances, there would be *no chance whatever*. In short, I believe that my life has been damned from the beginning, and that it will *always* remain so.

．　　．　　．　　．　　．　　．　　．

Charles

In a letter to the poet Desnoyers, Baudelaire rather amusingly expresses his antipathy to romantic philosophy with its idealistic and pantheistic interpretation of nature. His letter is typical of his violent reaction to the sentimentality which he despised and reveals his strong belief that the spiritual essence of man is of far greater importance than anything to be found in nature. His depreciation of nature's exuberance recalls his belief in the superiority of a disciplined art to an undisciplined nature.

To Fernand Desnoyers

[January 1855]

My dear Desnoyers,

You ask me for some verses for your little anthology, verses about *Nature*, I believe, about forests, great oak trees, verdure, insects—and perhaps even the sun? But you know perfectly well that I can't become sentimental about vegetation and that my soul rebels against that strange new religion which to my mind will always have something shocking about it for every *spiritual* person. I shall never believe that the *souls of the Gods live in plants*, and even if they did, I shouldn't be much concerned and I should consider my own soul of much greater value than that of sanctified vegetables. I have always thought, even, that there was something irritating and impudent about *Nature* in its fresh and rampant state. Since it is impossible to satisfy you completely in accordance with the strict terms of your project, I am sending you two poetic fragments which represent just about the sum total of the reveries that have come to me in the twilight hours [*Le Crépuscule du Matin* and *Le Crépuscule du Soir*]. In the depths of the woods, overshadowed by vaults like those of sacristies or cathedrals, I think of our astonishing cities, and the stupendous music that rolls overhead seems to me the translation of human lamentations.

C. B.

With the publication of the Poe translations Baudelaire was beginning to be recognized in the literary world, though he was still comparatively unknown to the general public. The opening of the *Exposition Universelle*, which included a vast exhibition of paintings from all over the world, gave him another opportunity to return to art criticism, a field in which he excelled.[57] It is interesting to note that in his three essays dealing with the exhibition Baudelaire completely ignored the work of Courbet who was holding a special exhibit of his

own. The omission is all the more striking, since the exhibition contained Courbet's famous *L'Atelier*, a huge canvas which contained,
among a group of well-known figures, a portrait of Baudelaire. Jeanne
was originally represented standing behind the poet—so it is thought,
at least—but she was later nearly effaced when the artist repainted that
area of the canvas before exhibiting the picture to the public.[58]

Baudelaire's failure to comment at length on Courbet's work was
undoubtedly the result of his antipathy to the whole realistic movement. It is true he devoted a few friendly lines to the painter from
Ornans in his article on Ingres, but even here his praise was nearly
nullified by severely critical remarks. A few months later he started to
compose an attack on Courbet, entitled *Puisque Réalisme il y a*, but the
study never got beyond a few pages of notes.

In addition to his articles on the *Exposition*, Baudelaire published on
July 8 another important essay, *De l'essence du rire*, in which he presented his theory of the comic in the arts. Based on the theological
doctrines of man's fall and of original sin which he had adopted from
de Maistre, his closely reasoned theory of the comic is both arresting
and provocative. In her admirable study, *Baudelaire the Critic*, Margaret
Gilman points out that the theory, though original in many ways with
the poet, contains elements drawn from varied sources. 'There is an
extraordinary skilful weaving together—conscious or otherwise—of
what would seem at first irreconcilable elements; Stendhal, de Maistre,
Maturin fused into one.' [59]

On June 1st, 1855, Baudelaire experienced a moment of triumph
when the *Revue des Deux Mondes*, bulwark of French romanticism
since 1830, published a selection of his poems in its pages. Shortly
before their appearance Baudelaire wrote a letter to one of the editors
of the *Revue*, Victor de Mars, in which he submitted for approval an
epilogue intended to serve as a fitting conclusion for the verses. The
epilogue was not accepted. In fact, the distinguished periodical was
never again to publish any of the poet's work.

It is in the letter to de Mars that Baudelaire uses for the first time in
his correspondence the title, *Les Fleurs du Mal*, suggested to him by
Hippolyte Babou.

To Victor de Mars

April 7, 1855

My dear M. de Mars,

I am preparing a very fine *Epilogue* for the *Fleurs du Mal*, which I
hope will be ready in time. Regardless of the poems you may choose,
I wanted to say that I am very anxious to arrange their order *with you*,

so that they will form a sequence, so to speak, just as we did for the first group.

I shall bring you the *Epilogue* on the evening of the 9th, or the 10th at the very latest.

The Epilogue (dedicated to a lady) reads something like this: *Let me find rest in love.—No, love will not give me rest.—Innocence and goodness are revolting.—If you wish to please me and to stimulate my desire, be cruel, deceitful, lascivious, debauched and thievish; and if you do not wish to be all of those things, I shall beat you without mercy, in cold blood. For I am the true representative of irony, and my malady is an incurable one.*—As you see, that makes a fine explosion of monstrosities, *a true Epilogue* worthy of the *prologue to the reader*, a real Conclusion.

Yours,

Ch. Baudelaire

Baudelaire's pleasure in having his poems published in the *Revue des Deux Mondes* was soon marred by the indifference with which they were received. No mention of them was made by any critic until five months later when Louis Goudall published a scathing review in *Le Figaro* for November 5. In a vicious attack Goudall excoriated the poetry of Baudelaire and predicted that the author would henceforth be considered among the 'dried fruits of contemporary poetry'.

Though Baudelaire had been encouraged by the fact that Michel Lévy had bought the rights to two volumes of translations from Poe (*Histoires Extraordinaires* and *Nouvelles Histoires Extraordinaires*), the incident with *Le Figaro* only deepened his depression which had been growing more pronounced with the years.

To make matters worse, Baudelaire was once again at odds with his mother. Disgusted by his weakness in going back to Jeanne and by his failure to earn a living, Mme. Aupick refused to see him or even to open some of his letters. When it was necessary to communicate with him, she did so through Ancelle, much to her son's disappointment and chagrin. On one occasion (letter of October 4, 1855) when Baudelaire was compelled to ask his mother for an advance, he found he didn't even know her address and that he was obliged to ask Ancelle to forward his letter. After telling Mme. Aupick that he intended to send her a de luxe edition of *Histoires Extraordinaires*, he concluded with a note of sadness: 'It is very hard and very painful to work in the midst of such cruel and trivial worries. And Ancelle ought to have given me this small advance on his own authority. Not that it is painful for me to write you. What is painful is never to have an answer from your pen.'

On another occasion (undated letter of 1855) when Mme. Aupick had sent him a package, Baudelaire thanked her while expressing his regret that the package contained no word from her. Without a hint of blame, but hungry for her affection, he ended: 'I don't want to bore you or tire you with my troubles. Let it suffice to say that not a day goes by without my seeing you in my thoughts in your little house!

'What emptiness around me! What blackness! What moral gloom and what fears for the future!

'I embrace you and I love you.'

Baudelaire's despair and fears for the future were hardly exaggerated. His penury, his loneliness hardly augured well for the years ahead. In one month, as he told his mother in an earlier letter (April 5, 1855), he had been obliged to move six times, 'living with bare walls, sleeping with bed-bugs . . . driven from pillar to post'. It was especially ironical that he who so loved beauty and luxury, who had lived surrounded by favourite paintings and elegant furniture, should have to live in the ugliest and shabbiest of hotel rooms. Perhaps it was as an escape from his dreary surroundings that he wrote the lovely *L'Invitation au Voyage* in which he dreamed of a country where all was 'luxury, calm, and sensuous delight'.

By December Baudelaire felt he could go on no longer. In a letter to his mother in which he makes no attempt to hide his bitterness and hurt, he begs for the assistance necessary to start life anew, away from the ugliness he has come to dread.

To Madame Aupick
Thursday, December 20, 1855

My dear mother, I have a great many things to tell you, and M. Ancelle, who will give you this letter, already knows all about them. Thank God, he and I have talked and argued about them quite often, not only on many occasions in the past, but especially in the last two months.

More than anything else, I want to see you. For more than a year now you have refused, and I really think your justifiable anger should be satisfied. In our relationship there is something absolutely abnormal, absolutely humiliating for me which you surely cannot wish to maintain. If you do not feel satisfied by this entreaty, at least be generous. I am not really old, but I may soon become so. It seems to me impossible that you should insist on maintaining this state of affairs; I am overwhelmed by humiliations of every kind; the least I can hope is not to suffer any from you. And as I was saying, if it is without pleasure and without confidence on your part that you allow me to effect this reconciliation, at least let it be with a sort of charity. Yesterday, thinking I was to leave (*it will be tomorrow*), I began to put a lot of papers in order. I found a pile of letters from you, written at different times and in various circumstances. I tried to re-read several; they were all filled with a deep concern that was purely material, it is true, as if debts were everything, as if pleasures and spiritual satisfactions were nothing. But since they were motherly above all, they started me down the road of the saddest of all thoughts. All these letters represented years that had slipped by, and slipped by amiss. Reading them soon became unbearable. Nothing is more odious, in certain cases, than the past. And thinking of it more and more, I told myself that this situation was not only monstrous and shocking, but even dangerous. Just because my mind is constituted in a certain way, which evidently seems eccentric to you, you shouldn't conclude that I take a sickly pleasure in this complete solitude and in this separation from my mother. I think I told you just now that I may become old; but there is something worse. One of us may die, and really it is painful to think that we run the risk of dying without seeing each other. You know how much I despise sentimentality of any kind. I know I have wronged you, but whenever I feel something deeply, my fear of exaggeration forces me to express it as coldly as I can. You will not be mistaken then in reading between the lines a warmth and an intensity of desire which my habitual reserve does not always let me fully express.—But above all, as I said before, grant me this one thing: even if you were to give me everything else, by that I mean material satisfactions, I should not be entirely happy. For quite a long time now, I have been somewhat ill in body and mind, and I want everything, everything at once, a complete rejuvenation, an immediate satisfaction of body and mind. The years accumulate without my attaining either, and really it is hard to bear.

Ancelle will tell you of my wish, or rather of my firm resolution to move permanently into lodgings that I chose two months ago. So almost immediately on moving in I am going to have rent to pay, since I took the rooms two and one half months ago and couldn't occupy them for lack of money.

I am utterly weary of living in cheap restaurants and shabby hotel rooms; it tires me to death and poisons my life. I don't know how I have stood it.

I am tired of colds and migraine headaches, and of fevers, and especially of the need to go out twice a day in the snow, and the mud, and the rain.—I tell him this constantly; but he wants your authorization before complying with my wish.

I lack everything; it is a matter therefore of a greater sacrifice or of a larger advance than usual. But in return I shall gain—and almost immediately—immense advantages; above all, no more waste of time. That is my affliction, my greatest affliction; for there is a condition even more serious than physical suffering, and that is the fear of seeing exhausted, consumed, and destroyed in the midst of this terrible, agitated existence, the admirable poetic faculty, the clarity of ideas, and the power of hope that in reality constitute my capital.

My dear mother, you know so little about a poet's life that doubtless you will not understand this argument very well; nevertheless, that is what constitutes my chief fear; I don't want to die like a dog in obscurity, I don't want to see old age approach without a settled existence, I shall NEVER resign myself to it; and I think my own self is quite valuable, I shall not say more valuable than others, but valuable enough for me.

To come back to the question of my moving, I lack everything; furniture, linen, clothing, even cooking utensils, a mattress, and my books which are scattered about among several binders, I need everything, everything immediately. Ancelle cannot undertake such complicated things, and I have made him realize that. Moreover, all these expenses are connected with one another. My moving depends on the possibility of leaving the place where I am. My peace of mind depends on having my quarters properly equipped.—Several things have been ordered. In three days everything will be ready. Tomorrow I must leave the rue de Seine, or else leave all my things there (and the book I am working on?—and the printer! and the publisher!); assuming I have the money today, I shall sleep on the floor two or three days and I shall work where I can; for I cannot stop.

I chose my lodging in the district of the Boulevard du Temple, 18 rue d'Angouleme; the house is beautiful and above all quiet; I shall be living like a decent man; at last!—and that, as I was telling you, will be a real rejuvenation, for I have need of an absolutely secret life and of complete chastity and sobriety.

My two volumes are finally going to appear, and during the new year I shall be able to live decently with what I get from the *Revue des Deux Mondes* and from Ancelle. I am not worried about that. At last I shall be in my own place. Thereafter you will no longer have to submit to similar importunities. There will no longer be any need for that.—I have taken every precaution to see that this new mode of life is protected from misfortune.

Oh, good heavens, I forgot to mention the amount of money. With fifteen hundred francs everything will be done in three days. To be frank, the life of a poet is well worth that: no more, no less; I have figured and re-figured fifty times. It is not much, but it is just what I need. I have strongly urged Ancelle not to embarrass me with his caution, with his fears, not to invent ways to give me the money in small installments, which would take away all its value and its usefulness; I have to act so quickly, so quickly! Moreover, as I was saying, all these expenses are closely associated with one another like a series of actions. As for the simple question of pride and decorum, I need say no more.

When I think of all that I'm obliged to spend, uselessly, unavoidably, without pleasures, without profit, I become exasperated. I have just counted all that I have received this year *from you, from Ancelle, from Le Pays, from the Lévy publishing company*; it is enormous; and yet I have lived like a wild animal, like a bedraggled dog. And this will last eternally until my imagination vanishes with my health, unless I immediately make the important decision in question.

This very morning I said something to Ancelle which I consider quite sensible. I said to him: would you prefer that I do what is done by so many men of letters, who have less pride than I, and what I have never done under any minister, under any government? To ask a government official for money horrifies me, and yet it has become almost a custom; there are funds for that. As for me, I have a pride and a discretion which have always made me repudiate methods of that sort. Never will my name appear on filthy government paper. I prefer to owe money to everyone, I prefer to argue with you and to torment my mother, however painful that may be.

You will not be offended if you receive my volume after everyone else. I want to give you a beautiful copy. And I shall have three special copies printed.

As for my small literary projects—but you are not very interested in them—I shall tell you about them another time.—Besides, for the new year I have the same projects as for the one which has just passed, projects which my horrible life has prevented me from accomplishing. —A volume of *criticism* (completed), *poetry* (completed) and almost sold,—a novel and a long play.—I embrace you—I shall not say: I beg you,—I shall say: have a little boldness and confidence.

Charles

Tomorrow I must leave; I ought to have left this neighbourhood today.

On the whole, everything considered, I have so seldom hidden anything in my life from M. Ancelle that I thought it wise to show him this letter before giving it to him to bring to you. I presume you will not find anything offensive in this conduct. He pointed out that the expression of my earnest wish to see you again was perhaps not accompanied by sufficient apologies. But my regrets, my excuses can be guessed; they are quite obvious: I have expressed them twice in two letters that you have not read. There are thoughts that can be seen, so to speak. Could you imagine that it made me happy to offend you and to give you an even worse opinion than you have of me?—I earnestly beg you once again, be generous and you will be satisfied. —Who prevents us, once I am leading a regular life, from seeing each other or meeting each other at least once a week? In that way I shall be able to keep you informed about my life, and, thanks to this further kindness of Ancelle, there will no longer be any question of misunderstandings.

Baudelaire's letter to his mother resulted in another reconciliation and enabled him to move to better quarters as he had requested. To Ancelle, however, Mme. Aupick confided her doubts and fears: 'Charles' condition breaks my heart; in order to reassure him at once you may write and tell him that I consent to this new sacrifice of 1500 francs. *That's what is important for him.* Don't promise anything else. He has offended me so deeply, his attitude toward me is so far from what it should be that I feel very little disposed to renew our relations. I have never paid him a visit without returning dissatisfied, my advice irritates him, and then he shows a lack of respect. You can realize that that is not tolerable. But in spite of my sulking, I am very much concerned about that poor forsaken boy, and there is nothing I would not do to improve his position. Unhappily, what can I do!

Economize on my pension, that's all, and yet that accomplishes nothing, changes nothing in his horrible life! How discouraging!' [60]

As Baudelaire grew older and more embittered, he became even more confirmed in his belief in original sin and in his distaste for the theory of indefinite progress, ideas which to a great extent he had derived from his reading of de Maistre and Poe. Reminiscent of his essays on the American writer is his letter to the naturalist Toussenel in which he reiterates many of the ideas that constitute his aesthetic and philosophical doctrines. Perhaps none of these ideas is more typical of his thinking than his conception of the rôle of the imagination and his acceptance of the theory of correspondences. It was in his sonnet *Correspondances*, to which all modern poetry is indebted, that Baudelaire gave magnificent poetic expression to his conception of universal analogy.

To Alphonse Toussenel

Monday, January 21, 1856

My dear Toussenel, I am most anxious to thank you for the gift you made me. I must bluntly and ingenuously confess that I did not realize the worth of your book [*Le Monde des Oiseaux*].

The day before yesterday I experienced a misfortune, a rather serious shock—serious enough to prevent me from thinking—so much so that I interrupted an important piece of work.—Not knowing how to distract myself, I picked up your book this morning—very early this morning. It held fast my attention, it restored my equilibrium and my peace of mind, as all good reading will always do.

For a long time I have rejected almost all books with a feeling of disgust.—For a long time too I have not read anything so utterly informative and entertaining.—The chapter on falconry and on the birds that serve man in hunting is a book in itself.—There are phrases which resemble the phrases of the great masters, cries of truth, irresistible philosophical accents, such as: *Every animal is a sphinx*, and in regard to analogy: *how the mind finds repose in a sweet quietude under the protection of a doctrine so fruitful and so simple, in which nothing is a mystery among the works of God!*

There are likewise many other things that are philosophically stirring, both the love for outdoor life and the honour paid to chivalry and to women.

What is undeniable is that you are a poet. For a long time I have said that the poet is *supremely* intelligent, that he is *intelligence* par excellence—and that *imagination* is the most *scientific* of the faculties, because it alone understands *universal analogy*, or what a mystic religion calls *correspondence*. But when I wish to have these things printed, I am told that I am crazy—and above all crazy about myself— and that I hate pedants only because my education is at fault.—What is very certain, however, is that I have a philosophical bent of mind which makes me see clearly that which is true, even in zoology, although I am neither a hunter nor a naturalist.—Such at least is my claim; don't do as my friends do and laugh about it.

Now, since I have gone further in my discussion and in my familiarity than I should have allowed myself, had your book not inspired in me so much sympathy, let me say everything.

What is *indefinite Progress*? What is a *society* that is not *aristocratic*! It is not a society, it seems to me. What is meant by man in a state of *natural* goodness? Where has he been known to exist? A naturally good man would be a *monster*, I mean a *God*.—In short, you can guess the order of ideas which shocks me, or rather which offends reason written since the beginning of time on the very surface of the earth.— Pure *quixotism* of a beautiful soul.—

And for a man like you to casually insult, like any journalist writing for *Le Siècle*, *de Maistre*, the great genius of our time—*a seer!*—And last of all a slangy and colloquial style which always mars a beautiful book.

From the beginning of the book I was struck by the idea that you are a man of genuine intelligence led astray by a sect. In short—what do you owe to Fourier? Nothing, or rather very little.—Without Fourier, you would have been what you are. *Rational man* did not wait for Fourier to appear on earth to realize that Nature is the *Word*, an allegory, a mould, a *repoussé*, if you wish. We know that, and it is not through Fourier that we know it;—we know it through ourselves and through the poets.

All the heresies to which I referred just now are, after all, only the consequence of the great modern heresy, of an *artificial* doctrine replacing a natural doctrine—I mean the suppression of the idea of *original sin*.

Your book awakens in me many dormant ideas—and in connection with *original sin* and with *form moulded on idea*, I have often thought that maleficent and loathsome animals were perhaps only the vivification, the corporealization, and the hatching into material life of man's *evil thoughts*.—Thus all *nature* participates in original sin.

Do not be vexed with me for my audacity and my bluntness, and be assured that I am

Faithfully yours,
Ch. Baudelaire

Early one morning in March, after waking from a strange dream, Baudelaire sat down at his desk and in a letter to a friend recounted the dream as he remembered it. Charles Asselineau, to whom the letter is addressed, was Baudelaire's closest and most loyal friend. Writer, bibliophile, and during the last years of his life director of the Bibliothèque Mazarine, he was introduced to the poet in 1845 by the painter Deroy. With his fine, sensitive mind, his critical judgement, his self-effacing nature 'the gentle Asselineau' came to know Baudelaire better than any of his other friends and to appreciate his genius. It was he who stood by him in his last illness as he had in life and who afterwards acted as a son to Mme. Aupick.

With Banville he edited the posthumous edition of Baudelaire's works in 1868 and in the following year published a moving biography of the unhappy poet.

To Charles Asselineau

Thursday, March 13, 1856

My dear friend,

Since dreams amuse you, here is one that I am sure will not displease you. It is five o'clock in the morning, so it is very fresh in my mind. Of course, it is only one of the thousand types of dreams by which I am beset, and I don't need to tell you that their utter strangeness, their general character which is absolutely foreign to my pursuits and to my amorous adventures, lead me to believe that they are a language of hieroglyphics whose key I do not possess.

It was two or three o'clock in the morning (in my dream), and I was walking alone in the streets. I met Castille, who had, I think, several errands to do, and I told him that I would accompany him and that I would make use of the cab to do a personal errand. And so we took a cab. I thought it a sort of *duty* to present a book of mine, which had just been published, to the procuress of a large house of prostitution. When I looked at the book which I held in my hand, *I discovered* it was an obscene book, which explained the *necessity* of offering the work to that woman. Moreover, in my mind this necessity was in reality a pretext, an occasion to give a passing kiss to one of the girls of the house; all of which implies that without the necessity of presenting the book, I shouldn't have dared to go into such a house.

I said nothing of all this to Castille. I had the cab stop at the door of the house, and I left Castille in the cab, promising myself not to keep him waiting a long time.

Immediately after ringing and entering, I noticed that my p . . . was hanging out of the fly of my unbuttoned trousers, and I felt it was indecent to appear that way even in such a place. Moreover, feeling my feet to be very wet, I noticed that *they were bare* and that I had stepped in a pool of water at the foot of the stairway. Bah! I said to myself, I shall wash them before getting a kiss and before leaving the house. I went upstairs.—From then on, there was nothing more about the book.

I found myself in huge adjoining galleries—badly lighted—dreary and faded in appearance—like old cafés, or old reading rooms, or ugly gambling houses. The girls, scattered through these vast galleries, were talking with men, among whom I noticed some students.—I felt very sad and very intimidated; I was afraid they would see my feet. I looked at them, I noticed I had a shoe on *one* of them.—Some time later I noticed that I had shoes on both feet.—What impressed me was that the walls of these huge galleries were decorated with drawings of all kinds, in frames. All of them were not obscene. There were even some drawings of buildings and some Egyptian figures. As I felt more and more intimidated and as I didn't dare approach a girl, I amused myself by carefully examining all the drawings.

In a remote corner of one of these galleries I found a very strange series.—In a large number of small frames I saw drawings, miniatures, photographic prints. They represented bright coloured birds with very brilliant plumage, each with one eye that was *alive*. Sometimes only half a bird was pictured. In some cases they represented images of creatures that were strange, monstrous, almost amorphous, like meteorites.—In a corner of each drawing there was a note: *Such and such a girl, aged   , has given birth to this foetus, in such and such a year*. And other notes of this kind.

The thought occurred to me that such drawings were not very conducive to suggesting ideas of love. Another thought was this: there is really only one newspaper in the world, and that is *Le Siècle* which could be stupid enough to open a house of prostitution and at the same time include in it a sort of medical museum.—Indeed, I said to myself suddenly, it is *Le Siècle* which has furnished the capital for this speculation in brothels, and the medical museum is explained by its mania for *progress, science,* and the *diffusion of knowledge.* Then I thought to myself that modern stupidity and folly have a mysterious usefulness and that evil-doing is often transformed into good through spiritual mechanics.

I admired the accuracy of my philosophic reasoning. But, among all these creatures there was one that was alive. It was a monster which was born in the house and which stood endlessly on a pedestal. Although alive, it was nevertheless a part of the museum. It was not ugly. Its face was even pretty, very tanned, of an Oriental colour. There was a lot of rose and green in it. It was crouching, but in a strange and contorted position. There was moreover something blackish which was twisted several times around it and around its limbs, like a large snake. I asked him what it was; he told me it was a monstrous appendage which grew out of his head, something elastic like rubber, and so long, so long that, if he were to roll it around his head like a braid of hair, it would be much too heavy and absolutely impossible to wear;—that, hence, he was obliged to twine it around his limbs, which, moreover, made a finer effect. I talked with the monster at great length. He told me about his troubles and his sorrows. For several years he had been obliged to remain in this room, on this pedestal, because of the curiosity of the public. But his chief worry occurred at dinner time. Since he was a living being, he was obliged to dine with the girls of the establishment—to walk tottering, with his appendage of rubber, to the dining-room, where he had to keep it twined around him or place it on a chair like a bundle of rope, for, if he let it drag on the floor, it would pull his head backwards. Further-more, he was obliged, small and dumpy as he was, to sit beside a tall and well-built girl.—What is more, he gave me all these explanations without any bitterness.—I didn't dare to touch him, but I was interested in him.

At this moment, (this is no longer a part of the dream), my mistress made a noise in the room with a piece of furniture and woke me. I awakened, tired, broken, with my back, legs, and hips aching all over. —I presume I was sleeping in the contorted position of the monster.— I don't know if all this will seem as amusing to you as to me. Good old Minet would have a hard time, I think, getting a moral out of this.

Yours,
Ch. Baudelaire

Baudelaire's letter to Asselineau constitutes a fascinating document for those who are interested in the psychological factors motivating the behaviour of so complex and baffling a personality. In his book, *L'Echec de Baudelaire*, Dr. René Laforgue has attempted to use this very dream as a means of better understanding the poet and his work. From it he deduces that Baudelaire showed a strong feeling of sexual inferiority, that the house of prostitution represented his mother's house, and that with his book he really wanted to realize the equivalent of incest. The monster in the dream, affirms Laforgue, is Baudelaire himself, while the appendage growing out of his head symbolizes Jeanne who was, so to speak, attached to him for life.

Without accepting Laforgue's analysis in its entirety, it is apparent even to the layman that Baudelaire suffered a marked sense of sexual inferiority. Nadar in his *Charles Baudelaire intime*, sub-titled *Le Poète vierge*, has gone so far as to insist that Baudelaire never lost his virginity though he has failed to offer any real proof to substantiate his case. The fact that the poet had contracted syphilis would alone seem to discredit Nadar's claim.

What appears most probable is that Baudelaire lacked the virility necessary to make him a successful lover, or, as Turnell suggests, that excessive cerebration sometimes resulted in temporary impotence. Baudelaire himself lends credence to the latter idea by an observation he makes in his *Journaux intimes*: 'The more man cultivates the arts, the less he copulates. The divorce between the intelligent man and the brute becomes more and more apparent. Only the brute copulates well, and sexual union is the lyricism of the people.'

It may be remembered also that Samuel Cramer, the prototype of his creator, considered love as being 'above all admiration and desire for the beautiful' and that with him 'sensual reverie' was 'perhaps better than love as it is understood by the ordinary man'.[61]

Baudelaire's feeling of sexual inferiority arising from his inadequacy could explain both his fear of Mme. Sabatier and his predilection for women such as Louchette or Jeanne. With Mme. Sabatier, who never lacked a choice of lovers, he naturally feared unfavourable comparisons or the thought of appearing ridiculous. And so he turned to women who, either because of their ugliness or their own perversity, would tolerate his inadequacies or perhaps even accept abnormal expressions of sexual passion.

That Baudelaire found some sort of sexual satisfaction with Jeanne is evidenced by the erotic poems which she inspired as well as by the deep attachment he felt for her even after their final separation. His gratitude to her, which he often voiced to his mother and to Ancelle, could hardly have sprung from any spiritual or intellectual kinship. It must rather have been the tender gratitude felt by a sensitive, unhappy man for a woman who, though possessed of undeniable exotic beauty, could still make him forget his inhibitions and give him the only sensual pleasure he had known.

Laforgue's idea that Baudelaire's dream signified an unconscious incestuous desire has been advanced by other critics, notably François Porché. Porché maintains with great plausibility that Baudelaire's libido was dominated by the subconscious struggle against incestuous passion that made him reject a woman who in any way resembled the mother image. A letter written by Baudelaire to his mother in 1861 gives substance to this idea, as will be seen.

*   *   *

Anxious to have the powerful support of Sainte-Beuve's pen, Baudelaire wrote to him on March 19, humbly suggesting that the eminent critic write a review of his first volume of translations from Poe, *Histoires Extraordinaires*. It was in this rather brief note that Baudelaire expressed his often quoted intention in regard to Poe: '*It is necessary*, or rather I desire that *Edgar Poe*, who is of little consequence in America, become a great man in *France*.'

In his reply dated the 24th of March Sainte-Beuve promised to write 'something rather short. . . . You are a subtle translator,' he added, 'and your style in certain passages which I have read has a singular beauty.'

Two days later Baudelaire answered Sainte-Beuve in a grateful and exhilarated mood. He explains the character of the book and summarizes the ideas contained in the preface. Actually the preface was only a re-wording in abbreviated form of his 1852 article. It is not known whether or not he wrote to the German scientist, Humboldt, to whom Poe's *Eureka* had been dedicated. As for the poems of Poe, Baudelaire translated only four: *The Raven* (in prose), *To my Mother*, *The Haunted Palace* and *The Conqueror Worm*. It was left for Mallarmé and for others to make Poe's poetry available in French.

Unhappily for Baudelaire, Sainte-Beuve failed to keep his promise and thus deprived his struggling friend and admirer of the help which he so desperately needed.

To Sainte-Beuve
Wednesday, March 26, 1856

You were right in thinking that I would be delighted with that fine short story. Lalanne [editor of *L'Athenaeum français*] has been fore-warned by Asselineau, and the book is to be given to someone else only in case you are not able to write a review. Lalanne has received a copy.

In reply to your letter, I can give you some details which you may find interesting.

There will be a second volume and a second preface. The first volume is designed to catch the attention of the public: *tours de force, speculations, hoaxes,* etc. *Ligeia* is the only important item which morally belongs to the second volume.

The second volume contains a more elevated kind of fantasy: *hallucinations, mental illnesses, the pure grotesque, supernaturalism,* etc.

The second preface will analyse works that I shall not translate, and what is most important will give an account of the *scientific* and *literary* opinions of the author. In regard to that matter I must write to Humboldt to ask his opinions about a small book, *Eureka,* that is dedicated to him.

The first preface, which you have seen, in which I tried to include an emphatic protest against Americanism, is nearly complete from the biographical standpoint. The critics will pretend to consider Poe as nothing but a *clever technician,* but I shall stress in particular the supernatural character of his poetry and of his stories. He is American only in his *technical cleverness.* In other respects his thought is almost *anti-American.* Furthermore, he mocked his compatriots in every way possible.

Next, the fragment to which you refer is part of the second volume. It is a dialogue between two souls after the destruction of the globe. There are *three dialogues of that type* which I shall be happy to lend you at the end of the month, before delivering my second volume to the printer.

And now let me thank you with all my heart; it is so kind of you to be running great risks with me. After the Poe, there will be two volumes of my own, one of criticism [published in 1868], the other of poetry. And so I am excusing myself in advance; besides I am afraid that when I am no longer speaking through the voice of a great poet, I will seem to you a very importunate and very disagreeable person.

Yours,

Ch. Baudelaire

At the end of the second Poe volume I shall include some examples of his poetry.

I am sure that a man as meticulous as you will not mind if I call attention to the spelling of the name (Edgar Poe). No d, no diaeresis, no accent.

To Baudelaire the year 1856 was, in his own words, 'the most cruel of all'. His disappointment at not receiving the recognition for which he had hoped and waited, the frustration caused by his misunderstandings with his mother, by his ever-increasing debts, and by his endless conferences with Ancelle ('the road to Neuilly, whose every stone I know by heart, has filled me with horror for several years') only increased his gloom and irascibility and doubtless led him to quarrel more bitterly with Jeanne. This time it was Jeanne who decided to go her own way. The poet, almost insane with grief and anger, once more turned to his mother and, in spite of their strained relations, confessed his whole desperate situation.

To Madame Aupick
Thursday, September 11, 1856

My dear mother, I beg you not to answer me as you did in your last letter. I have recently experienced too much torment, humiliation, and even anguish to make it worthwhile for you to add your share. A few days ago—about ten perhaps—I wanted to write and ask you, Ancelle being absent and travelling around in the South, to send me a little money, no matter how little, enough to permit me to leave Paris, to divert myself, to kill time: but I should have had to give an explanation, and I shall tell you in a moment why I didn't do so. However, since time has elapsed and since the adventure I underwent has so broken my strength that I can no longer work, it is not now a question of pleasure or of distraction, but of need, and of an urgent need. I have begun to work again in order to numb myself. But you know how irritating wrangling and discussions with brutes can be; now Ancelle will perhaps not be here for another eight or ten days, and this man, my landlord, is pestering me about a trifling two hundred and some francs. Michel Lévy is making me wait from day to day for the signature of our third contract, my desk is covered with uncorrected proof, consequently it is a bad moment to borrow money from him. The man here would like to have his money tomorrow. Mind you I could pacify him with less, with one hundred francs or one hundred and fifty, but I have taken it into my head to use the rest to go and see you, not for long, a day or two, not at your place, of course. I would simply go to the hotel, you would come and greet me, and I would leave again. Besides I have to work hard and I don't plan to be away long. Obviously, I was intending to borrow money from Ancelle on his return. In case you should send me some, I wouldn't take any from him, to make up for it, and I would tell him what I had done.

As I have just told you, I didn't write, although I had the keenest desire to do so, and although I thought you were still in Paris at that time, because the explanations that I would have had to give would have caused you joy, a sort of maternal joy, which I couldn't have endured. My state of mind must have been very obvious, for Michel Lévy, seeing me in that state, now of despondency, now of rage, asked no questions, left me alone, and didn't even urge me to work any more. My liaison with Jeanne, a liaison of fourteen years, is broken. I did all that was humanly possible to prevent the break. The wrench of separating, the struggle lasted two weeks. Jeanne always answered me imperturbably that I had an intractable disposition and that moreover some day I myself would thank her for her decision. That's a woman's crude, bourgeois wisdom for you! As for me, I know that, no matter what enjoyable experience, pleasure, money, or honours may befall me, I shall always miss that woman. Lest my grief, which perhaps you cannot understand, appear too childish, I shall confess that, like a gambler, I had put all my hopes on that head; that woman was my only distraction, my only pleasure, my only comrade, and, in spite of all the mental torment of our stormy relationship, the idea of an irreparable separation had never clearly entered my mind. Even now—and at present I am quite calm—I catch myself thinking while looking at some beautiful object, a lovely landscape, or anything pleasant: why isn't she here to admire this with me, to buy this with me? You see I do not hide my wounds. I assure you it took me a long time, so violent was the shock, to understand that work might possibly bring me pleasure and that, after all, I had duties to perform. I had before my mind an everlasting: what's the use? not to mention a dark veil before my eyes and a constant ringing in my ears.—This lasted quite a long time, but finally it has gone. When at last I realized that it was really *irreparable*, I was seized by a nameless rage: I was sleepless for ten days, vomiting all the time, and obliged to hide, because I wept constantly. My fixed idea was a selfish one moreover: I saw before me an interminable succession of years without a family, without friends, without a mistress, endless years of loneliness and troubles—and nothing to fill my heart. I couldn't even draw consolation from my pride. For all this was my own fault: I used and abused her; I enjoyed torturing her, and now I have been tortured in my turn. Then I was seized by a superstitious terror, I imagined you were ill. I sent someone to your home; I learned of your absence and that you were well, at least I was told that, but tell me so again in your letter.

Why continue this account which no doubt seems only strange to you? I should never have believed that moral suffering would cause such physical torture and that, two weeks later, I could go about my work like any other man. That I am alone, all alone forever, is more than probable.—For from the *moral standpoint* I can no longer put confidence in trollops, *any more than I can in myself*; henceforth I shall have to occupy myself with only my interests in money and fame, without any enjoyment other than literature.

I wasn't able to see Ancelle before his departure. I knew that he would go through Bordeaux and I wrote him in care of *general delivery*. I simply told him that on his return I would perhaps ask him to help this unfortunate woman to whom I am leaving only debts and that, after all, having only myself to think of, I could afford this sad extravagance. His reply seemed unfavourable. It is a question which can easily be postponed to a later date.

The second and third volume of Poe will appear almost simultaneously.

Answer me quickly; for you must understand that it is not merely a vulgar question of money, however annoying it may be, that has prompted me to write to you. To make matters worse, I think that the lawyer who is replacing Ancelle has also left for the South. I still have difficulty in concentrating on my work and I am bored to death. There are still moments when everything seems empty to me.

I embrace you with all my heart.

Charles

Hotel Voltaire, quai Voltaire

Baudelaire's distress clearly indicates how deeply attached he was to Jeanne. Moreover, it becomes evident that his attachment at that late date was largely the result of his need for some companionship and of the horror he felt at the thought of the lonely years ahead; 'I saw before me an interminable succession of years without a family, without friends, without a mistress, endless years of loneliness and troubles— and nothing to fill my heart.' His words recall the expression of abandonment and rejection that is to be found in his letter to Ancelle in 1845 at the time he attempted suicide: 'She [Mme. Aupick] has her *husband*, she possesses a *human being*, an affection, a *friendship*. I have only *Jeanne Lemer.*'

It is interesting to note that Baudelaire no longer blames Jeanne for the separation, as he had done in 1853, but that he accuses himself unsparingly in language that echoes the poem *L'Héautontimorouménos*, which may well have been written at this very time.

The knowledge that he now had only his mother at once increased his fears for her and left him terrified lest he should somehow lose her forever. From this time on his affection for her becomes more apparent in all that he says and does.

Two months after his separation from Jeanne, Baudelaire seems to have recovered his equilibrium and to have experienced a burst of energy and a triumphant self-confidence seldom revealed in his correspondence. In the back of his mind, however, there still lingers the thought of Jeanne and his fears about her future.

To Madame Aupick

November 4, 1856

My dear mother, I don't want to let this day slip by without sending you a few lines to show that I never forget you.—Only a few lines; for you know my tendency to procrastinate which always results in my being forced into precipitate activity later on.—That is my situation now. However, I believe that at present you may have full confidence in my destiny.—The fears that you expressed are foolish.— If the financial questions are hard to solve, my moral health, which is the important thing, is excellent.—The incident which at first depressed me so much, trifling for those lacking imagination, but frightful for me, subsequently gave me an inordinate taste for life.—I am in the process of writing the second preface or in other words the *introduction for Nouvelles Histoires Extraordinaires*, which you will receive in a few days.—As for the third volume [*Arthur Gordon Pym*], you will read it in daily installments, since you get *Le Moniteur*.

Will you let me laugh a little, just a little, at your everlasting desire to see me *like everyone else*, and to have me worthy of your old friends whom you complacently mention? Alas, I haven't come to that yet, and my destiny will be quite different. Why don't you talk a little about marriage to me, like all mamas?

To speak quite frankly, the thought of that girl has never left me,

115

but I am so inured to the business of living, which is nothing but vanity and empty promises, that I feel myself incapable of ever falling into the same inextricable entanglements of love.—The poor child is ill now, and I have refused to go and see her.—For a long time she fled me like the plague, for she knows my frightful temperament compounded of ruse and violence.—I know that she is to leave Paris, and I'm very glad, although I must confess that I feel sad when I think that she is going to die far away from me.

To sum up briefly, I have a diabolical thirst for pleasure, for glory and for power. Often, but I'm afraid not often enough, my dear mother, it is joined to the desire to please you.

In the future be careful not to send me people as tiresome as that bailiff from the Senate, the Tony who is a bill collector. He installed himself in my room for three hours and bored me with his vulgar conversation. I had to be rude in order to get rid of him.

I embrace you with all my heart.

Charles

Please tell me something about your health.

PART FIVE

Les Fleurs du Mal

Exiled on earth in the midst of jeers,
His giant wings keep him from walking.

Les Fleurs du Mal

In December 1856 Baudelaire had signed a contract with his good friend Poulet-Malassis arranging for the publication of his volume of poems, *Les Fleurs du Mal*, as well as a volume of art criticism, *Curiosités esthétiques*. Far from being a good business man, Malassis was an artist who enjoyed publishing limited editions of well printed books.[62] At the time he began work on Baudelaire's volume of verse, Malassis had had little experience and, what was worse, he could ill afford to gamble on so unpopular a writer. The book did not come off the press until June, delayed by the numerous changes made by the author and by his meticulous proofreading. During the months that the volume was in the press, the poet kept up a steady stream of letters to Malassis in which he discussed every possible subject from punctuation to the type of paper and size of the print. Though Malassis often became impatient with Baudelaire's passion for perfection, their friendship survived the strain and is said to have been even strengthened by their literary venture.

A note which Baudelaire wrote to Malassis in March shows the poet hard at work translating Poe, organizing a book of art criticism, and preparing the first edition of *Les Fleurs du Mal*. Since Gautier, the 'magician' to whom the book was dedicated, had advised against the use of the original dedication in which Baudelaire referred to 'this miserable dictionary of melancholy and crime', the poet wrote a second which he had printed at his own expense.

To Poulet-Malassis

March 9, 1857

My dear friend, here is your balm in the form of:

3 galley proofs, in which one poem is to be eliminated;

2 poems to be inserted;

your first sheet of proof which you have not re-read, since I found some strange mistakes;

the new dedication, discussed, agreed upon and accepted by *the magician* who explained to me very clearly that a dedication should not be a profession of faith which, moreover, would have the disadvantage of attracting attention to the scabrous aspect of the book and could lead to its being denounced.

I

By all means *Curiosités Esthétiques* [as a title].

I have only six more installments [of *Arthur Gordon Pym*] to finish. *You know what that means.*—Those frightful columns that have to be ready at 11 o'clock in the morning are hard on my nerves.

Yours,

Ch. Baudelaire

A year after having vainly asked Sainte-Beuve for a review of his first volume of Poe translations, Baudelaire wrote to the critic announcing the publication of his second volume, *Nouvelles Histoires Extraordinaires*. Inspired in large measure by Poe's *Poetic Principle*, the introduction to the second volume constitutes Baudelaire's most interesting essay on Poe, as well as one of his most important critical studies. Disappointed by his previous experience, Baudelaire is rather diffident in calling attention to his new book. Though Sainte-Beuve indicated his intention of writing a review, he failed once more to carry out his promise, either because he lacked sympathetic appreciation of the subject or because he hesitated to support so controversial a figure.

To Sainte-Beuve

March 9, 1857

My dear friend,

You are too indulgent to be offended at the impertinent question mark that I put after the word *remember* in the copy of *Nouvelles Histoires Extraordinaires* left for you yesterday at the office of *Le Moniteur*. If you can do me a service, I shall find it quite natural: you have spoiled me.—If you can't, I shall find that very natural also.

This second volume is more elevated and more poetic in character than two-thirds of the first.—The third volume (now being published in *Le Moniteur*) will include a third preface.

The story about the end of the world is called *Conversation Between Eiros and Charmion*.

A new printing of the first volume, *in which most of the misprints have been eliminated*, has just come off the press. Michel [Lévy] knows that a copy is to be reserved for you. If I don't have time to bring it, I'll have it sent.

Yours affectionately,

Ch. Baudelaire

After the death of General Aupick in April 1857, Mme. Aupick decided to retire to Honfleur where several years earlier she and her husband had built a small cottage by the sea. Since the general had always held it a matter of principle to spend all the salary paid him as a public official, Mme. Aupick was left with only the pension of a general's widow and the money bequeathed her by her first husband.

With the death of his stepfather, Charles seemed to undergo a change. Drawn more closely to his mother in her sorrow, he assumed a tender, protective air quite different from his selfish, demanding attitude of the past. When Mme. Aupick attributed his solicitude to a feeling of filial duty, Charles, hurt and almost angry, vigorously protested in a kindly, but frank letter. After informing his mother of the 32,000 francs brought by the sale of her husband's furniture and effects, he goes on to explain the reasons for his change in conduct.

To Madame Aupick

June 3, 1857

My dear mother,

. . . .

—A short time ago you complimented me in a most insulting way about my change of attitude toward you, which goes to prove that, though you are my mother, you don't know me very well. The sale, your momentary debts, your loneliness, everything is of interest to me; whether great or small, important or trivial, let me assure you I am passionately concerned, and not just as a matter of filial duty.

I wish to indicate very briefly the reasons explaining my feelings and my conduct since the death of my stepfather; in a few words I hope to clarify my attitude in this great misfortune as well as my future conduct:—this event has been something very solemn for me, like a recall to duty. I have sometimes been very hard and very rude to you, my dear mother; but after all I could think that someone was concerned with your happiness—and the first idea that struck me at the time of the death was that from now on, I was the one who naturally had that responsibility. All the things I had permitted myself, indifference, egoism, extreme rudeness, which are always the result of disorder and loneliness, all that is forbidden.—Everything that is humanly possible *will be done* to create a new sort of happiness in the last years of your life.—After all, it is not such a difficult matter, since you attach so much importance to the success of all my projects. In working for myself, I shall be working for you.

Don't worry too much about my wretched debts and about the fame which until now I have sought with such indolence and which hereafter will be all the more difficult to achieve. If every day one does a little of what should be done, all human difficulties resolve themselves naturally. I ask only one thing of you (*for myself*), that you make an effort to keep well and to live for a long time, as long as possible.

. . . .

Charles

It was undoubtedly as a result of this letter that Mme. Aupick wrote a few days later to her daughter-in-law: 'Tell Alphonse that I am very pleased with his brother, at least as far as his good intentions are concerned; as for his leading an orderly life, I don't know if he will ever change . . . When the Emons go to visit their daughter, I shall take advantage of the time I am alone to have Charles come and spend a few days with me.' 63

Baudelaire was by no means ignorant of his mother's deference to the opinions of the Emons, nor was he unaware of their efforts to influence her against him in every possible way. They had so completely convinced her that living with Charles would result in her complete financial ruin that she decided to remain alone at Honfleur and even hesitated to ask her son to spend a few days with her in her delightful retreat by the sea. Charles, who had hoped to enjoy with his mother some of the happiness he had known during her first widowhood, was deeply disappointed, but too proud to plead his own cause.

In his letter of July 9th Baudelaire makes no effort to hide his dislike of his father's old friend and associate. He insinuates that his decision not to visit Mme. Aupick at Honfleur was partly prompted by his knowledge that Mme. Aupick would fear the disapproval of M. Emon. Then, having opened the subject, he unburdens his heart and reveals the misery and humiliation he had experienced on the day of his stepfather's funeral when, to please his mother, he had bought a suit of mourning and attended the ceremony. The hostile reception he had received was seared on his memory for years to come. Only M. Jaquotot, an old friend of his own father and a member of the family council that met in 1844, had spoken to him with kindness and understanding. As a result of their encounter at the funeral, Charles renewed his friendship with M. Jaquotot and turned to him on several occasions for help and advice.

To Madame Aupick
Thursday, July 9, 1857

I can assure you that you need have no worry about me; it is you, rather, who cause me the gravest anxiety, and your letter, so filled with grief, has certainly done nothing to allay it. If you give way to your sorrow so completely, you will become ill and that will be the worst of misfortunes and for me the most unbearable kind of worry. I not only want you to seek diversion, but in addition I want you to have new pleasures.—Madame Orfila certainly seems to me a very sensible woman.

As for my silence, don't ascribe it to anything but one of those periods of lassitude which, to my shame, sometimes overpower me and prevent me not only from doing any work, but even from carrying out the simplest duties. Moreover, I wanted to write a letter, send you your prayer book and my book of poetry all at the same time.

The prayer book is not entirely finished; craftsmen, even the most intelligent, are so stupid. There are a few small things to rectify. I have had a little trouble about it, but you will be pleased.

As for the *Poetry* (published two weeks ago), at first I had no intention of showing it to you, as you know. But as I thought about it further, it seemed to me that modesty on my part would be as foolish as prudery on yours, since, after all, you would hear the book talked about, at least in the reviews that I'll send you. I received 16 copies on ordinary paper and 4 on fine paper. I have saved one of the latter for you and, if you haven't received it yet, it's because I wanted to have it bound.—You know that I have never thought of literature and the arts as pursuing any moral end and that for me beauty of conception and style are sufficient. But this book, whose title *Fleurs du Mal* says everything, is clothed, as you will see, with a cold and sinister beauty; it was created with passion and deliberation. Moreover, all the unfavourable things said about it are proof of its positive value. The book enrages people.—In fact, appalled, as I was, by the horror that I was going to inspire, I removed a third of the book while it was in the press.—They deny me everything, imagination and even a knowledge of the French language. I care nothing about all those imbeciles and I know that the book with its faults and merits will take its place in the memory of the literary public beside the best poems of V. Hugo, of Th. Gautier and even of Byron.—I have one request: since you are always with the Emons, don't let the book fall into the hands of Mlle. Emon. As for the priest, whom you doubtless entertain, you may show it to him. He will think that I am damned and he won't dare tell you.—A rumour has spread that I am going to be prosecuted, but nothing of the kind will happen. A government that has the terrible Paris elections on its hands doesn't have time to prosecute a madman.

A thousand pardons for all the childish effusions of my vanity. I had seriously thought of going to Honfleur, but I didn't dare say anything to you about it. I had thought of cauterizing my sloth, of cauterizing it once and for all, at the seashore, by a period of intense work, far from all frivolous preoccupations, either on my third volume of *Edgar Poe*, or on my first play to which I must give birth, come what may.

But I have work to do that can't be accomplished in a place without libraries, prints and museums. First of all I must finish *Curiosités Esthétiques*, the *Poèmes nocturnes*, and the *Confessions du Mangeur d'opium*.

The *Poèmes nocturnes* [later called *Petits Poèmes en Prose*] are for the *Revue des Deux Mondes*; the *Mangeur d'opium* is a new translation of a magnificent writer [De Quincey], unknown in Paris.[64] It is for *Le Moniteur*.

But I had to think of M. Emon (why not be perfectly frank!). He is your friend, and I insist on not displeasing you. Nevertheless, do you think I can forget his inferiority and his rudeness, or the churlish manner with which he accepted my handshake on that cruel day when, to please you, and only for that reason, I humiliated myself even more than you have humiliated me for so many years?

—Ancelle is well; *I have seen him only twice since you left*. He is as absent-minded as ever; his mind still works slowly, and he still loves his wife and daughter without being ashamed of it.

I am returning the letter from the gentleman I don't know. I have no idea who M. Durand is.

When I went to visit the tomb of my stepfather, I was quite surprised to find myself in front of an open grave. I went to see the caretaker who informed me of the transfer, and who gave me this little piece of paper as a guide.—Our wreaths, faded by heavy rains, had been carefully moved to the new burial place. I added some others.

I embrace you very affectionately, dear mother.

C. B.

Les Fleurs du Mal had gone on sale on June 25th and not long afterward the ominous rumblings of an approaching storm could be heard. On July 5th there appeared in *Le Figaro* a review by Gustave Bourdin in which Baudelaire was subjected to another brutal attack and his poetry assailed in a most flagrant manner. Bourdin went so far as to express doubt about the poet's sanity and to call his book 'a hospital open to all the aberrations of the human mind and to all the putrescence of the human heart'.

When it became evident that prosecution was imminent, Baudelaire wrote in haste to Poulet-Malassis warning him to take prompt measures and chiding him for his delay in selling out the edition. Only a few hundred copies had been put together; the rest still remained in sheets.

To Poulet-Malassis

July 11, 1857

Quickly, hide the whole edition and *hide it carefully*; you must have 900 copies in unbound sheets. There were still a hundred at Lanier's; the gentlemen there seemed quite surprised that I wanted to save 50. I put them in a safe place, and I signed a receipt. There are thus 50 left to feed the Cerberus of Justice.

That's what comes of sending copies to *Le Figaro*!!! That's what comes of not wanting to *launch* a book seriously. At least we would have had the consolation, if you had done all that should be done, of having sold the edition in 3 weeks, and we would have had nothing but the glory of a lawsuit, from which, moreover, it is easy to extricate oneself.

You will receive this letter in time, I hope; it will leave tonight. You will have it tomorrow at four o'clock. The seizure hasn't yet taken place. The information came to me from M. Wateville through Leconte de Lisle who, unfortunately, had allowed 5 days to elapse.

I am convinced that this mishap comes only as a result of the article in *Le Figaro* and from ridiculous gossip. Fear has done the harm.

Don't talk too much; don't frighten your mother or de Broise [Malassis' brother-in-law and partner], and come quickly so we can reach an understanding.

I'm going to write you a predated, *official* letter whose envelope you will destroy.

I have just seen Lanier and Victor, more changeable than the wind; they think themselves dishonoured and they were so spineless as to turn over the bookshop to the *inspector general of the press* in order to win his favour!!!

Yours,
Charles Baudelaire

I told M. Lanier that, since the 50 copies that I left him had to be considered a total loss, he at least ought to send them out as quickly as possible to the various shops which as yet had not received any. But he refused; he thinks that the inspector, while buying his copy, checked the remaining number with an eagle's eye.

On the 12th of July a second denunciatory article appeared in *Le Figaro* and this time Baudelaire knew that his chances of escaping prosecution were slim indeed. What he badly needed was the salutary effect of an article coming from the pen of the highly respected Sainte-Beuve, but there seemed little likelihood of such good fortune. It is true the critic had praised *Les Fleurs du Mal* in private, but he was far too cautious to risk defending the poet in public. In speaking favourably of *Madame Bovary* he had already offended the Minister of the Interior and had provoked an article in *L'Univers* suggesting that he be dismissed from the staff of the government-supported *Moniteur*. And Sainte-Beuve was hardly made of heroic stuff or capable of sacrifices, even for a close friend.

Though Sainte-Beuve failed to come to the defence of Baudelaire, he did ask his colleague Thierry to write a review. Thierry wrote a highly complimentary article, comparing the poet to Dante and praising the manner in which he had dared to look evil in the face like an enemy. Baudelaire and Asselineau, who had spent the entire night standing outside the press office anxiously waiting to see if the review would escape government censure, found their relief but momentary. The Minister of Justice, all the more infuriated by Thierry's defence and encouraged by another defamatory article in the *Journal de Bruxelles*, took action and confiscated the printed sheets in Alençon on July 16th.

On the advice of his friends, Baudelaire chose as his lawyer Chaix d'Est Ange who drew up a line of argument based in part on the suggestions of Sainte-Beuve.[65]

Harassed as he was by anxiety over the impending prosecution, Baudelaire still found time two days before the trial to write to Mme. Sabatier and send her a copy of *Les Fleurs du Mal*. So long a time had elapsed since his last letter (May 8, 1854) that this sudden re-awakening of his affection precisely two days before the trial seems somewhat surprising. Although the incident to which he refers in his letter had no doubt aroused his resentment, this was a strange time in which to patch up a petty quarrel.

It would seem quite possible that Baudelaire was simply 'using' Mme. Sabatier, though in a slightly different sense than that implied by him in a previous letter to her. He had sought every means of avoiding prosecution. Now that no escape seemed possible, he remembered

Mme. Sabatier's attractions and her ability to charm and sway all those within her reach. The very fact that he admits he needs her help and that he even carefully lists the judges seems proof of his hope that in some way she could influence at least one of them in his favour.

It is not necessary to believe that the letter is altogether insincere. It was perhaps the result of Baudelaire's remembrance of past emotions rather than a correct statement of his state of mind at that moment.

To Madame Sabatier

Tuesday, August 18, 1857

Dear Madame,

You didn't believe for a single moment, did you, that I had forgotten you? I reserved for you, from the date of publication, a copy printed on special paper, and if it is not attired in a garb worthy of you, the fault is not mine, but rather that of the binder from whom I had ordered something much more gay and distinctive.

Would you believe that the wretches (I am referring to the examining magistrate, the prosecuting attorney, etc.) have dared to condemn, among other poems, two of those composed for my beloved Idol (*Tout Entière* and *A Celle qui est trop gaie*)? The latter is the one which the venerable Sainte-Beuve declares the best in the volume.

This is the first time that I have not disguised my handwriting. If I were not overwhelmed with business and with correspondence (the hearing is day after tomorrow), I would take this opportunity to ask your pardon for so much foolishness and childishness. But still, haven't you more than evened the score, especially through your little sister? The little monster! She froze me with horror one day when we met, by laughing heartily in my face and saying: *are you still in love with my sister and do you still write her superb letters?*—I understood first of all that when I tried to hide, I succeeded very badly, and second that beneath your charming face you hide an uncharitable heart. Rakes are *lovers*, but poets are *worshippers*, and your sister, in my opinion, is hardly the sort to understand eternal things.

Permit me then, at the risk of amusing you also, to renew the declarations which so highly delighted the little vixen. Imagine an amalgam of dreams, affection, and respect, with a thousand childish fancies filled with seriousness, and you will come close to understanding that very sincere something which I feel unable to define more clearly.

It is impossible to forget you. They say there have been poets who have lived all their lives with their eyes fixed on a beloved image. In fact, I believe (but I am too directly involved) that *fidelity is one of the signs of genius.*

You are more than an image dreamed of and cherished, you are my *superstition.* When I do something utterly stupid, I say to myself: My Heavens! What if she knew! When I do something that is good, I say to myself: *That's something that brings me nearer to her—in spirit.*

And the last time that I had the happiness (in spite of myself) of meeting you! for you do not know how carefully I avoid you!—I said to myself: it would be strange if that carriage were waiting for her; perhaps it would be well for me to take another street.—And then: *Good evening, sir!* with that beloved voice whose tone delights and fills me with pain. I went away, repeating all along the street: *Good evening, sir!* trying to imitate the sound of your voice.

I saw my judges last Thursday. I shall not say that they are not handsome; they are abominably ugly; and their souls must resemble their faces.

Flaubert had the Empress on his side. I need a woman's help. And a few days ago the bizarre thought struck me that possibly you, through perhaps complicated connections and channels, could succeed in setting right one of those blockheads.

The hearing is for the morning after tomorrow, Thursday.

The names of the monsters are:

President	Dupaty.
Imperial attorney . . .	Pinard (formidable)
Judges	Delesvaux.
——	De Ponton d'Amécourt.
——	Nacquart.

6th Magistrate's Court.

I want to put all these trivialities aside.

Remember that someone is thinking of you, that there is never anything crass in his thought, and that he bears you a slight grudge for your mischievous gaiety.

I beg you most fervently to keep to yourself hereafter everything that I may confide to you. You are my constant companion and my secret. This intimacy, in which I have been giving myself the cue for so long a time, is what has given me the courage to assume so familiar a tone.

Goodbye, dear Madame, I kiss your hands with deep devotion.

All the poems included between page 84 and page 105 belong to you.

Charles Baudelaire

It was on the 20th of August that Baudelaire was finally brought to trial. Seated with the timid de Broise (Malassis had been unavoidably detained in Alençon) and surrounded by petty criminals, Baudelaire was subjected to the mortifying experience of facing the curious onlookers who had come attracted by the sensational aspects of the case.

The judges were not long in reaching a decision. Although Baudelaire was acquitted of the charge of offending religious morality, he was condemned, on the basis of the sordid realism of his poetry, of having offended public morality.

In a letter to Flaubert, Baudelaire cites the penalties imposed by the court and lists by their numbers the poems that had been banned. The poems to which he refers were: *Les Bijoux, Le Léthé, A Celle qui est trop gaie, Lesbos, Femmes Damnées*, and *Les Métamorphoses du Vampire*.

To Gustave Flaubert

Tuesday, August 25, 1857

Dear friend, I am hastily writing you a note before five o'clock, solely to prove my repentance for not having thanked you for your kind wishes. If you only knew the abyss of puerile activities into which I have been plunged! And the article on *Madame Bovary* has been postponed again for several days![66] What an interruption in one's life a ridiculous event like this can be!

The comedy was played on Thursday; it lasted a long time!

The result, 300 francs fine, 200 francs for the publisher, suppression of numbers 20, 30, 39, 80, 81, and 87. I shall write to you at length this evening.

Yours, as you know,
Ch. Baudelaire

Far from thinking she was being used in any sense of the word, Mme. Sabatier was deeply touched by Baudelaire's respectful and worshipful letter. Either because she had really come to love him, or because she pitied his shyness and sensitivity and misinterpreted the nature of his love, she decided to take the initiative and immediately wrote asking him to meet her. It is uncertain where the meeting took place or exactly what occurred. What is certain is that Mme. Sabatier and Baudelaire met on August 30th and that, as a result of that meeting, their relationship was 'completely upset'.

To Madame Sabatier

August 31, 1857

I have destroyed the deluge of childish explanations piled up on my desk. I did not consider them serious enough for you, my dear beloved. —I take up your two letters and I make a fresh attempt to answer them.

I need a little courage for that; for my nerves are so badly on edge that I could scream and I woke up with the inexplicable feeling of anxiety with which I left you last night.

. . . complete lack of modesty.

It is for that very reason that you are even more dear to me.

It seems to me that I have belonged to you since the first day I saw you. You may do what you like with me, but I am yours in body, mind and soul.

I urge you to hide this letter carefully, my poor dear! *Do you really know what you are saying?* People are put in prison for not paying their debts, but they are never punished for the violation of oaths of love and friendship.

And so I said to you yesterday: You will forget me; you will deceive me; he who amuses you will soon bore you.—And today I add: he alone will suffer who, like a fool, takes matters of the heart seriously.— You see, my most beautiful darling, that I am *horribly* prejudiced against women.—In short, I lack *faith.*—You have a lovely soul, but it is a woman's soul.

You see how in a few days' time our relationship has been completely upset. In the first place we are both fearful of hurting an honest man who has the good fortune still to be in love with you.

Then we are afraid of our own stormy natures, for we know (I, especially) that there are knots difficult to untie.

And finally, finally, a few days ago you were a divinity, which is so convenient, so beautiful, so inviolable. Now you are a woman.—And if, unfortunately for me, I acquire the right to be jealous! how frightful even to think of it! but with someone like you whose eyes are full of smiling charm for everyone, I would suffer martyrdom.

The second letter bears a seal whose solemnity would please me, if I were sure that you understood it. *Never meet or never part!* That clearly means that it would be better never to have met, but that once having met, we should never part. On a farewell letter this seal would be very ironic.

Finally, come what may, I am something of a fatalist. But what I realize only too well is that I abhor passion, because I know it for what it is with all its ignominy;—and then suddenly the image of my beloved which transcends everything in my life becomes too desirable.

I do not dare re-read this letter; I should perhaps feel obliged to change it; for I am afraid of hurting you; it seems to me that I must have revealed something of the disagreeable side of my nature.

It seems to me impossible to have you come to that filthy rue J. J. Rousseau. Yet I have many other things to tell you. You must write me then and tell me how it can be done.

As for our little project, if it becomes possible, give me a few days advance notice.

Goodbye, my dear beloved; I bear you a slight grudge for being so charming. Remember that when I carry away with me the perfume of your arms and your hair, I also carry with it the longing to return to you. What an intolerable obsession!

Charles

I have made up my mind to take this letter myself to the rue J. J. Rousseau, for fear you may go there today. It will get there sooner.

Baudelaire's letter to Mme. Sabatier has been subjected to much scrutiny and guesswork. There are many who believe that the words 'a few days ago you were a divinity . . . now you are a woman' imply that Baudelaire must have been her lover, at least for the moment. Yet the poet might also have been referring to the fact that, by offering herself to him, Mme. Sabatier had destroyed the illusions which he had built up around her.

The absence of any tragic undertones in the letter, the subtle reasons cited for not becoming more intimate seem to suggest what Mme. Sabatier herself quickly divined—that Baudelaire did not really love her. 'Do you want me to tell you what I really think, a cruel thought which hurts me very much. It is that you do not love me. Hence your fears, your hesitations at forming a liaison which, under such conditions, would become a source of annoyance to you, and to me an endless torture.' [67]

It is of little consequence whether absence of love on Baudelaire's part resulted from an unresolved Oedipus complex, from his love for Marie Daubrun, or from his timidity and fear of inadequacy. The fact remains that from the very beginning of their friendship he had emphasized the idealistic nature of his affection and that after 1854 his interest in Mme. Sabatier must have diminished, as the lack of letters from 1854 to 1857 would suggest. From that day on Baudelaire did his utmost to put their friendship on a more formal basis. For a time he ceased to attend her Sunday dinners, in spite of the fact that he had been one of her most regular guests. His letters are more impersonal, though still filled with gracious and affectionate compliments. Finally he came to sign his letters with the conventional endings that he might have used for the most casual acquaintance.

Crépet and Blin have suggested that the key to Baudelaire's relationship with Mme. Sabatier may be found in his prose poem, *Laquelle est la vraie?* Since almost everything that Baudelaire wrote tends to be autobiographical in nature, the possibility is a very strong one, especially since the first paragraph of *Laquelle est la vraie?* is very closely allied in spirit to his poem *Hymne*, composed in honour of Apollonie. If such were the case, the prose poem would seem to indicate that Baudelaire had experienced a rude awakening from a beautiful dream, that the woman he had worshipped for her spiritual beauty was after all 'only a slut' and that the poet remained inextricably trapped with one foot caught in the grave wherein his 'ideal' lay buried.

Though Baudelaire appeared calm and resigned in his letter to Flaubert, he was in reality much upset and in fact never fully recovered from the blow. Asselineau tells how he had asked the poet immediately after the trial: 'And did you think you would be acquitted?' In astonishment Baudelaire had answered: 'I thought they were going to make amends for the wrong done to my honour!' [68]

The unhappy writer was finally persuaded to accept the verdict of the court and on the advice of his friends went to see Pinard, the prosecuting attorney, who treated him with the greatest sympathy and consideration. It may have been Pinard who suggested that he write directly to the Empress Eugénie. As a result of his letter, the fine was reduced from three hundred francs to fifty.

To The Empress

November 6, 1857

Madame,

It requires all the prodigious presumption of a poet to dare to occupy the attention of Your Majesty with a case as trivial as mine. I have had the misfortune to be condemned for a volume of poems entitled: *Les Fleurs du Mal*, since the horrible frankness of my title did not serve as sufficient protection. I believed that I had produced a great and beautiful work, above all a clear work; it has been judged so obscure that I have been condemned to re-do the book and to strike out several poems (six out of a hundred). I must say that the Ministry of Justice has treated me with admirable courtesy, and that the very terms of the judgement imply the recognition of my pure and high intentions. But the fine, increased by expenses that are unintelligible to me, exceeds the resources of the proverbial poverty of poets and so, encouraged by so many proofs of esteem that I have received from highly placed friends, and at the same time, convinced that the heart of the Empress is open to pity for all tribulations, spiritual as well as material, I have conceived the idea, after a period of indecision and timidity that lasted ten days, of appealing to the gracious goodness of your Majesty and of entreating your intercession with the Minister of Justice.

Deign, Madame, to accept the homage of the feelings of profound respect with which I have the honour of being

the very devoted and very obedient

servant and subject

of Your Majesty,

Charles Baudelaire

19, quai Voltaire

Baudelaire's discouragement grew more marked as the year drew to its close, a year which should have brought him the greatest joy and pride, but which had only ended in disaster and humiliation. The condemnation of his book, the painful incident with Mme. Sabatier, his wretched health, and finally his loneliness 'without affection and without work', all combined to increase the inertia and moral lassitude which he struggled in vain to throw off. On Christmas Day he had written his mother telling her he was sending a small package that included, among other things, some articles about *Les Fleurs du Mal*, that book in which, as he said, 'I wanted to put some of my anger and sadness, and . . . which you so strangely spurned when you thought it best to add your reproaches to the insults which overwhelmed me on all sides.'

On the 30th of December Baudelaire wrote again and this time he made no attempt to hide what was hurting him most of all—his mother's refusal to accept him in her own home.

To Madame Aupick

December 30, 1857

I certainly have much to complain about in myself and I am quite surprised and alarmed by my state. Do I need a change? I have no idea. Is it physical illness that weakens my mind and will, or is it spiritual sloth that fatigues the body? I have no idea. What I feel is an immense discouragement, an unbearable sensation of loneliness, a perpetual fear of some vague misfortune, a complete lack of confidence in my powers, a total absence of desires, the impossibility of finding anything to distract my mind. For a while I found interest in the strange success of my book and in the hatreds it aroused, and then after that I experienced a relapse. You see, my dear mother, that that is a rather serious state of mind for a man whose profession it is to invent and give substance to works of the imagination.—I constantly ask myself: what's the good of this? what's the good of that? That is truly mental depression of the most serious kind.—Of course, recalling that I have already experienced similar states and that I have shaken them off, I should not be too alarmed; but also I don't remember ever having sunk so low or having my ennui drag on so long. Add to that the never ending despair caused by my poverty, by constant wrangling and by interruptions in my work occasioned by old debts (*don't be uneasy, this is not an alarming appeal to your weakness*).

. . . .

I am going to tell you very briefly not what prevented me from going to Honfleur, (I wasn't able to do so), but what prevented me from answering you. I was afraid both of hurting you and of not being understood. The day after the death of my stepfather, you told me that I was disgracing you, and you forbade me (before I dreamed of making such a request) to ever think of living with you. Further, you obliged me to make a humiliating show of friendliness with M. Emon. Be fair and grant, dear mother, that I bore that with the humility and the gentleness demanded by your unhappy situation. But later when, after writing me letters filled with scolding and bitterness and after reproaching me for that cursed book which, after all, is only a very defensible *work of art,* when you invited me to come and see you, making it clear that M. Emon's absence made my visit to Honfleur possible—as *if M. Emon were in a position to open or to close my mother's doors to me*—when finally you carefully enjoined me not to incur any debts in Honfleur—well, good heavens, I was so nonplussed, so astonished that I may very well have become unjust.—You see what a lasting impression that letter left in my memory. I didn't know what to decide or what to answer; after reading it, I felt an unexpressible agitation, and finally, after two weeks of not knowing what to do, I resolved not to do anything at all.

To tell the truth, my dear mother, I believe that you have never realized my intolerable sensibility.—At present we are very much alone and very defenceless, for I don't think my brother really counts. Suppose we try once and for all to be happy for each other's sake?

I must call your attention to a disagreeable little matter; I would gladly have kept it from you, if it weren't an indication that other similar mistakes may have been made. Doubtless the credit goes to M. Emon.—Some months ago I discovered one of my father's paintings in a shop in the Passage des Panoramas (a nude figure, a nude woman in bed who sees two nude figures in a dream). I had no money, not even enough to make a deposit, and since then the unendurable torrent of daily futilities has made me neglect the matter.—Do you think that several such blunders have been committed?—My father was a wretched artist; but all these old things have a moral value.

Goodbye, dear mother, tell me what your expectations are with regard to your health, whether living there suits you, and that you consider it important to live a long time for my sake.

I embrace you, and in my imagination I feel your embrace.

Charles

Mme. Aupick was genuinely moved and perhaps a bit conscience-stricken by her son's frank and revealing letter. She had finally begun to read *Les Fleurs du Mal*, encouraged by what Charles had told her in a letter written January 11th: 'You haven't noticed that in *Les Fleurs du Mal* there are two poems concerning you or at least alluding to intimate details of our former life, going back to that time of your widowhood which left me with such strange and sad memories—one: *I haven't forgotten, near the city* . . . (Neuilly), and the other which follows: *The greathearted servant of whom you were jealous* . . . (Mariette)? I left those poems without titles and without any further clarification, because I have a horror of prostituting intimate family matters.'

To her great astonishment and delight, Mme. Aupick found, as she wrote to her stepson Claude, that the book contained in addition to some horrible and offensive descriptions, 'some marvellous verses of great purity of language and simplicity of form that produce a wonderful poetic effect'. [69]

In the meantime, in spite of the remonstrances of the Emons, she invited Charles to come and live with her. Baudelaire's joy at receiving the invitation is clearly reflected in his reply.

To Madame Aupick
Friday, February 19, 1858

Dear mother, three weeks ago you wrote me a very charming letter (the only one with that tone in many years)—and I haven't yet answered. You must have been very painfully surprised. As for me, when I read that letter, I realized that you still love me, more than I had thought, and that many things could be put right, and that much happiness was still possible for us.

You may have been a little unjust in the various ways by which you doubtless tried to explain my silence. The truth is that your letter, so very kind and maternal, almost hurt me. It pained me to see how much you really wanted me to be with you, and to think how I would have to grieve you, since I was still not ready to leave.

First of all, I don't have enough confidence in Michel Lévy to leave Paris while my book is in the hands of one of his printers. You know how terribly meticulous I am about everything. I would be uneasy, and I would have good reason to be. (The book has 8 signatures, and I am on the 5th; the rest can be done in 10 days, if I work hard at it.)

In addition, think of the horrible existence I am leading, which leaves me so little time for work, and of all the questions to be settled before my departure. (At the beginning of the month, for example, I was forced to lose 6 days while I was hiding to keep from being arrested. Unfortunately, I had left my books and manuscript at home. That is only one of a thousand small details of my life.)

To have happiness so close, almost in one's hands, and not to be able to grasp it! And to know not only that one is going to be happy, but that one is going to bring happiness to someone to whom it is owed!

And then to all that suffering add this one, which perhaps you will not understand: when a man's nerves are very much weakened by an accumulation of anxieties and afflictions, the Devil, in spite of all resolutions, slips into his head each morning with this thought: Why not rest today and forget everything? Tonight I can do everything that is urgent.—And then night comes, the mind is horrified by the multitude of tasks that have been postponed; overwhelming melancholy brings a kind of paralysis, and the next day the same comedy is repeated in good faith, with the same confidence and the same pangs of conscience.

I am genuinely eager to get away from this cursed city where I have suffered so much and where I have lost so much time. Who knows if my mind will not be rejuvenated there with the aid of happiness and peace?

I have in my mind some twenty novels and two plays. I don't want a respectable and commonplace reputation; I want to amaze people, to achieve a towering position like Byron, Balzac or Chateaubriand. Is there still time? Ah! if I had known, when I was young, the value of time, of health and of money! And those cursed *Fleurs du Mal* that I have to begin again! I need peace of mind for that. To become a poet again artificially by an act of will, to return to a path that I believed had been cut once and for all, to treat anew a subject that I thought was exhausted, and all that in order to obey the will of three judges, one of them a *Nacquart* [son of Balzac's doctor and one of the judges in Baudelaire's trial].

In all seriousness and without exaggeration, I believe that, by assiduous work at home, I can pay all of my debts in two years, that is to say, earn three times as much as here. How unfortunate that you didn't offer me this marvellous arrangement almost a year ago, at a time when I was not plunged in such monstrous difficulties!

About *Les Fleurs du Mal*, no more compliments, you have given me four times as many as I asked.

. . . .

And then to return to the story of my plans for happiness, I shall be able to *read* and *read* and *read* without hindering my productivity. All my days spent in refurbishing my mind! For I must confess, my dear mother, that my unfortunate education has been sadly and cruelly interrupted by all my follies and tribulations. My youth is vanishing, and I often think with terror of the flight of the years; they are, however, made up of only hours and minutes, but in wasting time one thinks only of the fraction of time, and not of the sum total.

. . . .

In reading my letter, I don't want you to think that I am prompted only by my selfishness. Much of my thought is this: *My mother doesn't know me, she has scarcely known me; we haven't had time to live together. We must nevertheless find a few years of happiness together.*

. . . .

Goodbye. It is half-past four. I embrace you with all my heart. This letter is atrociously scrawled. But I have scribbled in big letters, hoping it would tire your eyes less.

Charles

Before going to Honfleur, Baudelaire felt he had to pay some of the most pressing debts that were hanging over his head. Knowing that his earnings were far too meagre to permit such a luxury and not wishing to borrow from his mother, he conceived the plan of getting an advance of his yearly income amounting to 2,400 francs.

So irritated had he become by what he considered Ancelle's intrusion in his personal affairs and by his endless delays that he could no longer bear to consult him. Remembering M. Jaquotot's kindness at his stepfather's funeral, he appealed to him and begged him to intercede with his mother. To his great astonishment and almost pathetic joy, Mme. Aupick agreed, and Baudelaire at once began making plans to leave for Honfleur.

But his joy was shortlived. Mme. Aupick had failed to tell Charles that, instead of ordering Ancelle to carry out the transaction, she had merely consulted with him. Baudelaire was ill with disappointment. He knew Ancelle would insist on a thorough investigation lasting for weeks or perhaps even months. And so he wrote his mother to tell her that his dream of happiness had come to an end.

To Madame Aupick

February 20, 1858

I have had three days of real joy; that is always something gained, for joy is so rare. In spite of everything, I thank you for it. But it was only a beautiful dream.—I am not giving up the idea of going to Honfleur. My wish to do so will grow stronger from day to day. But I shall go with my own money, and when I shall have been able to extricate myself by my own efforts.

I beg you, dear mother, not to get angry. I'll certainly go to Honfleur, but when? I don't know. I shall do everything necessary for that purpose.—I received your fatal letter this morning, so that the letter that I sent you yesterday, with its detailed explanations, is worthless.

I am obliged to provide quickly for the difficulties into which I am going to be plunged. They are more serious than they were previously, for, as I told you, I have made appointments with several people for the coming week, and I have refused money offered me elsewhere. It's enough to make me lose my mind.

But however appalling it may be, that still isn't the worst of it. Ancelle, to whom you have no doubt already written, is going to come and pester me to death with his services, and when he sees me refuse his money, he will want to do me a favour against my will. He is going to weary me with his odious conversation. I am so much in need of peace. He is going to force himself upon me here, he will try to worm his way into my business, to forcibly drag from me an account of my difficulties. Just thinking about his visit turns my pain into anger. Seeing my determination to refuse everything, he will try to do me the greatest possible harm with the usual pretext of being helpful. I can't leave Paris in order to avoid him; the remedy would be worse than the disease. He is going to force his way into my affairs, as he did at the hearing when I was prosecuted. He insisted on entering into conversation with my friends whom he didn't know at all, for he has such a passion for making acquaintances and for meddling in everything, and my friends would ask me who that tall gentleman was who seemed to know me so well. I anxiously kept my eye on him all the time, afraid that he would compromise me or make me appear ridiculous.—I hope that gives you an idea of his behaviour.

. . . .

I beg you, dear mother, not to be offended if I prefer my hell to an intervention that has always been disastrous for me. The usurer would have been better; but it's too late.

I hope I can count on you to keep Ancelle from meddling in any way. *In refusing his money, I have the right to refuse his services.*

I have never had any really serious quarrel with him, and I have never insulted him. That might happen; I should be ashamed and grieved about it, but the harm would have been done.

Remember that one of my great pleasures in going to Honfleur was to escape him.

I embrace you very tenderly.

Charles

In the meantime Baudelaire's fears proved well founded. In an effort to protect the best interests of his ward, the conscientious, but bungling Ancelle decided to investigate the matter for himself. He came to the hotel where Baudelaire owed a large debt and questioned the proprietor at length. Baudelaire, who was given a garbled version of the interview by the landlord, became enraged. Completely misunderstanding Ancelle's kindly intentions, he felt he was being spied upon and that his guardian was trying to pry into his personal life. His excitement and his anger assumed an almost pathological character. On one Saturday afternoon he wrote his mother no less than six letters, threatening in each one to avenge himself on his guardian. In one of the six, he told Mme. Aupick how Ancelle had asked if he came in late at night and if he entertained women in his room. He concluded with a paragraph that is almost comic in its display of childish hysteria: 'Ancelle is a wretch and I am going TO SLAP him before HIS WIFE and his CHILDREN. I am going to SLAP him at 4 o'clock (it is now half past two) and if I don't find him, I shall wait. I swear that this will have an end, and a terrible end.'

That night and the next day Baudelaire was ill with fever, neuralgia and spells of vomiting. A few days later, M. Jaquotot, at the request of Mme. Aupick, succeeded in making peace and in convincing Charles of his discourtesy to his guardian. The imperturbable Ancelle, accustomed by now to his ward's tantrums, went on as if nothing had happened.

When at last Charles received his money and paid his creditors, it was already well into March. In the meantime, his work had accumulated to such an extent that it was not until October that he finally got away to Honfleur, and then it was only for a few days.

Les Aventures d'Arthur Gordon Pym, the third volume of Poe, appeared in May 1858, but met with a rather indifferent reception from a public grown tired of the macabre. Even Baudelaire's friend and admirer, Barbey d'Aurevilly, writing for *Le Reveil*, was so reserved in his praise as to cause a slight rift between the two.

In June Baudelaire was so bitterly attacked by Jean Rousseau in *Le Figaro* that for the first time in his life he felt impelled to answer. Dignified as was his reply, its only result was to provoke another caustic article by Rousseau which accompanied Baudelaire's letter in *Le Figaro* for June 13. Rather ironically, it was the very next day that Baudelaire read Sainte-Beuve's laudatory review of Ernest Feydeau's trite novel *Fanny*. It was hardly surprising that he should have felt a wave of jealousy or that he should have made another effort to get the support of his old friend Sainte-Beuve.

Sadly enough, Sainte-Beuve remained deaf to his friend's plea and thus for the fourth time deprived the poet of his invaluable aid.

To Sainte-Beuve

June 14, 1858

Dear friend, I have just read your article on *Fanny*. Need I tell you how charming it is, and how surprising it is to see a mind at once so full of health, a Herculean health, and at the same time of the greatest delicacy, the greatest subtlety, the greatest femininity? Speaking of *femininity*, I wanted to obey you and read the stoic's book.[70] In spite of the respect that I must have for your authority, I most emphatically do not wish the suppression of gallantry, chivalry, mysticism, heroism, in short superabundance and excess (they are what is most charming, even in uprightness).

With you one should not hesitate to be perfectly frank, for you are too shrewd to be taken in by any pretence. Well, that article inspired in me a frightful jealousy. So much has been said about Loève-Weimars [the translator of Hoffmann] and about the service he has done for French literature! Shall I ever find a decent fellow who will say as much about me?

By what sort of coaxing shall I obtain that from you, my powerful friend? Yet what I am asking of you is not unreasonable. Didn't you half promise me that at the beginning? Isn't *Arthur Gordon Pym* an excellent pretext for a *general* survey? You who love to venture into all kinds of depths, won't you plunge into the depths of Edgar Poe?

You can guess that my request for this favour is associated in my mind with the visit I was to make to M. Pelletier. When one has a little money and when one goes out to dinner with an old mistress, one forgets everything; but there are days when the insults of a lot of idiots make one's blood boil, and then one begs for the help of his old friend Sainte-Beuve.

These last few days I have been literally dragged through the mud, and (pity me, it is the first time that I failed to stand on my dignity) I was weak enough to answer.

I know how busy you are, and how assiduous about your articles, about all your tasks and all your duties, etc. But if at times one weren't overly generous and kind, who could be considered a hero of kindness? And if one didn't praise decent people more than they deserve, how would they be consoled for the insults of those who only wish to speak ill of them?

Be that as it may, I shall say that whatever you wish will be satisfactory.

Yours. I like you even more than I like your books.

Ch. Baudelaire

The year 1858 was a particularly unfruitful one for Baudelaire. With the exception of *Arthur Gordon Pym*, published in May, and of

Haschisch, which began to appear in serial form in the month of September, he published nothing. A letter to Calonne, editor of the *Revue contemporaine,* indicates, however, that he was at work composing additional poems to be included in the second edition of *Les Fleurs du Mal.*

To Alphonse de Calonne
Wednesday, November 10, 1858

Dear Sir,

. . . .

I have begun the new *Fleurs du Mal;* however, I shall not send you any poems until I have enough to fill a whole page. The court asks that only six be replaced. Perhaps I shall do twenty. Protestant pedants will be pained to note that I am an incorrigible Catholic.[71] I shall be sure to make myself well understood—sometimes plunging very low, and then rising very high. Thanks to this method, I shall be able to descend to even the baser passions. Only those persons who are absolutely dishonest will fail to understand the deliberate impersonality of my poems.

As for my dilettantism in doing three different things at the same time, don't worry about that; it is my method.

Yours,
Ch. Baudelaire

On February 20, 1859, Baudelaire was deeply disturbed on reading in *La Revue française* an article, *De l'Amitié littéraire,* written by his friend Babou. Hoping to do Baudelaire a good turn or perhaps merely to vent his spite on Sainte-Beuve, Babou had attacked the great critic for his failure to recognize publicly the merits of *Les Fleurs du Mal* and to distinguish between greatness and mediocrity in his critical reviews. Without ever mentioning Sainte-Beuve by name he concluded his indictment: 'To take foolish risks by acting in accordance with the demands of virtue and conscience would be in his opinion foolhardy and quixotic. That fine gentleman can praise *Fanny* and can remain silent about *Les Fleurs du Mal.'*

It was perfectly obvious to everyone, including Sainte-Beuve, that Babou was referring to him. The critic was infuriated and, surprisingly enough, Baudelaire was almost equally vexed. He quickly wrote to Sainte-Beuve disclaiming any responsibility for the attack and expressing his annoyance at Babou's interference.

To Sainte-Beuve

February 21, 1859

My dear friend, I don't know whether you receive *La Revue française*. But fearing you may read it, I protest against a certain passage (referring to *Les Fleurs du Mal*) on page 181, where the author who, moreover, has a good deal of intelligence, is guilty of an injustice to you.

In a newspaper I was once accused of ingratitude towards the early leaders of Romanticism *to whom I owe everything*, as that infamous sheet judiciously added.

This time, on reading that unfortunate passage, I said to myself: My heavens! Sainte-Beuve who knows my loyalty, but who knows that I am a friend of the author, will perhaps think that I was capable of having suggested that passage. It is just the contrary. I have often quarrelled with Babou trying to persuade him that you have never failed to do all that you should and could do.

Not long ago I was talking to Malassis about the great friendship with which you have honoured me and to which I owe so much good advice. The monster wouldn't give me any peace until I gave him the long letter you sent me at the time of my trial which may serve as a plan for the formulation of a preface for *Les Fleurs du Mal*.

. . . .

Charles Baudelaire

From letters written to Asselineau and Poulet-Malassis it is clear that Baudelaire was perfectly sincere in what he had told Sainte-Beuve. Though he could hardly have failed to concur with Babou's sentiments, he was genuinely fond of Sainte-Beuve and may well have sympathized with the selfish motives that prevented the critic from supporting him. Moreover, he clearly considered it unwise to antagonize 'uncle Beuve'.

Three days later he wrote to Asselineau: 'Babou has played a cruel trick on me. He thinks that the pen is meant for playing jokes. I have just received a long letter from Sainte-Beuve. Even when one is sure of possessing the truth, it should be kept hidden if one foresees that it may cause trouble for a friend. Babou knows very well that I am deeply attached to uncle Beuve, that I greatly value his friendship, and that even *I* take pains to hide my opinion when it is at variance with his.'

And to Poulet-Malassis Baudelaire wrote on the 28th of February: 'Ah, you had guessed the Sainte-Beuve–Babou affair. A few days ago I received a frightful letter from Sainte-Beuve. It seems he was deeply wounded by the blow. I must do him this justice that he didn't believe I had ever insinuated such a thing to Babou. I told him that you had in your keeping the compliments and the advice he gave me at the time of the trial and that we had the idea of using the material in our preface for the second edition.

'Either Babou wanted to help me (which implies a certain degree of stupidity), or he wished to play a trick on me; or without worrying about my best interests, he wanted to gratify a mysterious spite.

'I told Asselineau of my annoyance and he answered that I had nothing to complain about, since it brought a long letter from uncle Beuve.'

* * *

When in January Baudelaire went to live with his mother in Honfleur, he left Jeanne at 22 rue Beautreillis where he had been staying with her since November 1858. In April 1859 Jeanne suffered a paralytic stroke which necessitated taking her to a hospital, the Maison Dubois. This was undoubtedly the 'serious mishap' which had cost Baudelaire so much time and to which he refers in his letter to Poulet-Malassis.

To Poulet-Malassis

Friday, April 29, 1859

My dear friend,

. . . .

I have finally completed *L'Opium*; it's going to appear [in the *Revue contemporaine*]. We must also publish as a brochure *L'Opium et le Haschisch*; subtitle: *L'Idéal artificiel*; to be composed of five installments from the *Revue*, almost a book. We can be *sure of the sale of such a brochure*, and then we will likewise get rid of those wretched *Curiosités* which will thus be largely composed of articles dealing with the fine arts and which, before being printed, are awaiting only the appearance of the *Salon de 1859* (finished and ready to be delivered this evening or tomorrow), of *Peintres espagnols*, and of *Peintres idéalistes* which I shall do in May.[72]

I shall be happy to have your opinion about the *Gautier* [brochure on Gautier]. Remember that there are some errors in the version published by *L'Artiste*. . . .

In Paris I read some letters from you which show your discouragement. If you become downhearted, then you are running a real risk. I don't want you to lose your head for so trifling a matter, and remember that this is not just egoism speaking, but friendship. There have been times when your position was excellent. That can be true again, and without much difficulty.

. . . .

And now something serious as a postscript: I came back here in order to work rapidly and to compensate for the time which an unfortunate mishap caused me to lose in Paris.

You will receive this letter and this promissory note on Saturday the 30th. On May 3 I must pay 120 francs to the hospital, plus 30 francs to the nurse. I can't go to Paris. Take advantage of Saturday (tomorrow) to cash this note, payable here at my mother's (where it will never be challenged) and no later than Sunday send 150 francs (a note for 100 and one for 50, or a money order) to the director of the municipal hospital, 200 Faubourg Saint-Denis. In your letter explain that you are sending the money on behalf of M. Baudelaire in payment of the bill for Mlle. Jeanne Duval, that 120 francs are for her room and board, and that 30 are to be given to the patient herself for her nurse. The receipt is to be given to Mlle. Duval.

Even if all this should cause you a lot of inconvenience, I am counting on your friendship. I don't want my poor paralysed patient to be put out of the hospital. She herself might be glad, but I want her to be kept until all methods of cure have been tried.

It is understood that you will send the letter by *registered mail*. Leaving Sunday, the letter will arrive in Paris the 2nd, the day before the bill for room and board falls due.

. . . .

Yours,

Ch. Baudelaire

The concern which the poet felt for Jeanne's welfare, his feeling of responsibility, reveal a deeper side of his nature, often neglected in favour of the more bizarre aspects of his life. A more selfish man would have quickly forgotten Jeanne, once she had lost her beauty and had become ill and infirm. Not so, Baudelaire. Though passionate love had long since died away, though he was well aware of her faults and vices, he continued to feel for her an affection that was almost paternal. To his mother he wrote a few months later (Oct. 15–20, 1859): 'Now I am obliged to play the rôle of father and guardian, (which is rather painfully comic). It is not merely a question of spending money; I also have to think for a person whose mind is somewhat weakened.'

Baudelaire had evidently written Jeanne at the same time that he wrote Poulet-Malassis, asking her whether she had received the money. When she replied that the money had not arrived, Baudelaire was deeply upset and wrote at once to Malassis, asking him to make an investigation. Fearing Jeanne would be put out of the hospital, he urged his friend to write the Director without further delay: 'I hope your letter will result in placating the director of the Hospital for a few hours until the money is found. This mishap is all the more unfortunate since the doctors have just decided that the patient is in no condition to leave. If I had had the money, I would have sent a telegram.'

Four days later Baudelaire wrote Malassis a letter of apology and an explanation of what had taken place.

To Poulet-Malassis

Sunday, May 8, 1859

My dear fellow, I apologize profoundly for my stupid complaint. I was deceived by a letter from that terrible woman (not written by herself, since she would not have been able), telling me that she had received nothing.—In her unhappy mind dulled by illness, she had conceived the ingenious plan of getting money twice, without realizing how easy it would be for me to check. On the 4th, my mother, from whom I immediately tried to borrow 150 francs until your money should be found again, made a terrible scene, and I retaliated. As a result my mother is ill. And I have been in bed since the 4th with my stomach and intestines upset and a neuralgia which moves about according to the changes in weather and prevents me from sleeping with its stabbing pain.

Such are the results of anger and worry. This must end, for work, money and time are one and the same thing.

Your translation of that Austrian book is an excellent idea; tell me if it sells well; don't forget that; don't forget your frontispieces for *Emaux et Camées* either.

Yours,
C. B.

Jeanne remained in the hospital until May 19 when she returned to her apartment on the rue Beautreillis. After his return to Paris from Honfleur in the month of June, Baudelaire lived much of the time in Jeanne's lodgings, though he also kept a room for himself at the Hôtel de Dieppe, 22 rue d'Amsterdam. Made more compassionate by Jeanne's illness and by his own unhappiness, he seemed to have forgiven his mistress for her sorry attempt to extort money from him during her stay at the hospital.

At Christmas Baudelaire wrote Jeanne a kindly letter apologizing for his inability to entertain her and instructing her to obtain from Ancelle a small sum of money which he wished to give her as a present. The fact that Jeanne presented the letter to Ancelle, as she had been directed, is responsible for its preservation today. It is the only letter that remains of those written her by the poet.

To Jeanne Duval
Honfleur, December 17, 1859

My dear girl, you must not be angry with me for having suddenly left Paris, without going to see you and entertaining you a little. You know how exhausted I was by anxiety. Moreover, I was very worried by my mother, who knew that, out of the terrible debt of five thousand francs which is due, two thousand were payable in Honfleur. Besides she is lonely and bored. Everything turned out all right, but just imagine, the very day before, I was short sixteen hundred francs. De Calonne [editor of the *Revue contemporaine*] acted very generously and helped us out of our scrape. I swear I shall return in a few days; I must come to an understanding with Malassis, and besides I left all my boxes at the hotel. Hereafter I don't want to make any more of those enormously long stays in Paris which cost me so much money. It is better for me *to come often and to stay only a few days*. Meanwhile, since I may be away for a week and since I don't want you, in your condition, to be without money even for a day, speak to M. Ancelle. I know I have overdrawn a little on next year, but you know that in spite of his misgivings he is quite generous. This small sum will suffice until I come, and the beginning of the New Year will bring me some money. Put this letter in another envelope and, since you don't feel equal to writing with your left hand, have your servant write the address.

Don't forget to put *Avenue de la Révolte opposite the chapel of the Duke d'Orléans*. You know he is constantly on the go. Hence there is no use sending anything to him, unless it is *very early*.—You will receive this Sunday, but it is wiser not to send it to him before *Monday*, because of Mass and because he goes out with his family on Sundays.— I know that Malassis will be in Paris Wednesday. Therefore I am in a hurry.

I found my room quite changed. My mother, who cannot rest a

moment, re-arranged and beautified (she thought she had beautified) my room.—I shall be coming back then and, if as I think, I *have some money* in my pocket, I shall try to entertain you.—Since I lack paper, I am adding a word here *for Ancelle.*—*I have glanced through the catalogues of the exhibition and I have not* yet found the address of *his painter.* If you would rather not have him read all this, tear it in two and leave only the receipt.—As for me, it makes no difference.— With these slippery streets, do not go out without someone to AC- COMPANY you.—DO NOT LOSE MY POEMS AND MY ARTICLES.

Received from M. Ancelle the sum of forty francs for Madame Duval.

Ch. Baudelaire

PART SIX

De Profundis Clamavi

Prayer

Do not punish me through my mother and do not punish my mother because of me.—I commend to you the souls of my father and of Mariette.—Give me the strength to do my duty promptly every day and thus to become a hero and a Saint.

De Profundis Clamavi

THE same compassion and generosity that Baudelaire showed his decrepit mistress can be seen in his attitude toward many struggling artists with whom he came into contact. In the *Salon de 1859* Baudelaire had enthusiastically praised a poor and obscure artist whose sombre and mysterious etchings of Paris had strongly appealed to the author of *Tableaux Parisiens*. The etchings were those of Charles Méryon, who had become a printmaker only because colour blindness kept him from becoming a painter.

Baudelaire's praise deeply touched Méryon and he called to express his gratitude. Subject to intermittent attacks of insanity, he had recently returned from a stay in the asylum at Charenton. In fact, Méryon was to spend his last days at Charenton and to die there in 1868, a year after the death of his benefactor.

To Poulet-Malassis

Sunday evening, January 8, 1860

What I am writing you this evening is worth being written.

M. Méryon sent me his card and he came to see me. He said to me: 'You live in an hotel whose name, I presume, must have attracted you, since it is in harmony with your tastes.' When I looked at the envelope of his letter, I noticed the address was: Hotel de *Thebes*, and yet his letter reached me.

In one of his large plates he has replaced a small balloon by a cloud of birds of prey, and when I pointed out that it was unreasonable to put so many eagles in a Paris sky, he replied that the idea was not without basis, since *those people* (the Imperial government) had often released eagles in accordance with the rite in order to study the omens —and that all this had been printed in the papers, even in *Le Moniteur*.

I must say that he makes absolutely no secret of his respect for all kinds of superstitions, but he explains them badly, and he sees the cabal in everything.

In another one of his plates he showed me that the shadow, falling from a part of the masonry of the Pont Neuf on to the side wall of the quai, formed the exact profile of a sphinx; he explained that that had been entirely involuntary on his part, and that he hadn't noticed the peculiarity until later, recalling that the design had been done a short time before the Coup d'État. Now today the prince is the person who, by his actions and appearance, most resembles a *sphinx*.

He asked me if I had read the stories of a certain Edgar Poe. I replied that I knew them better than anyone else, and for a good reason. Then he asked me very emphatically whether I believed in the reality of this Edgar Poe. I, in turn, naturally asked him to whom he attributed all his stories. He told me: *To an Organization of writers who were very clever, very powerful and well informed about everything.* And this is one of his reasons: '*La Rue Morgue.* I did a design of the *Morgue.* An *Orang-outang.* I have often been compared to an ape. That ape assassinated *two women, a mother and her daughter.* I too, I have morally assassinated *two women, a mother and her daughter.* I have always taken the story as an allusion to my misfortunes. I should be very pleased if you could discover for me the date when Edgar Poe (always supposing he had no help from anyone) wrote that story, to see if that date coincides with my experiences.'

One of his chief preoccupations is cabalistic science; but he interprets it in so strange a fashion that it would make a cabalist laugh.

Don't laugh about all this with unkind boors. I wouldn't want to harm a man of talent for anything in the world.

After he left, I asked myself how it happened that I hadn't gone crazy, since I have always had in my mind and nerves everything necessary to make me go crazy. In all seriousness, I offered heaven the thanks of the Pharisee.

Guys and I are completely reconciled.[73] He is a charming man, full of wit, and he isn't ignorant as all literary men are.

C. B.

Soon after his talk with Méryon, Baudelaire tried to persuade Poulet-Malassis to publish an album of the artist's views of Paris, for which he himself would write short poems or prose reflections. On March 9th he wrote Malassis a business letter to which he added as a postscript: 'I turn my letter over to ask you very seriously if you would be interested in publishing the Méryon album (which will be enlarged) and whose text I am to write. You know that unfortunately the text will not be what I would like. . . . Méryon doesn't know how to take care of himself; he knows nothing about life. He doesn't know how to sell, he doesn't know how to find a publisher. His work is very easily saleable.'

Méryon was too unbalanced to appreciate the value of Baudelaire's kind offer, and the poet, out of pity for the deranged artist, agreed to write mere catalogue descriptions for each view. On the 11th of March he wrote again to Malassis to explain what had happened:

> Méryon has rejected with a kind of horror the idea of a text made of twelve short poems or sonnets; he has refused the idea of poetic meditations in prose.[74] So as not to hurt him, I have promised to make, in return for three sets of good prints, a text in the manner of a guidebook or a manual, unsigned. . . . The thing came to my mind very simply. On the one hand, an unfortunate madman who doesn't know how to take care of his affairs and who has produced a beautiful work; on the other, you whom I want to have publish as many good books as possible. As the journalists say, I thought you might have the twofold pleasure of combining good business with a good deed.

Unfortunately, the project was never carried out. Baudelaire did succeed, however, in persuading the government to purchase several sets of Méryon's prints. He also acquired several sets for himself, including one for his mother and another for Mme. Sabatier.

*   *   *

For some time Baudelaire's health had been causing him concern. On January 15 he wrote his mother about a sudden illness which may well have been a slight stroke:

> The day before yesterday I experienced a strange attack. I was away from home and I had eaten almost nothing. I believe it was something like a cerebral congestion. A kind old woman revived me by using some rather strange methods. But when I recovered, another attack occurred. Nausea, and such weakness and dizziness that I couldn't climb a step of the stairway without thinking that I was going to faint. At the end of a few hours, it was all over. I came home yesterday evening; I am perfectly well, but as tired as if I had taken a long journey.

> .   .   .   .

> A rather comic detail of my sad adventure . . . is that I didn't lose consciousness for a moment and that I was worried at the thought that people would think me drunk.

Saddened by his inexplicable attack and by his mother's reproaches for his prolonged stay in Paris, Baudelaire wrote Mme. Aupick at the end of January in an effort to gain her understanding.

To Madame Aupick

[January 20–25, 1860]

. . . .

You do your best to prove that your health ought to be very important to me. Good heavens! I know that only too well! Sometimes I tremble with terror at the thought of the loneliness into which I shall some day be plunged. Even if fame should come, nothing will compensate for the lack of that normal family affection which I have so much desired and which I have never known.

However that may be, and however disorganized you may consider me, please notice that I have reached that point so difficult to understand in one's youth, where one realizes that in order to excel in a profession it is necessary to sacrifice everything to it, even passions and pleasures. I am completely resigned on that score. Finally, you have given me *two years* to pay my debts. It is true that only one year remains, but I feel that this year is starting well; I feel myself master of my tools, master of my thought, and my mind is well disciplined. If I could succeed through my own efforts in *being truly inspired* every day, I should be the first of men.

Your anger made you forget to tell me whether *L'Opium* makes a favourable impression on you and whether it is intelligible.

You are completely mistaken in what you say about the health measures necessary for me. It isn't a matter of indigestion. It was my brain that was affected. Although I understand all this in only a confused way, I am convinced that some day my heart or my bile will cause me serious trouble.

—Goodbye, I embrace you tenderly.—I am working as hard on my *Opium* as if it were a *punishment* imposed by a schoolmaster.

C. B.

Though Baudelaire had praised Wagner as early as 1849 when, in a letter written July 13, he had stated that in the future Wagner would be 'the most illustrious among the masters', his opinion could well have been influenced by those of Gérard de Nerval and Champfleury, both of whom were ardent admirers of the German composer.

In 1860, however, Baudelaire's enthusiasm for Wagner was suddenly transformed into a passion resembling that which he had felt for Poe. The great composer himself had come to Paris to direct several concerts, hoping to win for his music a more favourable reception than it had previously received. On January 25 and on February 1 and

February 8 he gave three concerts at the Salle Ventadour. He was greeted by a mixture of enthusiasm and opposition reminiscent of the reception given *Hernani* thirty years before. Baudelaire was ecstatic. A week later (February 16) he wrote to Poulet-Malassis: 'I don't dare speak about Wagner any more. Everyone has made too much fun of me. That music has been one of the great joys of my life; I haven't been carried away like that for more than fifteen years.'

Angered by the hostile criticism given the concerts by the greater part of the press, Baudelaire rose to the defence of Wagner's genius and wrote him a letter expressing his admiration in terms that recall the spiritual and aesthetic experiences described in the poems *Elévation* and *Correspondances*.[75]

To Richard Wagner

Friday, February 17, 1860

Sir,

I have always imagined that no matter how accustomed to fame a great artist might be, he would not be insensible to a sincere compliment, when that compliment was an expression of gratitude, as it were, and I have likewise imagined that such a compliment could have a *special* value coming from a Frenchman, that is to say from a man little prone to enthusiasm and born in a country where poetry and painting are scarcely any better understood than music. First of all, I want to tell you that I owe you *the greatest musical enjoyment that I have ever experienced*. I have reached an age when one scarcely finds pleasure in writing to famous men, and I would have hesitated even longer to express my admiration by letter, had I not noticed every day outrageous, ridiculous articles in which every possible effort is made to defame your genius. You are not the first man, sir, who has given me occasion to suffer and to blush for my country. In short, indignation has impelled me to express my gratitude. I said to myself: I want to be distinguished from all those imbeciles.

The first time I went to the Théâtre des Italiens to hear your works I was not favourably disposed and, to tell the truth, I was even badly prejudiced; but I deserve to be excused; I have been duped so often; I have heard so much music by insufferably pretentious charlatans. By you I was conquered at once. What I felt is indescribable, and if you will be kind enough not to laugh, I shall try to express it to you. At first it seemed to me I was familiar with that music, and later in thinking about it, I understood how this illusion came about; it seemed to me that the music was *mine*, and I recognized it as every man recognizes the things he is destined to love. To anyone except an intelligent man, this sentence would seem utterly ridiculous, especially coming from someone who, like me, *does not know music*, and whose whole musical education is restricted to having heard (with great pleasure, to be sure) some beautiful works of Weber and Beethoven.

Next the quality which most impressed me was that of grandeur. It possesses greatness and it makes one experience greatness. I have encountered everywhere in your works the solemnity of the great sounds, the great aspects of Nature, and the solemnity of the great passions of man. One feels himself immediately carried away and subjugated. One of the strangest parts and one which gave me a new musical sensation is that which is intended to portray religious ecstasy. The effect produced by the *Introduction des invités* and by the *Fête nuptiale* is tremendous. I felt all the majesty of a life that is more ample than our own. And something else: I often had a feeling, somewhat strange in nature, of pride and of joy in understanding, in being possessed, in being overwhelmed, a truly sensual pleasure like that of rising in the air or being tossed on the sea. And at the same time the music now and again breathed pride of life. Generally those profound harmonies seemed to me like stimulants which accelerate the pulse of the imagination. Finally, I also felt, and I beg you not to laugh, sensations which probably derive from my bent of mind and from my habitual preoccupations. Throughout there is something exalted and exalting, something aspiring to mount higher, something excessive and superlative. For example, to use comparisons borrowed from painting, I imagine before my eyes a vast expanse of dark red. If this red represents passion, I see it pass gradually, through all the transitions of red and rose to the incandescence of a fiery furnace. It would seem difficult, even impossible to achieve anything more intense; and yet a final flash appears, cutting an even whiter streak than the white that serves as a background. It is, if you like, the supreme cry of a soul in a paroxysm of ecstasy.

I had begun to write a few thoughts on the passages from *Tannhaeuser* and *Lohengrin* which we had heard; but I realized the impossibility of saying everything.

I could continue my letter indefinitely. If you have been able to read this far, I thank you. I have only a few more words to add. From the day I first heard your music, I have said to myself constantly, especially

in my bad moments: *If only I could hear a little Wagner this evening.*
There are doubtless other men like me. In short, you must have been
satisfied with the audience whose instinct was far superior to the poor
knowledge of the journalists. Why could you not give additional concerts and include some new compositions? You have given us a fore-
taste of new pleasures; have you the right to deprive us of the rest?—
Once again, Sir, I thank you; in an hour of discouragement you have
recalled me to my real self and to the truly great.

Ch. Baudelaire

I am not adding my address, because you might think I have a
favour to ask of you.

In spite of the fact that Baudelaire did not give his address, Wagner
sought him out, sensing in his correspondent 'an extraordinary intelligence which pursued with enthusiastic ardour and to their final
consequences the impressions he had received from my music'.[76]
On February 28 Baudelaire wrote to Champfleury: 'I am writing at
once to M. Wagner to thank him with all my heart. I shall go to see
him, but not immediately. Some rather troublesome business is taking
all my time. If you see him before I do, tell him that it will be a great
honour for me to shake the hand of a genius, insulted by all the
frivolous-minded rabble.'
Not long after this (March 4), Baudelaire wrote to Mme. Sabatier,
offering excuses for his absence from her Sunday dinners. To her he
confided: 'I am so unhappy and so worried that I shun every distraction. Very recently I even refused a charming invitation from Wagner,
in spite of my wish to meet him.'
The two men finally met and became good friends. Though Wagner
never seemed to realize the greatness of his admirer's genius, he did
express grateful appreciation for the encouragement and praise offered
him by the author of *Les Fleurs du Mal*. It is said that when he learned
of Baudelaire's death seven years later he was deeply grieved.
As for Baudelaire, one of the greatest comforts he knew during
the last years of his life and especially during his final illness was to
hear the music of Wagner, played for him by sympathetic friends who
sought to make his days less bleak and cheerless.

*   *   *

Early in 1860 Armand Fraisse, scholar, critic, and journalist living
in Lyons, sent Baudelaire copies of his articles on *Les Fleurs du Mal*,
La Légende des Siècles, and *Sonnets humoristiques*, written by Soulary,
a friend of Fraisse who had recently risen to fame.

Grateful for the appreciative remarks of Fraisse and pleased by the literary acumen which he had shown, Baudelaire replied with a long letter which reveals some of his literary ideas and judgements.

To Armand Fraisse

February 18, 1860

Sir,

Your articles and your letter obviously call for an answer. First let me thank you for personal reasons; several times already you have spoken about me and always *very intelligently*, I mean in a very flattering way and at the same time with a sagacity that surprises me.—Re-reading my sentence, I find it impertinent, and even laughable. It seems to be saying that you are sagacious because you compliment me.—In your article about Hugo, it seems that you have been intimidated, confused. You have not sufficiently distinguished between *the quantity of eternal beauty* in Hugo and the comic *superstitions* introduced into his work by issues such as modern stupidity or *wisdom*, belief in progress, the salvation of humanity by balloons, etc. . . . As it is, your article is the best and the wisest I have read.—In general, Hugo's friends are as stupid as his enemies; as a result, the truth won't be told. Here, except for Villemain, my friend D'Aurevilly, sometimes M. E. Renan, no one has critical perspicacity or wisdom. Only once have I heard a clear and just opinion expressed about the *Légende des Siècles*; it was given by Théophile Gautier at a dinner. Never have the most obscure questions of esthetics been so well clarified; never have the so-called *merits* and *faults* been so well defined. But unhappily, as a result of the times and circumstances, those remarks will never be printed.—I am giving the copy of the *Salut Public* to *M. Paul Meurice*, who will certainly see that it reaches Guernsey; it is all the more probable since Madame Hugo is now in Paris.

Coming back to M. Soulary. Your study is excellent and full of charm. You are a true *dilettante* in your feeling for poetry. That is the way it should be felt. From the word that I have underlined you can guess that I was somewhat surprised by your admiration for De Musset. Except at the age of one's first communion, in other words at the age when everything having to do with prostitutes and silken ladders produces a religious effect, I have never been able to endure that *paragon of lady-killers*, his spoiled child's impudence, invoking heaven and hell about hotel room adventures, his muddy torrent of mistakes in grammar and prosody, and finally his utter incapacity to understand the work through which a reverie becomes a work of art. Some day you will find that you are enthusiastic only about perfection and you will scorn all those effusions of ignorance. I ask your pardon for speaking so sharply about certain things; incoherence, banality and carelessness have always caused me an irritation that is perhaps too acute.

. . . .

That M. Soulary is a great poet is evident to everyone today, and that was evident to me from the time that I first read his verses. Who is the imbecile anyway (perhaps he is a famous man) who speaks so lightly of the Sonnet and does not see its Pythagorean beauty? Because the form is constraining, the idea is all the more intense. Everything is appropriate for the Sonnet, buffoonery, gallantries, passion, reverie, philosophical meditation. In it is to be found the beauty of well worked metal and mineral. Have you noticed that a bit of sky, seen through a vent, or from between two chimneys, two rocks, or through an arcade, etc., gives a more profound idea of infinity than a great panorama seen from the top of a mountain? As for long poems, we know what to think of them; they are the expedients of those who are unable to write short ones.[77]

Everything which goes beyond the span of attention that human beings can give to a poetic form, is not a poem.

Allow me to say that you did not understand what I wrote you about that resemblance *of which I was so proud. Everything that you tell me on that subject, I already believed and I already know.* Otherwise, what would be so piquant, curious and amusing about it? I can tell you something even more strange and almost unbelievable. In 1846 or 1847 I happened to see some stories by Edgar Poe. I experienced a peculiar emotion. His complete works not having been collected in a single edition until after his death, I patiently set about making the acquaintance of Americans living in Paris, in order to borrow copies of the magazines which Edgar Poe had edited.[78] And then, believe me if you will, I found poems and short stories which I had conceived, but vaguely and in a confused and disorderly way, and which Poe had been able to organize and finish perfectly. Such was the origin of my enthusiasm and of my perseverance.

. . . .

Very sincerely yours,
Ch. Baudelaire

After the publication of *Les Paradis artificiels* in May, Baudelaire was too proud to ask Sainte-Beuve for a review, much as he needed his support.[79] Only when an editor of *Le Moniteur* advised him to approach the well-known critic, did Baudelaire write his friend and almost apologetically solicit a review. On July 3 Sainte-Beuve replied, saying that he was too busy to attempt a review, but describing the book as 'very clever, very ingenious, and very subtle'.

Far more enthusiastic in his praise was Flaubert who wrote to Baudelaire congratulating him on the excellence of his most recent publication. In the eyes of Flaubert, however, the work had one fault which he felt impaired its validity: 'Here is my only objection (to have done with the *buts*). It seems to me that in such a work treated on so high a level, in a study which is the beginning of a natural science, in a work based on observation and induction, you have insisted (and several times at that) too much (?) on an *Evil Spirit*. One feels, so to speak, a Catholic leavening here and there. I would have preferred you not to blame haschisch, opium and excess.'[80]

In reply to Flaubert's objection Baudelaire reiterates his belief in the objective existence of evil.

To Gustave Flaubert

June 26, 1860

My dear Flaubert, my warmest thanks for your excellent letter. I was struck by your observation and, after plumbing very carefully the depths of my past reveries, I realized that I have always been obsessed by the impossibility of accounting for some of man's sudden acts and thoughts except by the hypothesis of the intervention of an evil force outside himself.[81] That is a tremendous admission for which I won't blush even with the whole 19th century standing against me. Note that I am not renouncing the pleasure of changing my mind or of contradicting myself.

One of these days, if you will allow me, I shall stop at Rouen on my way to Honfleur; but since I presume that, like me, you hate surprises, I shall warn you some time in advance.

You tell me that I work a great deal. Is that a cruel jest? Many people, not counting myself, think that I am not doing very much.

To work means to work ceaselessly: it means to forsake one's senses, to forgo reverie; it means being a pure will constantly in motion. Perhaps I shall achieve that.

Sincerely, your devoted friend,

Ch. Baudelaire

I have always dreamed of reading *The Temptation* [*of Saint Anthony*] in its entirety, and another singular book, of which you have not published even a fragment (*November*). And how is *Carthage* [*Salammbô*] going?

To Armand Fraisse, who had written a favourable review of *Les Paradis artificiels* and who, in a personal letter, had signified his intention of experimenting at least once with the use of narcotics, Baudelaire sent a word of warning. He himself was well aware of the danger involved. Like many of his literary contemporaries, he had begun experimenting with drugs as a very young man. In his early care-free years at the Pension Bailly and at the Hôtel Pimodan his use of drugs had been primarily a means of procuring sensuous pleasure and of enlarging his experience. As he grew older, particularly after 1858, he came to rely on them more and more, either as a palliative to relieve pain and discomfort or as a means of escape.

Though he may have been taking drugs during the period when he was composing *Les Paradis artificiels*, it is clear from the work itself that Baudelaire considered the practice as dangerous and demoralizing. In his preface to *Haschisch* he had even cited as one aspect of his study the 'implied immorality in this pursuit of a false ideal'.

To Armand Fraisse
[about August 15, 1860]

... Beware of all drugs ... I know a terrible story, although it has nothing to do with opium. It is about a society woman who experienced an inexplicable melancholy and physical depression simply as the result of having drunk champagne with her husband at lunch and dinner in place of ordinary wine. You can guess what happened: it was impossible for her to return to a normal state without champagne. Now champagne is a very innocent corrupter compared to Indian hemp, laudanum and morphine.

I have a horror of all stimulants because of the manner in which they amplify time and magnify everything. A continued spiritual orgy makes it not only impossible to be a business man, but even a man of letters.

.   .   .   .

With the approach of autumn Baudelaire's depression and melancholy grew more marked. His thoughts turned to religion, but, unable to pray for himself, he wrote to his mother (October 8) asking for her prayers: 'I am horribly unhappy. I am too weary to explain anything at all. And if you think a prayer can have any efficacy (I am speaking quite seriously), pray hard for me; I need it.'

A few days later he wrote her a much longer letter in which he poured out the thoughts which tormented him day and night.

To Madame Aupick

October 11, 1860

Alas, I have only very little to say in reply: My debts have doubled as all debts inevitably double *after a certain amount of time*. All those who have studied these questions know that. I first owed M. Arondel ten thousand francs; for several years now I have been owing him fifteen thousand. In order to make payments, I borrow; and to give you another example, the money earned from the publication of my works in the past 16 months has all gone into interest on a debt of 3,000 francs incurred in order to move to Honfleur. Furthermore, the total sum increases because of the difficulty of working in the midst of such tortures, while expenses go on and on. You rack your brains, you think of a thousand and one fantasies in an effort to understand, instead of saying to yourself: *the legal guardianship!* That frightful mistake which has ruined my life, blighted all my hopes and coloured all my thoughts with hate and despair. *But you do not understand.*

—Now I am going to speak seriously and without exaggeration about some very sad thoughts. In spite of the diabolical courage which has sustained me so often, I may die before you. What has held me back for 18 months is the thought of Jeanne. (How would she manage to live after my death, since you would have to pay everything that I owe with what I would leave?) There are still other reasons: leaving you alone! and leaving you the horrible trouble of extricating yourself from the chaos that I alone can understand!

The mere idea of the preparatory work needed to facilitate an understanding of my affairs is enough to make me continually postpone the carrying out of what I would consider the most sensible act of my life. I must tell you everything—I am sustained by pride and by a savage hatred of all men. I always hope to be able to dominate, to avenge myself, to be able to say whatever I wish without fear of the consequences —and other childish ideas.—Finally, although I do not wish to frighten you for any reason whatsoever, to distress you, or to cause you any remorse, I have the right to hope that some fine morning I shall give way to despair, I who am truly very weary, and who have never known joy or security. After your death, it is clear and certain that I shall not go on living; since the fear of hurting you while you are still alive may yet stop me; but after your death, nothing will stop me. In a word, to make everything perfectly clear, I am restrained by my concern for your welfare and that of Jeanne. Surely you will not be able to say that I go on living for my own pleasure. I am coming to the point. Whatever happens to me, if, after preparing a list of my debts, I were suddenly to disappear, you must, if you are still living, do something to relieve that once beautiful woman who is now an invalid. All of my literary contracts are in order, and I am convinced that a day will come *when everything that I have done will sell very well.* The proprieties oblige me to make you my heir. Besides, the *legal guardianship*, thank God, has not taken away my right to make a will! I repeat: if through accident, illness, despair or some other cause, I should be freed from the weariness of living, after the *very reasonable and very sordid* payment of my debts, what remained should be assigned to the aid of that woman; plus the income, however small, from the sale of my poetry, my translations and my prose works. But you understand nothing about business.

(A brother has turned up, to whom I have talked and who evidently would also help her; he doesn't have any money, but he is earning some.)

I have just re-read everything that I have written and frankly I think that, considering your frailty, it is abominable to send this to you. Nevertheless, I have the deplorable courage to do so. At least it *will serve to show you what my habitual thoughts have been all of my life.*

Practical news.

No word about the play [*Le Marquis du 1er Houzards*].[82] And yet *I am finally satisfied with my plan.* I would not have believed that I could master problems so new to me. I despise all these banalities, but I consider that a work of this type may bring 50,000 francs. To think that a letter from the director of the Théâtre du Cirque expressing his satisfaction would enable me to borrow *three thousand francs* in a month! As you know, my dream is to combine *literary qualities* with the spectacular setting of the boulevard theatre.

—My biography, with my portrait, is going to be published.[83] Another cause for annoyance. What information can I give except odious information? You know what I think of *public opinion*, which to you is so important. But still, like an actor, one must strike a proper pose.—As an homage and as a token of sympathy, I have sent my *Paradis* to that excellent M. Cardinne [Mme. Aupick's confessor].

I have rented a small apartment at Neuilly so I won't have to stay in an hotel any longer; I have had my furniture sent there. It is in bad condition, and I must admit that I had counted on your kind assistance to have it restored and to add a bed, a table, etc.

However, *I am still at the hotel.*

—*Les Fleurs du Mal* is in press. Terrible business. It is a book that will always sell, unless the court meddles again. 34 new poems have been added, nearly all of which you have seen. The others are going to be printed in *L'Artiste.*—But I am *very perplexed.* There is a prose introduction full of violent buffoonery. I hesitate to print it, and yet I'll never grow tired of insulting France.

. . . . . .

There still exists the question of that ridiculous Cross of [the Legion of] Honour. I certainly hope that the preface to the *Fleurs* will make that impossible forever. Besides I courageously replied to the friend who offered me the opportunity: '*Twenty years ago* (I know that what I am saying is absurd) that would have been fine! Today I want to be an *exception.* Let them decorate every Frenchman, *except me.* I shall never change my manners or my style. Instead of the cross, they should give me *money, money,* nothing but *money.* If the cross is worth five hundred francs, let them give me five hundred francs; if it is worth only twenty francs, let them give me *twenty francs.*' In short, I replied to boors *like a boor.* The more unhappy I become, the more my pride increases.

I embrace you very sadly. I love you with all my heart; you have never known it. Between us there is this difference: I know you by heart, but you have never been able to understand my wretched character.

Charles

Baudelaire either failed to realize or refused to admit that causes other than the legal guardianship were responsible for his despair and for his horror of life. Disappointment, frustration, hunger for understanding had led him to hate life and to hear the 'bitter laugh of defeated men' even in the 'enormous laughter' of the ocean. Certain poems published in 1860—*Obsession, Horreur sympathique, Les Aveugles, L'Alchimie de la Douleur, Hymne à la beauté,* and *L'Horloge* —constitute a painful autobiography which reveals the poet's state of mind as clearly as his frank letter to his mother. The weariness and the despair which they contain, the dread of time and its inexorable laws make understandable the author's desire for death, his longing for 'the emptiness, the blackness, and the nakedness' to be found only in a 'starless night'.

Baudelaire's thoughts of Jeanne, his wish to protect and to help her are typical of his attitude following her illness. He appeared to cling to her even more closely, now that death seemed to threaten them both. 'Death and Illness make ashes of all the fire which flamed for us,' he wrote in *Un Fantôme*, a sonnet sequence published in 1860 in *L'Artiste*, but 'Time . . . black assassin of Life and Art, you will never destroy in my memory one who was my pleasure and my glory!'

Perhaps Jeanne seemed all the dearer to Baudelaire since Marie Daubrun had chosen to nurse back to health the desperately ill Banville. Surely Marie must have been in Baudelaire's thoughts during the year 1860, for two of his poems published that same year, *A une Madonne* and *L'Amour du Mensonge*, were inspired by her. According to Feuillerat, it is in *A une Madonne* that the poet shows the anger, indignation, and grief that he felt on losing Marie, as he well knew, forever.

About December 15 Baudelaire moved to Neuilly where he joined Jeanne in the small apartment rented by him in July. Once again his hopes of escaping the dreary monotony of cheap hotels and of enjoying some semblance of family life were dashed to the ground. At Neuilly he found a situation that was completely intolerable. He bore it as long as he was able and when he could no longer conceal his unhappiness he wrote to his mother telling her of his misery.

To Madame Aupick

[about January 5, 1861]

My dear good mother, your letter made me weep, I who never weep. Poor mama, all alone, you must not grieve too much. Who knows if this year will not contain some pleasures? Pleasures, like pains, are so unexpected!

I shall tell you at greater length about all the anger and all the anguish that I have experienced. If I had had any money, I should have left immediately. Apart from financial annoyances, I have had troubles of an altogether moral nature, and unhappily they are not over.

You did well in writing to me. For I was extremely worried. You mustn't hold it against me if I am brief—or rather no—I prefer to tell you everything today.

You know or you can guess that, in order to put ideas or images on paper, a certain zest, a certain gaiety of spirit is necessary which is incompatible with great anxieties and towering passions. It follows that too many troubles make it impossible to earn money.

You know also that I came to Neuilly in order to spend less money and to be kind to a sick woman as well.

Now you are going to hear what happened and, above all, bear in mind that I was in a rage for 15 whole days.

When one has lived 19 years with and for a woman, one has something to say to her every day. Well, I found a brother here who had re-appeared a year ago and who remained in Jeanne's room from 8 o'clock in the morning until 11 o'clock at night. Not a second for confidences. Wishing to be considerate because of her condition, I restrained myself for a long time; finally one evening, at midnight, I told her with the greatest tact that I had come here for her sake, that I had no right to drive out her brother, but that since I was kept in the background, I was going to go and stay with my mother who also needed me—that I had no intention of depriving her of money, but that, since her brother left me out and took up all her time, it was only fair that he, who earns more than a writer and who does not owe 50,000 francs plus constantly increasing interest, should henceforth pay two-thirds or one-half of her expenses.—I expected an outburst of bad temper.—Nothing of the sort, but lots of tears. She told me that she knew my devotion, my worries, my anxieties, *that what I said was very just*, that she was going to urge her brother to start working again, but that she was very much afraid that my demand would be badly received, *since during so many years of absence he had never sent any money to his mother*.

—As a matter of fact, the next day she broached the question: 'You are here all day long. You keep me from living with Charles. Partly on my account he has gotten into inextricable difficulties; he is going to leave, but he is counting on you to be good enough to pay half of my expenses.'

You would never guess the reply, so stupid and so cruel that if it had been made directly to me I would have cut the man's face with blows from my cane.—'That I should be accustomed to straitened circumstances and troubles—that when one took responsibility for a woman, it was on the basis of knowing how to do it—that, as for him, he had never saved any money—and that even in the future no one should count on him.'

I asked Jeanne *what she thought of such a reply.* For my part, I imagined that perhaps there was something behind it, that she was deep in debt to her brother, as a result of which he believed himself relieved of responsibility. I questioned her gently on the subject. 'How much have you borrowed from your brother in the past year, while I was living at the hotel?'

'He has given me only 200 francs.' That was her reply.

In plain English that means he was in no hurry to go back to work, since he had a perfectly easy life living with his sister. It isn't surprising that she is so poorly dressed and doesn't have the money to pay her debts.

I was touched by all those tears on that aged face, by all the uncertainty of a feeble creature; my anger faded away. But I am in a state of constant irritation that external concerns are not calculated to decrease.

(To give you an idea, I need 4,000 francs on the 10th and I have 1,860.)

That's the way things stand.

When Jeanne needs to see me, she comes to my room. The gentleman does not go away—and if I decide to leave Paris, he will not help his sister.

Quite often I have justly accused myself of a monstrous egoism. But good heavens! mine has never gone that far.

. . . .

Charles

After Baudelaire left Jeanne in January 1861 and returned to the hotel life he hated so intensely, he felt ill and unable to work. He had no one in whom he could confide save his mother, and she was incapable of completely understanding her proud and sensitive son with his strange ideas and ways, so utterly different from her own. Try as she would, she could never comprehend his feeling for Jeanne, nor his insistence on helping the wretched creature who had done him so much harm. She suspected him of seeing Jeanne in spite of his assurances to the contrary and she added to his worries by her complaints of being neglected and by the expression of a wish to die.

Charles had hoped his mother would be pleased with the second edition of *Les Fleurs du Mal,* but as usual she trusted more in the opinions of others than in her own. Her confessor, the Abbé Cardinne, who Baudelaire thought would understand the real nature of his poems, had been shocked and infuriated, and the poet felt only helpless rage on learning of the priest's unfavourable reaction.

To make matters worse, Jeanne, whom Baudelaire had not seen for three months, came to him with a story that deeply upset him emotionally and physically and made him think once again of seeking release in suicide.

In the midst of all his troubles the poet's only solace was his consuming interest in the music of Wagner and his desire to publish the article to which he had devoted so much loving care.

To Madame Aupick
[February or March 1861]

Ah! dear mother, is there *still time* in which *we* may be happy? I no longer dare to believe it;—40 years of age, a legal guardianship, enormous debts, and finally, worse than anything else, my will power lost, ruined! Who knows if my mind itself has not been affected? I just don't know, I no longer have any way of knowing, since I have lost even the ability to make an effort.

Above all I want to tell you something that I do not tell you often enough, and that you doubtless do not know, especially if you judge me by appearances, and that is that my love for you keeps constantly increasing. It is shameful to admit that that love does not even give me the strength to lift myself up. I contemplate the years gone by, the horrible years, I spend my time reflecting on the brevity of life; nothing else; and my will continues to rust away. If anyone ever experienced spleen and hypochondria as a young man, it was certainly I. And yet I have a desire to live, and I should like to have a taste of security, fame, and satisfaction with myself. Something terrible tells me: *never*, and something else tells me: *try*.

Of so many plans and projects, piled up in two or three portfolios that I no longer dare open, what shall I carry out? Perhaps nothing, ever.

April 1, 1861

The preceding page was written a month ago, six weeks, two months, I no longer know when. I have fallen into a kind of perpetual nervous terror; frightful sleep, frightful awakening; impossibility of acting. My copies [of *Les Fleurs du Mal*] lay on the table for a month before I could find the heart to wrap them for the post. I haven't written to Jeanne, I haven't seen her for nearly three months; naturally I haven't sent her a penny, since it was impossible. (She came to see me yesterday; she has just come out of the hospital and the brother who I thought would help support her has sold part of her furniture while she was away. She is going to sell the rest in order to pay some debts.) In that horrible mental state of hypochondria and powerlessness, the thought of suicide returned; now that it is over, I can mention it; the idea haunted me every hour of the day. I saw in it absolute deliverance, deliverance from everything. At the same time for *three months*, by a strange, but only apparent contradiction I prayed *every hour of* the day (to whom? what definite being? I have absolutely no idea) for two things: for myself, the strength to live; for you, many long years. Let me add in passing that your wish to die is quite absurd and not at all charitable, since your death would be a final blow for me and would make happiness absolutely impossible.

Finally the obsession disappeared, driven away by an unavoidable and strenuous task, the article about Wagner, improvised in three days in a press room; without the pressure of a deadline, I should never have had the strength to do it.[84] Since then I have become ill again with lethargy, horror and fear. Two or three times I have been in rather poor health; but one of the things that is particularly unbearable for me is that when I am falling asleep, and even in my sleep, I distinctly hear voices, complete sentences, which are very trite and commonplace and which have nothing to do with my affairs.

Your letters came; they were not of a nature to relieve me. You are always ready to stone me with the crowd. That has been true since my childhood, as you know. How do you always manage to be the opposite of a *friend* for your son, except in financial matters, provided, of course—and that shows your character, at once absurd and generous —that they weigh on you alone? For your benefit I was careful to mark all the new poems in the table of contents. It was easy to see for yourself that they were all done to fit into the plan. A book on which I have worked for twenty years, and I am no longer free not to publish it!

As for M. Cardinne, that is a serious matter, but in a sense quite different from what you think. In the midst of all my troubles I will not have a priest struggle against me in the mind of my old mother, and I shall put an end to it, if I can, if I have the strength. The conduct of that man is monstrous and inexplicable. As for burning books, that isn't done any more, except by madmen who like to see paper destroyed by flames. And I who stupidly deprived myself of a precious copy in order to please him and to give him something he had been asking of me for three years! But you have always had to humiliate me before someone. Remember that used to be the case with M. Emon. Now it is a priest who doesn't even have enough tact to hide a thought that might wound you. And finally he didn't even understand that the book sprang from a Catholic idea; but that is quite another matter.

What saved me from suicide more than anything else were two ideas which will seem to you quite childish. The first was that it was my duty to furnish you with detailed notes about the payment of my debts, and that thus *it was necessary first to go to Honfleur*, where all my documents, intelligible only to me, are stored. The second—shall I confess it?—is that it was rather hard to end everything before having published at least my critical works, even were I to give up the plays (I am planning a second one), the novels, and finally a long book of which I have been dreaming for two years: *Mon Coeur mis à nu*, which I shall fill with all my anger.[85] Ah! if it ever sees the light, the *Confessions* of J. J. [Rousseau] will seem pale. You can see that I am still dreaming.

. . . .

Charles

Baudelaire's essay on Wagner, together with the *Salon de 1859* and *Le Peintre de la vie moderne*, represent Baudelaire at his best as a critic. His understanding and appreciation of Wagner's genius is all the more amazing since his knowledge of music was fairly slight. That he was fond of music and sensitive to its beauty is evident from his references to music, particularly that of Weber and Beethoven. 'Music engulfs me like the sea,' he had written in one of his well-known poems, *La Musique*. And in *Les Phares*, as well as in the *Salon de 1845*, he had compared the painting of Delacroix to a 'plaintive and profound' melody from Weber.

When technical knowledge was necessary, Baudelaire leaned rather heavily on Liszt's *Lohengrin and Tannhäuser* and on Wagner's own explanations. But the real greatness of his criticism lies not in his display of technical knowledge, but rather in his power to translate aesthetic experience, to 'transform pleasure into knowledge' and understanding, as he himself so aptly expressed it at the beginning of his article. It is in the sheer brilliance of this accomplishment that Baudelaire succeeds, as perhaps no other critic, in interpreting the genius of the great German composer.

His article on Wagner finished, Baudelaire tried desperately to earn enough money to appease his creditors and to enable him to return to

Honfleur to be near his mother whose love was all that remained to him. One crisis followed another until he could bear it no longer, and in a paroxysm of fright and despair he wrote her one of his most pathetic and revealing letters.

To Madame Aupick

May 6, 1861

My dear mother, if you really have any maternal feeling and if you are not too tired, come to Paris, come to see me, and even to take me home. For a thousand terrible reasons I cannot go to Honfleur to seek what I would so much like, a little courage and affection. At the end of March I wrote you: *Shall we never see each other again?* I was in the midst of one of those crises in which one sees the terrible truth. I would give almost anything to spend a few days with you, you the only being to whom my life belongs, a week, three days, a few hours.

You do not read my letters carefully enough, you think I am lying, or at least that I am exaggerating when I speak of my despair, of my health, and of my horror of life. I keep telling you that I should like to see you and that I cannot rush off to Honfleur. Your letters contain many false and erroneous ideas that conversation could correct and that volumes of writing would not suffice to destroy.

Every time I pick up my pen to explain my situation to you, I am afraid; I am afraid of killing you, of destroying your feeble body. And, without your suspecting it, I am constantly on the verge of suicide. I believe that you love me passionately, blindly; you have such strength of character! As for me, I loved you passionately in my childhood; later on, suffering from the weight of your injustice, I was guilty of a lack of respect, as if maternal injustice could justify a lack of filial respect; I have often regretted it, although I have said nothing, as is my habit. I am no longer an ungrateful and wilful child. Prolonged reflections on my destiny and on your character have helped me to understand all my faults and all your generosity. But nevertheless, the harm is done, done through your imprudence and my mistakes. We are evidently meant to love each other, to live for each other, to end our lives as honourably and as peacefully as possible. And yet in the terrible circumstances in which I am placed, I am convinced that one of us will cause the death of the other, and that finally we will succeed in killing each other. After my death it is obvious that you will not go on living. I am the only thing that keeps you alive. After your death, especially if you were to die from a shock caused by me, I would kill myself, that is beyond all doubt. Your death, of which you speak with too much resignation, would not improve anything in my situation; the legal guardianship would be maintained (why shouldn't it be?), nothing would be paid, and worst of all, I would have the *horrible sensation of utter loneliness*. For me to kill myself is absurd, isn't it? 'And so you are going to leave your old mother all alone,' you will say. My heavens! if, strictly speaking, I do not have the right, I believe that the amount of suffering I have undergone for *more than thirty years* would excuse me. 'And what about God!' you will say. I wish with all my heart (with what sincerity I alone can know) to believe that an exterior invisible being is concerned with my fate; but what can I do to make myself believe it?

(The idea of God makes me think of that cursed parish priest. In spite of the painful feeling that my letter will cause you, I do not want you to consult him. That priest is my enemy, perhaps only through sheer stupidity.)

To come back to the thought of suicide, an idea which is not fixed, but which returns at periodic intervals, there is one thing that ought to reassure you. I cannot kill myself without first putting my affairs in order. All my papers are at Honfleur, in great confusion. I would have to do a great deal of work at Honfleur and, once there, I would no longer be able to tear myself away from you. For you must understand that I would not want to dishonour your house with so abhorrent an act. What is more, you would go mad. Why suicide? Is it because of debts? Yes, and yet the problem of debts can be surmounted. It is inspired above all by a frightful fatigue resulting from an impossible and *too prolonged* situation. Each minute proves to me that I no longer have any taste for living. You acted very unwisely when I was a child. Your lack of judgement and my *past mistakes* weigh upon me and envelop me. My present situation is atrocious. There are people who greet me, there are people who flatter me, there may even be some who envy me. My literary standing is more than good. I can do what I wish. Everything will be published. Since I have an unpopular bent of mind, I shall earn little money, but I shall leave a great reputation, of that I am sure—provided I have the courage to live. But my spiritual health, execrable;—ruined perhaps. I have still more projects: *Mon Coeur mis à nu, several novels, two plays,* one of them for the Théâtre-Français—will all that ever be finished? *I no longer think so.* My financial standing, appalling—that is my worst trouble. Never any peace of mind. Insults, abuse, rebuffs of which you can have no conception and which poison and paralyse my imagination. I earn a little money, it is true; *even if I no longer had an inheritance*, I SHOULD BE RICH if I had no debts, just think of that. I could give you money, I could easily help Jeanne. I shall speak of her again. You are the one who has provoked these explanations.—All this money disappears in an extravagant and unhealthy existence (for I live very badly) and in the payment or rather the partial liquidation of old debts, in the expenses occasioned by bailiffs, legal documents, etc.

Very shortly I shall come to practical, that is to daily problems. For I really need to be rescued, and you alone can rescue me. I want to tell you everything today. I am alone, without friends, without a mistress, without a dog or a cat. To whom can I complain? I have only the portrait of my father, and it remains mute.

I am in that horrible state of mind which I experienced in the fall of 1844. A resignation worse than rage.

But my physical health, which I need for your sake, for mine, and for my work, that is another question! I must tell you about that, although you pay very little attention. I do not intend to speak of the nervous afflictions which are slowly killing me and destroying my courage—nausea, insomnia, nightmares, fainting spells. I have spoken of them to you too often. But with you there is no need of false modesty. You know that when I was very young I contracted a venereal infection which I later thought was completely cured. After 1848, it broke out again in Dijon. Once again it was checked. Now it has returned and has assumed a new form, spots on the skin and an extraordinary fatigue in all my joints. You can believe me; *I know what I am talking about.* Perhaps, in the sadness in which I am plunged, my fright has aggravated the disease. But I need to follow a strict regimen and I cannot do so in the life that I am now leading.

I want to put all this aside and resume my reveries; I find a certain pleasure in them before coming to the plan which I wish to suggest to you. Who knows if I shall ever again be able to open to you my whole heart *which you have never appreciated or known*! I write this without any hesitation, so well do I know it to be true.

There was a time in my childhood when I loved you passionately; listen and do not be afraid to read on. I have never told you so much. I remember a ride in a cab; you were leaving a nursing home where you had been sent and, to prove to me that you had thought of your son, you showed me some pen and ink sketches which you had made for me. Do you think I have a terrible memory? Later, the square of Saint André des Arts and Neuilly. Long walks, endless expressions of affection! I remember the quays which were so melancholy in the evening. Ah! those were for me the happy years of motherly love and affection. Forgive me for calling *happy* those years which doubtless were unhappy for you. But I was still living in you; you were mine exclusively. You were both an idol and a comrade. You will perhaps be astonished that I can speak with such intense feeling of so distant a time. I myself am astonished. Perhaps the desire for death, which I have once more experienced, makes the past stand out more clearly in my mind.

Later on, you know what an atrocious education your husband insisted on giving me; I am 40 years old and I cannot think of school without pain, any more than I can think of the fear which my stepfather inspired in me. Yet I loved him, and moreover I think that today I have enough wisdom to do him justice. But after all he was stubborn and inept. I want to hurry on, for I can see tears in your eyes.

Finally I left home, and since then I have been entirely forsaken. I thought only of pleasure, of constant excitement; travel, fine furniture, pictures, women, etc. I am paying a cruel price for it today. As for the legal guardianship, I have only one word to say: today I realize the immense value of money and I understand the gravity of all things that have to do with money; I grant that you thought you were acting wisely and that you were working for my interest, but one question nevertheless, a question which has always obsessed me: how does it happen that this idea has never occurred to you: 'It is possible that my son will never have the same sense of management as I, but it is also possible he may become distinguished in other ways. In that case what shall I do? Shall I condemn him to a dual, to a contradictory existence, a life honoured on one hand, odious and despised on the other? Shall I condemn him to bear an unfortunate stigma until his old age, a stigma which will prove harmful and produce only helplessness and sorrow?' It is obvious that if this legal guardianship had not been established, everything would have been squandered. I would have had to acquire a taste for work. The legal guardianship was established, *everything has been squandered and I am old and wretched.*

Is it possible to make a fresh start? That is the whole question.

All this looking back into the past had no other object than to show that I could offer excuses, if not complete justification. If you feel any reproaches in what I write, you can at least be sure that all this in no way alters my admiration for your kind heart and my gratitude for your devotion. You have always sacrificed yourself. You have a genius for sacrifice. Less through reason than through charity. I ask even more of you. I ask you at one and the same time for advice, moral support and a complete understanding between you and me to help me out of my difficulties. Please come, I beg you. I have exhausted my nervous strength, my courage, my hope. I see endless horror before me. I see my literary life hampered forever. I see a catastrophe. You can easily ask for a week's hospitality from some of your friends, from Ancelle, for example. I would give almost anything to see you, to embrace you. I foresee a catastrophe, and I cannot go to you now. Paris is bad for me. Twice already I have committed a serious mistake which you would describe more severely; I shall finally lose my head.

I ask you for my happiness and for *yours*, in so far as we can know *such a thing*.

You have permitted me to suggest a plan, here it is: I ask for a half-measure. Transfer of a large sum limited to 10,000 francs, for example, 2,000 to be turned over to me immediately; 2,000 in your hands to provide during a year's time for unforeseen and foreseen necessities, necessities of life, of clothing, etc., (Jeanne will go into a nursing home where the bare necessities will be paid). I shall speak more about her in a moment. It is you once more who have provoked me to it. And lastly 6,000 in the hands of Ancelle or of Marin, which will be spent slowly, wisely and in regular instalments so as to pay perhaps more than 10,000 and to avoid any commotion—any scandal at Honfleur.

That would mean a year of peace. I would be a great fool and a very great scoundrel not to profit by it to get a fresh start. All the money earned during this time (10,000, perhaps only 5,000) *will be put in your hands*. I shall not hide any of my business from you, nor any of my profits. Instead of supplying immediate needs, this money will also be applied to paying my debts.—And so on in the years to come. And thus *perhaps* I shall be able, through the fresh start effected with your knowledge, *to pay everything*, without diminishing my capital more than 10,000 francs, not counting, of course, the 4,600 of the preceding years. And the house will be saved. For that is one of the considerations always before my eyes.

If you adopted this plan in the interest of my complete happiness, I should like to be settled at the end of the month, immediately perhaps. You have my permission to come and get me. You must know there are a thousand details which a letter cannot include. I should prefer, in a word, that each amount be paid only after your consent, after a full discussion between you and me—in a word that you become *my real legal guardian.* Can one be obliged to associate so disagreeable an idea with the tenderness of a mother?

In the latter case I shall unfortunately have to renounce all the small amounts, 100, 200 francs here and there, earned in the daily routine of Parisian life. It would be a question of big speculations and of long books whose payments would be delayed over a period of time.— Consult only yourself, your conscience and your God, since you are fortunate enough to believe. Be on guard in expressing your ideas to Ancelle. He is good; but he is narrow-minded. He cannot believe that a headstrong scapegrace whom he has had to take to task is an important man. He will let me die like a dog out of sheer stubbornness. Instead of thinking only of money, think rather of fame, of peace of mind, and of *my life.*

In that case, I say, I should not stay with you for two weeks, a month or two months. I should stay with you forever, except when we should come to Paris together.

The work of reading proof may be done by post.

Another wrong idea of yours which should be corrected, an idea which you constantly express in your letters. *I am never bored in solitude, I am never bored with you.* I only know that I shall suffer because of your friends. I accept that.

Sometimes I have had the idea of calling a family council, or of appearing before a court. You may be assured I should have some good points to make, were it only this: *I have produced eight volumes under frightful conditions. I can earn my living. I am being driven mad by debts contracted in my youth!*

I have not done it out of respect for you, out of regard for your extreme sensitiveness. Have the goodness to be grateful to me for that much. I repeat, I have allowed myself to appeal only to you.

Beginning next year, I shall devote the income of the remaining capital to Jeanne. She will go into a nursing home somewhere so as not to be entirely alone. This is what has happened to her. Her brother shoved her into a hospital to get rid of her, and when she came out, she discovered he had sold part of her furniture and her clothing. In 4 months' time, since my flight from Neuilly, I have given her 7 francs.

—I beg you, peace of mind, give me peace of mind, work and a little love.

It is obvious that in the present state of my affairs certain things are extremely urgent; thus I have again made the mistake, in the course of these inevitable bank dealings, of appropriating for my own personal debts several hundred francs which did not belong to me. *I was absolutely forced to do it.* Needless to say, I thought I could repair the wrong immediately. A person in London refuses me the 400 francs which he owes me. Another who was to return 300 francs is away on a trip. Always the unforeseen.—Today I had the *desperate courage* to write a confession of my guilt to the person concerned. What sort of scene is going to take place? I have no idea. But I wanted to unburden my conscience. I hope that for the sake of my name and my talent no scandal will arise and that he will be willing to wait.

Goodbye. I am exhausted. To return to matters of health, I have neither slept, nor eaten for three days; I have a lump in my throat.— And I have to work.

No, I do not say goodbye; for I hope to see you again.

Oh, read this very carefully, do your best to understand.

I know that this letter will upset you, but you will certainly find in it a note of tenderness, of love and even more of hope, which you have too seldom heard.

And I love you.

Charles

Baudelaire's confession of the love and adoration which, as a small child, he had felt for his mother has been cited by critics as proof that he suffered from an Oedipus complex. There is perhaps much truth in their claim, for it seems fairly obvious that love and admiration for his mother coloured his whole life and perhaps even prevented him from responding to the attraction of women whose charm and femininity reminded him of her.[86]

But it must be admitted that the letter reveals more than these Freudian overtones. Baudelaire was frightened by the return of his old malady and by the dire consequences that it threatened. Like a man whom death stares in the face, he saw his whole life in retrospect and he felt impelled to assure his mother of the love which he had so often denied her. To recall the slightest incident of his childhood was to show her how much he loved her and, in a measure, to prove to her that his seeming indifference had been the result of either pride or misunderstanding. Certainly it confirms the shock he must have felt as a child on being thrust from the luxurious comfort of home into the rigorous military discipline of school life.

Baudelaire's criticism of the guardianship seems to have been, in part at least, a means of rationalizing his own failure and incapacity, for only two days later, in replying to his mother's offer of assistance, he admits for the first time the wisdom of her action: 'When I read your letter this morning, my first thought was to *fight* against the indolence and laziness that always follow a momentary relief; for, in such cases, one forgets future troubles; *that is one of the reasons that I myself would not wish to have my guardianship removed*, nor all of my debts paid *at once. The bliss would induce laziness.* In my view, the guardianship should not be abolished until one of us, either you or I, is morally certain that I can always go on working endlessly, even when it is not necessary.'

One of Baudelaire's most admirable traits is shown in his concern, even when he was ill and living in Brussels, to pay all the debts that had accumulated through the years. That he had sometimes used money not his own is not too surprising considering the circumstances. The person to whom he refers in his letter and to whom he had confessed his fault was undoubtedly Poulet-Malassis. Two days later Baudelaire wrote to his mother and told her of the meeting which he had arranged and of the understanding and forgiveness with which he had met.

Deeply disturbed by her son's state of mind, Mme. Aupick hastily sent him five hundred francs and began making preparations to go to Paris. In the meantime she informed Ancelle of Baudelaire's plight and of the plan which he had suggested to her.

Ancelle went to see Charles, but only succeeded in further exasperating his ward by what the latter considered his indifferent and casual attitude. After considerable deliberation Ancelle finally agreed to let Charles have four thousand francs. The sum was far from being satisfactory, but it sufficed to restore Baudelaire's hopes and to relieve his most acute anxiety.

In a calmer and more hopeful frame of mind Baudelaire wrote to his mother in June, expressing sentiments much like those to be found in *Fusées*: 'If, when a man acquired the habit of idleness, reverie, and sloth to the point of constantly postponing what is important until the morrow, another man woke him in the morning with the lashes of a whip and continued flogging him mercilessly until, unable to work out of pleasure, he worked out of fear, wouldn't this man—the flogger— really be his friend, his benefactor?'

DE PROFUNDIS CLAMAVI

To Madame Aupick

June 21, 1861

My dear mama,

Yesterday, in telling you about the first package that is being shipped, I forgot to answer your good letter—the latest one, at once so excellent and so laughable. Only mamas have the unusual privilege of making one laugh while inspiring respect and gratitude.

I am referring to the letter in which you explain that one must never put off until tomorrow what can be done today and that promptness always has its reward.

What touches me is your solicitude. What makes me laugh is that you are teaching me what I already know. I spend my life preaching to myself sublime, irrefutable sermons which have never cured me.— I am and I have always been both rational and full of faults.—Alas, perhaps I need to be whipped like a child or a slave!

I have finished almost all of my business; I am working hard on two or three things.

Considering my situation calmly, nothing is lost. I can become great, but I can also lose my way and leave nothing but the reputation of having been a strange man.

Everything depends on habit.

We shall talk at length.

I embrace you and I thank you profoundly for that warmth of heart that you offer me and that I have certainly never felt for the people who most deserve it.

I am writing you in one of those serious moments when I am my own confessor.

C. B.

In spite of all his efforts, it was clear to Baudelaire that his hopes of obtaining financial security were becoming more unrealizable. The fact that Poulet-Malassis was on the verge of bankruptcy made his situation even more precarious and set him to dreaming of some miracle by which he could be saved. The one thing that might prove a panacea for his ills was, he thought, membership in the French Academy. Such a miracle, as he called it in a letter to his mother, would have meant complete rehabilitation. It would have helped sell his books, it would have justified him in the eyes of the world, and most of all, it would have been a source of joy for his mother whom he longed to please before she died.

Baudelaire's decision to seek membership in the Academy was not as impulsive as it might seem. As early as July 10, he had casually mentioned to his mother that friends were encouraging him to apply for the seat left vacant by Scribe. On July 25 he warned her that he hoped to become a candidate in the near future and argued that 'membership in the Academy seems to me the only honour that a man of letters can solicit without blushing'. Finally on December 11 Baudelaire wrote to the secretary of the French Academy to announce his candidature. His announcement caused a great stir among the literary public and led many to believe that he was merely trying to play a trick or to create a scandal.

To make matters worse, he would have liked to succeed to the chair of Father Lacordaire, whose spiritual work he admired not only for its ideas, but also for its style. To Victor de Laprade, member of the Academy living in Lyons, Baudelaire wrote in lieu of paying the required visit: 'If I had dared, I should have chosen the chair of Father Lacordaire, because he is a man of the church and because he is a *Romantic*; but I was told that my candidature was scandal enough without adding that of wishing to succeed a monk . . .' In a somewhat dubious attempt to convince Laprade of his orthodoxy, Baudelaire went on to insist that he had always been a 'fervent Catholic' and that even his friend Chenavard, subtle though he was, had failed to 'sense the Catholic beneath *Les Fleurs du Mal*. Nevertheless, supposing the work is diabolical, could it be said that there exists anyone more Catholic than the Devil?'

A few days before writing Laprade, Baudelaire had paid a call on de Vigny, ill and dying of cancer. Though Vigny was in constant pain and could see few visitors, he received Baudelaire with the greatest courtesy and kindness and talked to him for more than three hours. Baudelaire, who had always admired the poetry of Vigny, was deeply touched by the poet's understanding and consideration. Grateful for the sympathy and the advice which the older poet gave him, he wrote immediately on his return home and sent him most of his published works.

To Alfred de Vigny

[December 12 or 13, 1861]

Sir:

I went home completely dazed by your kindness and, since I am most anxious to have you know my work, I am sending you somewhat more than you asked.

In the two booklets (*Richard Wagner*, *Théophile Gautier*) you will find some pages that will please you.

Here is *Les Paradis* to which I have the weakness to attribute some importance. The first part is entirely mine. The second is an analysis of De Quincey's book to which I have added here and there some ideas of my own, but with great modesty.

Here is the last copy of *Les Fleurs* on good paper. The truth is that it has been intended for you for a very long time. All the old poems have been revised. All the new ones are marked with pencil in the table of contents. The only praise I ask for the book is the recognition that it is not merely a collection of poems and that it has a beginning and an end. All the new poems have been composed to fit into a singular framework that I had chosen.

I am adding an old copy of a magazine in which you will find the beginning of a new endeavour [*Petits Poèmes en Prose*], which will perhaps interest you. Jules Janin and Sainte-Beuve found some relish in it. As for my articles about literature and the fine arts, I do not have a single available copy.

If I can find a copy of the old edition of *Les Fleurs*, I shall send it to you.

Finally, here are Poe's poems. I am not calling anything in particular to your attention; everything is equally interesting. Do not return the volume; I have another copy.

I thank you again, Sir, for the charming welcome you gave me. In spite of the lofty conception that I had formed of you, I did not expect it. You are new proof that immense talent always implies great kindness and an exquisite indulgence.

Charles Baudelaire

22, rue d'Amsterdam

Vigny was struck by the rare beauty of *Les Fleurs du Mal* and wrote a charming letter to Baudelaire expressing his admiration for the poems which he felt had been too little appreciated and too lightly judged. Realizing, however, the humiliation and disappointment that Baudelaire would have to face, he advised him to do nothing more about his candidature.

So occupied was Baudelaire in writing letters and in paying the required visits to the Academicians that he found it impossible to accomplish any work. On December 25 he wrote a long letter to his mother explaining the necessity of further postponing his return to Honfleur. In an effort to justify his candidature to her he indicated that the diversion of his campaign helped to dispel his thoughts of suicide:

'One cannot live without a driving obsession, without a hobby.' But it was mainly because of her, he continued, that he had made the attempt: 'I told myself that you attached great importance to public honours and that, *if by a miracle*, for that is the word that must be used, I succeeded, you would be overjoyed.'

The time had now come when Sainte-Beuve in his official capacity was obliged to make some mention of the candidates submitting them-selves for election and, in so doing, to speak of the work of Baudelaire. Whether through prudence, through a lack of sympathetic compre-hension, or through a feeling of incompetence, the critic condemned his friend more than he praised him and gave the impression of relegating him to the rank of a minor poet. With circumspection and damning praise he characterized Baudelaire's position in literature:

At first one wondered whether M. Baudelaire, in offering himself as a candidate, wasn't trying to play a trick on the Academy, to act out an epigram; whether he wasn't attempting by that means to notify its members that it was high time they thought of adding to their ranks that distinguished poet and writer, so adept in all forms of writing, Théophile Gautier, his master. More than one member of the Academy, completely ignorant of M. Baudelaire's existence, has had to be shown how to spell his name. It is not as easy as it might seem to prove to Academicians who are statesmen and politicians that in *Les Fleurs du Mal* there are poems really very remarkable for their talent and artistry, to explain that among the author's short prose poems, *Le Vieux Saltimbanque* and *Les Veuves* are two gems, and in short to show them that M. Baudelaire has succeeded in building for himself at the end of a promontory once considered uninhabitable and beyond the confines of Romanticism, a strange sort of kiosk, very ornate and exaggerated, but yet elegant and mysterious where Edgar Poe is read, where exquisite sonnets are recited, where the intoxicating effects of hashish are sought as a subject of rational analysis, and where opium and a thousand abominable drugs are drunk in precious porcelain cups. This strange kiosk made of marquetry with its studied and composite originality, which for some time has been attracting attention to the extreme point of the Kamchatka of Romanticism, I call *la folie Baudelaire* [Baudelaire's country pleasure-house]. The author is satisfied to have made something out of the impossible in a place where it was believed that no one could go. Does this mean that, when every-thing has been explained as well as possible to respectable and some-what astonished colleagues, that all this strange fare and these refinements appear to them sufficient qualifications for the Academy, and has the author seriously been able to convince himself of it? What is certain is that M. Baudelaire gains from being seen, that where one expects to see a strange, eccentric man, one encounters a polite, respectful, exemplary candidate, a nice young man, refined in his speech, a perfect gentleman in every sense of the word.

In his recent book *Sainte-Beuve, sa vie et son temps*, André Billy denies that the critic's attitude was motivated by envy or malice, as has been alleged by Fernand Vandérem in his monograph *Baudelaire et Sainte-Beuve*. In the opinion of Billy, Sainte-Beuve felt ill at ease in evaluating the younger generation of poets, fearing to be mistaken either through excessive praise or disdain. Moreover, the critic was undoubtedly shocked by the audacity of *Les Fleurs du Mal* as he had been by *Madame Bovary*. And looming above these considerations was his constant fear of being blamed in official circles for condoning what was considered the immorality of the poet. 'In outward appearance I seem to be brave,' he once told the Goncourts, 'but at heart, morally, I am very timorous.'

Apparently delighted at being discussed by Sainte-Beuve, Baudelaire seemed unaware of the dubious nature of the praise granted him. A few days after reading the article in *Le Constitutionnel* (January 20), he wrote to express his gratitude.

To Sainte-Beuve

[about January 25, 1862]

Another favour for which I am indebted to you! Will there be no end to it?—And how can I thank you?

I had missed the article. That explains my delay in writing you.

A few words, my dear friend, to describe to you the special kind of pleasure you have brought me.—For several years I have been very much hurt (but I said nothing about it) to hear myself called a bear, a surly and impossible man. Once, in a spiteful journal, I read some lines about my repulsive ugliness which were well calculated to alienate all sympathy (that was hard for a man who has so much loved the perfume of women). One day a woman said to me: 'It's strange, you are quite respectable; I thought that you were always drunk and that you smelled badly.' She had been taken in by the legend.

At last, my dear friend, you have set all that right, and I am very grateful to you for it—I who have always said that it isn't enough to be learned, but that above all it is necessary to be kind.

As for what you call *my Kamchatka*, if I often received encouragement as vigorous as that, I believe that I should have the strength to create an immense *Siberia*, but one that would be warm and populated.

. . . .

Promise me, I beg you, to take a few minutes to answer the following:

A great sorrow, the need to work, physical pains, among them an old affliction, have interrupted my work.

I finally have 15 copies of my chief books. My list of recipients [in the Academy], very limited in number, is completed.

I feel it a matter of good policy to seek election to the chair of Lacordaire. There are no literary men among the applicants. That was originally my plan, and if I did not carry it out, *it was in order not to disobey you* and not to appear too eccentric. If you think it a good idea, I shall write a letter to M. Villemain before next Wednesday, in which I shall state briefly that a candidate's choice of seat should not only be determined by his desire for success, but should also be a sympathetic homage to the memory of the deceased. Then too Lacordaire is a *romantic* priest, and I like him. Perhaps I shall slip the word *romanticism* into the letter, but not without consulting you.

. . . .

In spite of my tonsure and my white hair, I want to speak to you as a small boy. My mother, who is very bored, keeps asking me for *new publications*. I have sent her your article. I know what maternal pleasure she will get from it. Thank you for me and for Her.

Yours,
Ch. Baudelaire

22, rue d'Amsterdam

The 'great sorrow' which Baudelaire admits he had recently experienced was undoubtedly the same one to which he alludes in a letter to his mother on March 17. Crépet suggests that what the poet described to Mme. Aupick as a 'monstrous fact' was his discovery of Jeanne's inexcusable treachery and infidelity, his knowledge that the man posing as Jeanne's brother was a lover who, ironically enough, had been living at Baudelaire's expense.

Baudelaire's mention of 'an old affliction' may well have been a reference to the recurrence of the syphilitic condition described in an earlier letter to his mother. No doubt he was thinking of the attack suffered two days before, which he has left unmentioned save for a pathetic and memorable notation in his *Journaux intimes*: 'I have cultivated my hysteria with joy and terror. Now I suffer constantly from a feeling of dizziness, and today the 23rd of January 1862 I experienced a strange warning; I felt passing over me the wind of the wing of madness.'

From the very first Sainte-Beuve had tried to dissuade Baudelaire from seeking election to the Academy, as had other friends and acquaintances, including Lamartine and de Vigny. In answering his friend's letter the critic repeated his earlier advice and admonished him not to further shock the Academy by returning to the attack and seeking the place of a man such as Lacordaire.

Realizing that further struggle was useless and that he could count on little support even from his friends, Baudelaire sent a second letter to the secretary of the Academy announcing his withdrawal. Sainte-Beuve wrote at once to congratulate him on his decision and, by way of comfort, told him what a good impression the poet's letter had made on the Assembly.

In spite of later attempts to make light of his venture, Baudelaire was deeply hurt by his experience. Moreover there seemed no way for him to turn, no means by which he could retrieve his fortunes. The miracle for which he had hoped had not come to pass, and Baudelaire was left saddened and embittered by his failure.

*   *   *

It seemed that Jeanne would never cease to be a source of unhappiness to Baudelaire. Hoping to obtain more money, with which, no doubt, to buy alcohol and drugs, she had written Mme. Aupick in March telling her that she had been abandoned and left to starve. Shocked by her son's indifference, Mme. Aupick wrote him at once, reprimanding him for the neglect of his ill and helpless mistress. Baudelaire in turn hastened to defend himself, indignant and hurt that his mother should suspect him of such base conduct. To prove his innocence he was driven to tell her things that he had once sought to hide, though even yet he could not bear to explain the 'monstrous' fact which had made further association with Jeanne impossible.

To Madame Aupick

March 17, 1862

I do not need your advice about *integrity* any more than I need *to examine my conscience.*

Usually I hide my life, and my thoughts, and my anguish, even from you.

I cannot and I will not tell my grievances. First, they would fill at least 50 pages. Second, I would suffer for 50 pages.

I shall confine myself to saying this:

Given my character, which you know in part, sensitive, prodigal, violent, putting pride above everything else, *is it likely that I would commit a barbarous act out of pure avarice? Avarice!* What have I done for 17 years, but forgive? (I admit that, as long as the woman was beautiful, my indulgence could be attributed to selfishness.) But when illness and old age came upon her, what did I do for three years? I did what the egoism of man doesn't generally do. To charity I even added the zeal of pride.

Two days after the catastrophe I wanted to dismiss an insolent and scheming servant girl who was buying quack remedies and disregarding the doctor's orders. Jeanne indicated that I was the one to leave and that she would keep the girl. I left, and I continued to tramp the streets in order to get some money for her.

Another example: one day in Honfleur, nearly three years ago, I received a letter from her in which she complained that the hospital expenses had not been paid and that she might be put out.—Furious, I wrote to Malassis, who agreed to pay for me. He replied by sending me the *receipt* from the railroad office.—Then I wrote a very abusive letter to the institution. They responded by sending me a *receipt* signed by the director of the hospital. I was left in a ridiculous position. In her poor childish imagination Jeanne had invented that way of making me pay twice—without the least concern about the ridiculous position in which she was putting me, without any concern about the disputes in which she could involve me.

Women are that way; children are that way; animals are that way. However, animals have no books, no philosophy, no religion; hence, no honour. Therefore they are less guilty.

18 months ago I wheedled money from you and from Ancelle in order to set up an apartment in Neuilly; and when I went to live there, I found a brother who, in 18 years, had never come to the aid of his sister and who, by his persistent presence, made it quite clear he did not understand that I was poor. I am being moderate in my language. —Then I left.

Last January something monstrous happened that made me ill; I haven't said anything about it to anyone—and I don't want to say anything about it.—It would scorch my throat.

Several days ago Malassis told me that Jeanne came and asked him to buy some books and drawings from her. Malassis is not a second-hand bookdealer. He publishes new books. There are several hundred second-hand bookdealers in Paris. I vaguely suspect that she chose Malassis in order to intimidate me, to wound my vanity. Let her sell the souvenirs that every man gives a woman with whom he has lived for a long time; it makes no difference to me. But I had the humiliation of being obliged to give my publisher vague explanations like those you are constraining me to give you today.

The beginning of your letter makes me believe that you were almost duped; you claim to be more generous than I am. When I told Jeanne that she would have to count on someone else, I had just given her all that I had, trusting to my genius and to my star to get what I needed.

If you yield, here is the danger:—the next month, the following week, you will receive a new demand, and so on indefinitely. At the very time that I learned from Malassis that she was determined to harass and intimidate me, I was telling myself: 'If I can get together some money in the near future, I shall send HER something, but in such a strange and roundabout way that she can't possibly guess that it came from me. For if she guessed, she would take my weakness as encouragement and sanction.'

You can certainly see that I am not very ferocious.

Your innocence, your gullibility, your naiveté, your softheartedness make me laugh. Don't you realize then that, if I wished, I could ruin you and cast you into poverty in your old age? Don't you know that I have enough eloquence and cunning to do so? But I restrain myself and in each new crisis I say to myself: 'No, my mother is old and poor; you must leave her in peace; you must have the ingenuity necessary to extricate yourself from your difficulty.'

I know nothing more stupid than *pure feeling*, which is the sole inspiration of women and children.—Feeling impels a child, if he is very energetic, to kill his father for a pot of jam or, if he is 18, to buy lace for a prostitute; it impels a woman to kill her husband in order to buy jewels or to support a rascal—exactly as it impels a dog to push everything aside in order to seize a piece of meat.—As for this reasoning, which is so simple:—'My caprices and even the satisfaction of my needs must not interfere with the freedom of others'—it is only within the grasp of *men*.

I beg your pardon for acting like a pedant and a misanthrope with you. I am convinced of everything that I am saying. I have had a terrible education, and perhaps it is *too late* for me to save myself.

What has been proved to me is that women are interesting only when they are very old.

That brings me to Madame Batôn [a friend of Mme. Aupick]; she has three blessings and she is ungrateful. She is OLD; hence she is free from stupid passions. She is ALONE; hence she is not accountable to anyone. She is RICH; hence she has more opportunities for cultivating her mind. Let her adopt virile passions, charity or learning. Truly, I do not have time to be sentimental about imaginary troubles.

As for Madame de Montherot, I knew she was in Honfleur through one of my friends, the editor of *L'Illustration*. Since I know that you always want to rent my room, I expressed a certain amount of anxiety; he replied that I need have no fear, because Madame de Montherot was too much of a nonentity to be interested in examining books and prints.

I have just written to Jeanne. So don't reply. I am forced to postpone until another day the bother of talking about myself and about my affairs.

I persist in wishing to return to Honfleur; but how many things have to be done beforehand!

My impulsive candidacy has not done me any harm. Several things have happened that I'll tell you about.—It goes without saying that I'm not interested in the election to fill *Scribe's* chair, which has been postponed until April.

I feel no rancour toward anyone except M. Villemain; I am going to make him aware of that *publicly*.[87]

M. Biot is dead, and his place will be taken by M. Littré.

I am terribly behind in giving you the news.

My letter of withdrawal, before the *Lacordaire* election, produced a certain sensation in the *Academy—not unfavourable*.

I embrace you.—Charles

Baudelaire's attack on women and on the emotions which motivate their cruel and stupid conduct is reminiscent of certain scathing reflections to be found in the *Journaux intimes*:

'Woman is the opposite of the dandy.

For that reason she should inspire horror.

Woman is hungry and she wants to eat. Thirsty, and she wants to drink.

She is in heat, and she wants to be ——.

Fine virtues!

Woman is *natural*, that is to say abominable.

Moreover, she is always vulgar, that is to say, the opposite of the dandy.'

Though Baudelaire seems to have only scorn for the feminine sex, and especially for young girls, he makes an exception of older women who, he admits to his mother, alone are interesting. That he was sincere in his statement is obvious from his poem *Les Petites Vieilles* and his prose poem *Les Veuves* where he portrays them with a tenderness and pity that are undeniable.

If the *Journaux intimes* reveal Baudelaire's dislike of feminine behaviour, they also reveal his deep concern for the welfare of Jeanne. Various entries indicating his apprehensions about her future, his anxiety about her health are proof of the unselfish interest which he tells his mother he had long felt for his former mistress.

In a letter written to Asselineau after the death of Baudelaire Mme. Aupick came somewhat belatedly to the defence of her son and admitted the truth of his allegations: 'The Black Venus tortured him in every way imaginable! Oh, if you only knew! And how much money of his she devoured! In her letters, and I have a great many of them, I never see a word about love. . . . It is always money that she needs, and *immediately*!' [88]

*   *   *

On November 13, 1862, Poulet-Malassis was arrested on the complaint of a creditor and imprisoned for debt. Though Baudelaire owed him five thousand francs, he was unable to come to his rescue, for Malassis' bankruptcy and imprisonment left him without a publisher and at the mercy of other firms which were either uninterested in his works or waiting to buy them for little or nothing. That Baudelaire was intending to send part payment on his debt to the mother of Malassis is evident from a letter sent to Mme. Aupick on the very day that he wrote to the unhappy prisoner. As usual, his hopes failed to materialize.

To Poulet-Malassis

December 12, 1862

The man who had you put in prison, my dear friend, certainly played a cruel trick on me; for I was surely counting on you to manage my affairs. I am such a blunderer!

Hetzel made me a very fine offer for *two* works, one as a companion volume to the other. He wanted to *launch* them with care, but the offer was for only one printing; but that didn't answer my purpose.

And Michel [Lévy] is still keeping me on the string. Like the traditional dreamer, I recoil before every reality.

Why in the devil do you offer me someone to act as my agent? I have to learn to handle my business myself.

And how unfair you are to me! What can I do to make myself agreeable to you? You were asking me for a literary journal. Like all prisoners you believe that something is going on in the outside world. There isn't any news, unless you are alluding to the *Fils de Giboyer* [play of Augier with anti-Jesuit and anti-royalist sentiments]. But you know very well that I'm not interested in such smut.

As for *Salammbô*, a great, great success. A printing of two thousand sold out in two days. That is an absolute fact. A beautiful book, full of faults, and one which infuriates all the pests, particularly Babou. *There are those who reproach Flaubert for imitating ancient writers.* What Flaubert has done, he alone was able to do. Entirely too much bric-à-brac, but many splendours, epic, historic, political, even animal. Something astonishing in the gesticulation of all the living beings.

.   .   .   .

Champfleury and La Fizelière told me that you still weren't allowed to see anyone. So my remorse was groundless, for I was really conscience-stricken at not having yet gone to see you.

But when will this end? And when may we visit you? I am anxious to know. Tell me about your mother. I shall perhaps have to write to her in a month or two weeks. As for me, I am in very bad health, and all my ailments, physical and mental, are growing worse alarmingly.

I should have a doctor like Mesmer, Cagliostro, or the tomb of Pâris.[88a] I'm not joking.

Yours,
Ch. Baudelaire

I forgot something important which you could never guess. I saw Mme. Paul Meurice in connection with Legros who has done a very fine portrait of Hugo. She asked me about you, overwhelmed me with questions with a surprising emotion (like mine when I ask everyone about you); and then I saw her eyes fill with tears and the veins in her neck swell, and I really think she would have wept, if a visitor hadn't been announced.

I would be very proud indeed to excite so much interest *even in a white-haired woman.* As for her husband, invisible. He is plunged in some big new *production.*

Baudelaire was hardly exaggerating when he told Malassis of his inability to do without his help and advice. Though he had long dreamed of having his collected works published as a complete set, his efforts only resulted in disappointment and frustration. Hetzel confined his interest to *Les Fleurs du Mal* and to the *Petits Poèmes en Prose.* Michel Lévy was solely concerned with buying the rights to the Poe translations.

Though disappointed by his own lack of success, Baudelaire was still capable of genuine enthusiasm for Flaubert's recently published *Salammbô*. His accurate appraisal of the novel seems all the more amazing coming as it did immediately after the publication of the book. In 1862 Flaubert was one of the few writers for whom Baudelaire felt sincere admiration. To his mother he had written a few months earlier (October 10): '*I am an old man,* a mummy, and I am disliked for being less ignorant than other men. What decadence! Except for d'Aurevilly, Flaubert, Sainte-Beuve, I have nothing in common with anyone. Only Th. Gautier can understand me when I talk about painting. *I have a horror of life!*'

Baudelaire's anxiety about his poor health was well founded. In a letter written to his mother that same day he is more explicit about the nature of his ailments: 'None of my infirmities has left me; neither my rheumatism, nor my nightmares, nor my anxieties, nor that unbearable faculty of hearing every noise strike me in the stomach; nor especially fear; fear of dying suddenly, a fear of seeing you die; fear of going to sleep; and horror of waking up;—and that prolonged lethargy which makes me put off the most urgent matters for months—strange maladies, which somehow intensify my hate for everyone.'

Baudelaire's fear of sudden death may have been magnified by the death on April 14 of his half-brother Claude, who had suffered a stroke similar to that which was to paralyse the poet a few years later. It was after Claude's death that Baudelaire in writing to his sister-in-law had expressed his regret at not having gone to see his brother: 'It is a horrible vice of all men to postpone all their duties until another day. One always imagines that there will be *time*, and then *death*, that is the *irreparable*, arrives.'

To Etienne Carjat

October 6, 1863

My dear Carjat,

Manet has just shown me the photograph that he was taking to

Bracquemond; I congratulate you and I thank you. It is not perfect, *because perfection is impossible*; but I have rarely seen anything as well done.[89]

I am ashamed to ask so many things of you, and I do not know how I shall be able to thank you; but if you have not destroyed the plate, make *several* proofs for me. *Several* means *as many as you can!* And, if I am being indiscreet, I insist that you tell me—but not too harshly.

Manet has just told me the most unexpected news. He is leaving this evening for Holland from where he will bring back *a wife* [Suzanne Leenhof]. However, he has several excuses; for it seems that his wife is beautiful, very kind, and a very great artist [musician]. So many treasures in one woman is monstrous, don't you think?

Please reply, if this note reaches you.

Yours,
Charles Baudelaire

Manet was a comparatively unknown figure when Baudelaire first made his acquaintance about 1859. At a time when the artist was still being ridiculed by most French critics, Baudelaire recognized his extraordinary merit and came to his defence in two critical articles published in 1862, *L'Eau-forte est à la mode* and *Peintres et Aqua-fortistes*. In the years that followed the two men became close friends, and Baudelaire did his utmost to encourage Manet in the face of indifference and hostility.

It is hardly surprising that Baudelaire was pleased with the Carjat photograph. With its unforgettable, disquieting expression it produces a strangely moving effect which has made it the best known of all the photographs of the poet. The intense, almost savage bitterness reflected in the haunted eyes and in the tightly drawn lips reveals, better than anything Baudelaire ever wrote, the 'horror of life' which both repelled and fascinated him.

While on a visit to Paris in 1862, Swinburne picked up a copy of *Les Fleurs du Mal* and was so impressed by its beauty that he wrote an anonymous review for the *Spectator*. Ranking Baudelaire with Hugo, Browning, and Tennyson (in his lyrics), Swinburne had enthusiastically praised the colour and perfume of his verses, his perfect workmanship, his sensuous and weighty style. 'It has the languid, lurid beauty of close and threatening weather—a heavy, heated temperature, with dangerous hothouse scents in it; thick shadow of cloud about it, and fire of molten light.'

Less to Baudelaire's taste was Swinburne's claim that he was a moralist: 'There is not one poem of the *Fleurs du Mal* which has not a distinct and vivid background of morality to it. . . . Like a mediaeval preacher, when he has drawn the heathen love, he puts sin on its right hand and death on its left. It is not his or any artist's business to warn against evil; but certainly he does not exhort to it, knowing well enough that the one fault is as great as the other.' [90]

Though he sent Baudelaire a copy of the review accompanied by a letter, much to his surprise he received no answer from the poet. On several occasions when Swinburne was visiting Paris, the two writers sought to meet each other, but always without success.[91] Told by Whistler of Swinburne's disappointment, Baudelaire finally wrote the English poet a letter which his friend Nadar was to deliver in person on a trip to London.[92] He had already dispatched a copy of his article on Richard Wagner bearing the inscription: 'To M. Algernon C. Swinburne, kind remembrance and a thousand thanks.' As luck would have it, Swinburne never received the message. Nadar absent-mindedly put the letter into his briefcase and did not discover it until forty years later, three years after the death of Swinburne.[93]

To Charles A. Swinburne [*sic*]

October 10, 1863

Sir,

One of my friends, one of my oldest friends, is going to London— M. Nadar, whom I feel sure you will enjoy knowing. Will you please be good enough to do for him everything that you doubtless would have done for me, had I gone to make an appeal to the public of your country. Instructions, advice, publicity, he needs a great many things.

I am infinitely grateful to Nadar for having asked me for letters to my very few acquaintances in London; for he has thus forced me to repay a great debt which I owe you and which has gone unpaid for a long time. I am referring to the splendid article (on *Les Fleurs du Mal*) that you did in September 1862 for the *Spectator*.

Once M. R. Wagner flung his arms around me to thank me for a brochure that I had done about *Tannhäuser* and said: '*I would never have believed that a French writer could so easily understand so many things.*' Not being chauvinistic, I appreciated all the graciousness of his compliment.

Allow me, in my turn, to tell you: '*I would never have believed that an English writer could so well penetrate French beauty, French aims, and French prosody.*' But after reading the verses printed in the same issue

(*August*), filled with a feeling at once so real and so subtle, I was not at all surprised: only poets understand poets well.

Allow me, nevertheless, to say that you have carried my defence rather far. I am not so much a *moralist* as you obligingly pretend to believe. I believe simply (as you do, no doubt) that every poem, every work of art that is *well done*, naturally and necessarily suggests a *moral*. It is up to the reader. I even have a very decided hatred of every exclusively moral *intention* in a poem.

Please be kind enough to send me what you publish: I shall take a great deal of pleasure in it.—I have several books to publish; I shall send them to you as they appear.

Please accept, Sir, my very warm thanks and sympathy.

Charles Baudelaire

December found Baudelaire still in Paris, though he had been anxious to go to Brussels before the winter season began in order to arrange for a series of lectures and to find a publisher for his books.[94] Before he could leave he needed to pay some of his most pressing debts, but there seemed no way for him to find money. An effort to get a grant from the government for the avowed purpose of making a study of Belgian art proved fruitless. Income from his publications was almost negligible. Partly as a result of Malassis' bankruptcy, *Les Fleurs du Mal* and *Les Paradis artificiels* were selling for only one franc and his brochure on Gautier for only fifty centimes. The few things which he had succeeded in publishing during the first half of 1863 brought only a very small remuneration.

In a desperate attempt to pay some of his creditors, Baudelaire was finally obliged to sign a disastrous contract with Michel Lévy. For a mere 2,000 francs he rashly sold all future rights to his three volumes of Poe translations, to *Eureka* and *Histoires grotesques et sérieuses* on which he was still working, as well as to his three notices on Poe. Since the first three volumes of the translations had been bringing him an income of five hundred francs a year, the inequity of the contract seemed all the greater. To add to the irony, Baudelaire was not to receive as much as twenty francs from the sale, for Lévy had agreed to divide the money among the poet's creditors as soon as the fifth volume was delivered to him. *Eureka* was published at the end of November, but Baudelaire was to continue to struggle with *Histoires grotesques et sérieuses* until March 1865.

In November something happened which helped to somewhat counterbalance the disappointments of the year. Long an admirer of the drawings of Constantin Guys, Baudelaire had written about the artist a lengthy essay (sixty-one pages) entitled *Le Peintre de la vie moderne*. For more than two years it had lain in the drawer of Grandguillot, editor of *Le Pays*, who nevertheless became indignant when in disgust Baudelaire gave it to *Le Figaro*. On November 26, 28, and December 3 it was finally published, preceded by an introductory note written by Bourdin whose scathing review of *Les Fleurs du Mal* in 1857 had led the government to take action against the volume.

For Baudelaire the drawings of Guys represented a kind of modernity in subject and style that was lacking in Delacroix. The essay gave him an opportunity not only to praise the fashionable elegance of Guys' drawings, but also to introduce some characteristic digressions on modern artistic expression, on women, on the importance of the artificial (set forth in the chapter, *In Praise of Make-Up*) and on the ideal of the dandy. All his life Baudelaire had been preoccupied with dandyism in its physical and especially its moral aspects. In his drawings Guys seemed to Baudelaire to have expressed the true beauty of the dandy which to the poet 'consists above all in the cold air coming from the unshakable resolution not to be moved; one might call it a hidden fire which can be sensed, which would be able to glow, if it but chose'.[95]

That last day of December as he sat in his cold, dark room writing a New Year's letter to his mother, there was little he could offer either her or himself by way of hope for the future. Even the promise of *Le Figaro* to publish other prose poems that he might write could not dispel the feeling of gloom that oppressed him. In November he had written to his mother: 'But the days are so short. I have so much pain after my lunch and after my dinner, I feel so depressed in my unlighted room, I suffer so much from lack of *friendship* and *luxury*.' In the gay holiday season he must have been even more conscious of his loneliness and poverty.

To Madame Aupick

December 31, 1863

My dear good mother, there is nothing more disagreeable than to write to one's mother with one eye fixed on the clock; but I want you to receive tomorrow a few words of love and a few good resolutions, of which you may believe what you will. I have the execrable habit of putting off until the next day all my duties, *even the most agreeable*. Thus it is that I have put off until tomorrow the accomplishment of so many important things for so many years and that I find myself today in such a ridiculous position, as painful as it is ridiculous, in spite of my age and my name. Never has the solemnity of the year's end struck me as it has this year. So, in spite of the immense ellipses of my thought, you will understand perfectly when I tell you: that I beg you to *stay well*, to *take good care of yourself*, to *live as long as you can*, and to *grant me your indulgence for a little longer*.

All that I am going to do, or all that I hope to do this year (1864), I should have done and I should have been able to do in the one which has just passed. But I am afflicted by a frightful malady which has never ravaged me as much as this year, I mean *dreaming, depression, discouragement*, and *indecision*. Most emphatically, I consider the man who succeeds in curing himself of a vice as infinitely more brave than the soldier or the man who goes out to fight a duel. But how can one cure himself? How does one make hope from despair or will power from inertia? Is this illness imaginary or real? Has it become real after having been imaginary? Could it be the result of physical debility or of an incurable melancholy resulting from so many years filled with torment and spent without consolation in solitude and indigence? I have no idea; what I do know is that I feel complete disgust for everything, and especially for all pleasure (that is just as well), and that the only feeling which gives me a sense of living is a *vague* desire for fame, for vengeance, and for fortune.

But even for the little I have done, so little justice has been shown me!

I have found some people who have had the courage to read *Eureka*. The book will sell badly, but I had to expect that; it is too abstract for the French.

I am positively going to leave. I am giving myself *five* days, a *week* at the most, to collect some money from three newspapers, pay several people, and do my packing.

If only disgust for the Belgian expedition does not seize me as soon as I reach Brussels! And yet it is a serious matter. The lectures, which can bring me only a very small sum (1,000, 1,500, or 2,000 francs), supposing I have the patience to give them and the wit to please a lot of bumpkins, are only the secondary aim of my trip. You know the real one; it is a question of selling and of selling at a good price three volumes of *Variétés* to M. Lacroix, the Belgian publisher.

I shudder to think of my life up there. *Lectures, proofs coming from Paris to be corrected, proofs* for newspapers, and proofs for *Michel Lévy*, and finally, in the midst of all that, the *Poèmes en Prose* to be finished. I have the vague idea, however, that the change will do me good and will make me more active.

I have talked too much about myself; but I know you like that. Write me about yourself, *about your state of mind and health.*

I had wanted to have Hugo as an abettor in my plan. I knew that M. Lacroix would be at Guernsey on such and such a day. I had asked Hugo to use his influence. I have just received a letter from Hugo. The storms over the Channel upset my plan and my letter arrived *four days after the departure of the publisher.* Hugo says he will repair that by a letter, but nothing equals the *spoken word.*

I embrace you with all my heart.

C. B.

Before leaving, I shall send you some inexpensive New Year's gift, probably a book to your liking. It is already chosen.

PART SEVEN

Brussels

*One always imagines that there will be time,
and then* death, *that is the* irreparable, *arrives.*

Brussels

ON the 24th of April Baudelaire set out for Belgium where he planned to stay only long enough to give his lectures and to arrange for the publication of some of his books. Between May 2 and May 23 he was scheduled to give a series of five lectures under the auspices of the *Cercle artistique et littéraire*. His first lecture, devoted to Delacroix, seemed to be fairly successful and elicited a favourable review from the critic Frédérix in *L'Indépendance belge*. Baudelaire must have been especially pleased with the critic's comments on his 'aristocratic manner' and on his 'vigorous and sharp mind', and he wrote the reviewer a short note to express his appreciation.

The financial arrangements that he was obliged to make, however, must have disappointed him gravely and no doubt did much to increase his apprehensions about his future success in Belgium.

To Madame Aupick

Wednesday [Friday], May 6, 1864

My dear mother, I was obliged to spend two days in the country at the home of some women friends [perhaps Mme. Joseph Stevens and her daughter]. Yesterday evening I found your excellent letter which had arrived the evening of the third. Thus you'll have this one (which is going to leave this evening) tomorrow night. One night and one day.

Here is a review which appeared about my first lecture. It is called a great success. But between ourselves everything is going badly. I arrived too late. There is a lot of avarice here, infinite slowness in everything, and an enormous number of empty heads; in a word, all these people are more stupid than the French.

I am giving another lecture [on Gautier] next Wednesday. The club's funds for the winter season were depleted, I was told, and since the real purpose of my trip was to persuade the publisher Lacroix to buy three volumes, I accepted the price of 50 fr. a lecture (instead of 200 or 100). Unfortunately, Lacroix was in Paris. I have just requested permission to give three other lectures free of charge when he will be here, but I'm not telling anyone my reason.

I have had letters written to clubs in Antwerp, Bruges, Liége and

Ghent to inform them of my presence here. The replies haven't come yet.

. . . .

I love you with all my heart, and all the more because I feel how much I am making you suffer. I promise to write you often.

Charles

Even in Brussels Baudelaire could not escape being tormented by thoughts of Jeanne. A note scribbled to Ancelle reveals his concern and his distracted state of mind. It was the last time that Jeanne was to be mentioned in his correspondence. It is not known what became of her after the death of Baudelaire. The last time she was seen by any of his friends was one day in 1870 when Nadar caught sight of her as she hobbled along the street on crutches and slowly disappeared from view.

To Ancelle

[about May 10, 1864]

My dear Ancelle, I shall try to find time to write you this week. But I beg you to put 50 fr. in an envelope and send them to Jeanne (Jeanne Prosper, 17 rue Soffroi, Batignolles). I am leaving the money from my lectures untouched and I am keeping it for the proprietor of my hotel in Paris.

I have a lot of things to tell you. Impossible today. Another article appeared in *L'Indépendance*, but I don't have it at hand.

I think that poor Jeanne is going blind.

I shall write you more suitably in two or three days. I am frightfully busy.

I am sending you this receipt made out in advance to avoid all contact between you and her.

Charles

It was becoming clear to Baudelaire that his visit to Brussels would bring him only further disappointments. His health was growing noticeably worse, his nerves more frayed and weakened. Though he insisted on correcting proof for his *Histoires grotesques et sérieuses* with the same meticulous care that he had given his other publications, Michel Lévy often ignored his letters or refused to comply with his requests. 'I spend my life writing letters to which no one replies,' Baudelaire complained to Ancelle (June 1864). He was afraid to open the letters that he received, he continued, knowing that more often than not they were threats and demands from his creditors. 'I have just received a letter from him [the proprietor of his hotel in Paris], which I haven't opened, for there are days when I am incapable of opening a letter which can contain only disagreeable things, a nervous malady which keeps getting worse and saps all my strength.'

The fact that his lectures had gone badly and that he had had no success in finding a publisher increased Baudelaire's nervous condition. It seems possible that his frustration finally created an almost pathological condition and that he half believed the untruths which he told his mother in his letter of June 11.

To Madame Aupick

Saturday, June 11, 1864

My dear mother, you are not forsaken at all, but you are a woman, you are nervous. And as for me, I have a horror of writing you when I have only deplorable things to tell. Moreover, I am horribly busy; I am worried to death about the future, about Paris, *about a book* which is being printed *in my absence* [*Histoires grotesques et sérieuses*], whose proofs I receive *only irregularly*; finally, without counting my other tribulations, I have been constantly ill, *physically* and morally, for the past six weeks.

. . . .

I think my affairs are taking a turn that will oblige me to stay longer than I thought. I wanted to leave on the 20th; but since I am forced to earn my living and I can't go through Paris without distributing money, I have had the idea of turning my trip into a book divided into a series of letters which will doubtless appear in *Le Figaro*. Then I shall resell the book. That requires courage; but I must go to Antwerp, to Ghent, to Liége, to Namur, to Audenarde, to Bruges; I have to observe and question; and if you only knew what boors I have to deal with!

(Can you send me once more, without completely upsetting your budget, a small sum, 200 or 100 or even 50?)

Once we are together again, I want to do everything, everything possible to improve my lot and *to save myself*; for *I don't want any* more of the *legal guardianship*; I want to spend my life in working and in keeping you company, and *I don't want to die in poverty*.

Now here is the account of my sad epic (sad up to now) and you can judge for yourself if I am to blame.

I came because of *a publisher* [Lacroix], to offer him 3 vol. for five years, and to ask him 20,000 francs or the largest price possible for each printing, should there be a series of printings.

The five lectures were given for him. He received five invitations, he didn't come.

The lectures (the last took place the 23rd), although horribly long, twice the usual length, two hours instead of one, have been so successful that no one can recall anything like it previously. At first, I acted magnanimously when they spoke to me about terms: '*Arrange it as you wish; I don't understand such matters.*' That's what I said. They answered vaguely that it would be 100 francs. I was told they would write to clubs in Liége, Ghent, Antwerp and Bruges. Well, they have delayed so long that the good season has ended. On the 24th a functionary from the *club* came to me with 100 francs (instead of 500) plus a letter which, taking too literally my apparent scorn for money, informed me that at the end of the season the treasury was exhausted, but that I would be kept in mind and I would be compensated the next year. Just imagine society people, lawyers, artists, magistrates, people apparently well reared, who actually steal from a foreigner who is in their hands.

What can I do? No written contract! Here dishonesty does not dishonour anyone, it is an indication of cleverness. To have sent the money to the poor would have been to insult the *club* and to turn everyone against me. Besides, I was frightfully in need of money; and so I paid for my hotel the 24th and I was 3 pennies short.

Perhaps you think my troubles end there. By no means.

All of a sudden the rumour spread that I was a member of the *French police*!!!!!! That infamous gossip comes from Paris, it has been started by someone among Victor Hugo's followers who is well acquainted with Belgian stupidity and credulity. It is vengeance for a letter which I published in Paris in which I poked fun at the famous Shakespearean banquet.[96] —Perhaps you don't understand.—Now the publisher in question is V. Hugo's publisher, and I should be inclined to believe that, since he didn't come to the lectures, it was because he had been prejudiced against me.

However, I have to make an end of it and on Monday I want to stake everything on a *reading* that I have planned to give at the home of a stockbroker who is letting me use his salon.

I have just written a sixth invitation to the publisher Lacroix. I have also just addressed an invitation to the minister of the Royal Household at whose home, moreover, I have been well received. I want to have the best people there. I want visible amends for that stupid slander.

It has cost me a lot to write you all this. I love you and I embrace you.

Your last letter did not have enough stamps. Don't make me incur debts with the concierge.

You will have this letter tomorrow, Sunday evening; if you answer me Monday before five o'clock, I shall get your letter Tuesday evening.

Charles

In spite of his intentions, Baudelaire never succeeded in completing his book on Belgium. After his death it was found to be only a miscellaneous collection of bitterly savage notes filled with hatred and vituperation. It was his revenge against a country where he had known only disappointment and unhappiness. It was his way of evening the score with a people who, as he told Manet (May 27), were 'fools, liars, and thieves'.

The fiasco of his lectures was undoubtedly one of the factors that provoked Baudelaire to such blind fury. Though he boasted of his success to his mother, possibly to spare her needless pain, he could hardly have been unaware of his abysmal failure. It is true his first lecture on Delacroix had been fairly successful, but his second lecture on Gautier and the three that followed on *Les Paradis artificiels* were almost unattended. Camille Lemonnier has written movingly of hearing Baudelaire deliver his lecture on Gautier.[97] Though the audience grew smaller and smaller until only the youthful Lemonnier was left, Baudelaire went on speaking until he had finished reading the last line of his monograph. Then bowing to the youth as if to a great audience he left the stage and took his departure.

Remembering the success of writers such as Dickens and Thackeray, Baudelaire with his inordinate pride must have felt doubly humiliated. Perhaps to keep from breaking down completely, he sought escape from a reality he could no longer face by inventing stories of being tricked and cheated. Perhaps he actually believed his own lies, forgetting that a month earlier he had told his mother the truth about his financial arrangements with the club.

Baudelaire gave the party at which he hoped to meet the elusive Lacroix on Monday, June 13, in the luxurious rooms of M. Prosper Crabbe, wealthy stockbroker and art collector. An ironic reference to the affair in a note sent his mother three days later plainly indicated that things had not gone well: 'And the famous party!!! Ah, it was really funny, funny enough to make one die laughing.'

The following day he wrote a more detailed report of what had taken place. In the relentless objectivity of his account it is clear how deeply he had been hurt. He seems almost to be taking a masochistic pleasure in reliving his humiliation.

To Madame Aupick

Friday, June 17, 1864

My dear mother, it is six o'clock, I was wrong in not writing you this morning. I have made an important decision. I am no longer seeing anyone. The Frenchman [Malassis], one of my friends, with whom I could poke fun at these disgusting Belgians, has left. I am alone; I get up early; I work.

Thursday I shall know my fate.

Here is an account of the famous reception: 15 people invited by me, of whom 5 came, the best, but not influential—and of whom only two, the minister and the editor of *L'Indépendance belge*, wrote to send their regrets—15 people invited by the owner of the house, of whom 5 came. Can you imagine *three enormous rooms* lighted by *chandeliers, candelabras*, adorned with magnificent pictures, an absurd profusion of cakes and wines; all this for 10 or 12 *very dreary* people?

A journalist bending down beside me said: '*There is something* CHRISTIAN *in your works* which has not been sufficiently noticed.' At the other end of the room where some stockbrokers were seated, I heard some whispering. Those gentlemen were saying: 'He says that we are CRETINS!'

That gives you an idea of Belgian intelligence and manners.

Seeing I was boring everyone, I stopped my reading and began to eat and drink; my five friends were embarrassed and dismayed, I was the only one who laughed.

You were very thoughtful, as I have already told you: 100 francs for my hotel, 50 for a shoemaker who was dunning me (no credit is allowed here) and 50 francs set aside for small daily expenses.

My nervous condition is intolerable; but I think of the horrible future and I want to put God and fortune on my side.

I embrace you.

Charles

One of the shareholders of the Lacroix firm came to the lectures, to be sure, and he is the one who arranged an interview for me with Verboekoven which took place Thursday, i.e. yesterday. But I am afraid that Lacroix has the deciding voice.

If I carry out my study of Belgium, you will see some very amusing things which no one has dared to say.

Baudelaire was not too preoccupied with his own troubles to come to the defence of his good friend Edouard Manet when the latter was accused of a lack of originality by the art critic, Théophile Thoré. On June 15 Thoré, reviewing the Salon in Paris for *L'Indépendance belge*, had discussed intelligently and sympathetically the paintings that were being exhibited by Manet. Though Baudelaire concurred with Thoré's praise of Manet, he vigorously contradicted the critic's assertion that Manet's paintings were 'pastiches' of Velasquez, Goya, and El Greco. His defence of Manet's originality is of interest not only to admirers of the artist, but also to those concerned with Poe's relation to Baudelaire.

To Théophile Thoré

Brussels, Taverne du Globe

[about June 20, 1864]

Dear Sir,

I do not know whether you remember me and our former discussions. The years fly by so quickly! I read very assiduously everything that you write and I wish to thank you for the pleasure you have given me in rising to the defence of my friend Edouard Manet and in doing him a *little* justice. However, there are a few small things to correct in the opinions which you have expressed.

M. Manet, who is considered a fool and a madman, is merely a very honest and a very simple man, doing all he can to be rational, but unfortunately stamped by romanticism since his birth.

The word *pastiche* is not just. M. Manet has never seen any *Goyas*, M. Manet has never seen any *Grecos*, M. Manet has never seen the Pourtalès collection. This may seem incredible to you, but it is true.

I myself have been amazed by these mysterious coincidences.

At the time when we were enjoying the marvellous Spanish collection which the stupid French republic in its excessive respect for property returned to the princes of Orléans, M. Manet was a boy and was serving on board ship.

There has been so much talk about his *pastiches* of Goya that now he is trying to see some Goyas.

It is true he has seen some works by Velasquez, I do not know where. Do you doubt all that I am telling you? You doubt that such amazing geometric parallelisms can occur in nature. Well then, I want you to know that I am being accused, I, of imitating Edgar Poe!

Do you know why I translated Poe so patiently? Because he resembled me. The first time I opened one of his books, I saw with astonishment and delight not only subjects I had dreamed of, but SENTENCES which I had framed in my thoughts and which he had written twenty years before!

Et nunc erudimini, vos qui judicatis! . . . Don't be angry; but keep a kind memory of me in a corner of your mind. Every time you seek to do Manet a service, I shall thank you.

Charles Baudelaire

I am delivering this hastily scribbled note to M. Bérardi, so that it may be sent to you. I am determined to have the courage or rather the utter effrontery to speak my mind. Quote my letter, or at least a few lines from it.[98] I have told you the plain truth.

'Strangely weakened by four months of colic' and leading a 'vegetable existence', as he told Ancelle (September 2), Baudelaire was obliged to spend day after day shut up in his room, waiting for good news from Paris that never came. Only his mother and Ancelle never failed him, and Baudelaire began to appreciate their loyalty and affection more and more. His mother's love he had long since ceased to doubt, but it was only now that he came to fully understand his guardian's interest and concern. Ancelle's letters, filled with advice, with bits of news, or with clippings that might be of interest to his ward, helped to increase his liking and admiration for the old gentleman. More and more Baudelaire came to rely on him as an adviser and to confide in him as a close friend. The first indication of his change in attitude appears in a letter written on September 2 in which Baudelaire, after explaining his failure to come to Paris as he had been planning for some time, apologizes for his often churlish conduct in the past: 'I thank you very warmly for all the affection that you have shown me and that I have often repaid with gross discourtesy.'

Even to his mother Baudelaire no longer criticized Ancelle's sometimes bungling efforts. When he had to cancel a trip to Paris because his guardian had failed to send him sufficient funds he wrote (November 3): *'Don't write to M. Ancelle.*—That excellent man thought he was acting for the best in doing what he did; he blundered slightly, but his intentions were good.'

To Ancelle himself he wrote a long letter in October explaining his financial situation and recounting his experiences.

To Ancelle
Thursday, October 13, 1864

My dear Ancelle, there are several reasons for my very long delay in answering you. The first is that I've been ill again (but you mustn't let my mother know, in case you write her). This time it is no longer my stomach, but a fever which wakes me at about one or two o'clock in the morning and doesn't permit me to fall asleep again until about 7 o'clock. This daily affliction makes me see in the shadows a great many beautiful things which I would like to describe; but unfortunately it results in an extreme fatigue which lasts throughout the day.

The second reason is that, despite the charming and cordial tone of your letter and the kindness of your offer, *I was determined to get along without you.* Today it has been proved to me that that is impossible.— Understand: the fragments that I have done represent 1,000 francs. But I shall not let them be published *as long as I am in Belgium.*— Therefore I must go back to France to obtain money and I must have money in order to leave—and also to start again on a trip to Namur, Bruges and Antwerp (matters of painting and architecture; six days at the most).—All this makes a *vicious circle.* M. de Villemessant (*Figaro*) is impatiently waiting for my articles. To ask him for money and at the same time to tell him: *Don't publish yet,* would very frankly be taking advantage of his kindness.—And then the 1,000 francs that I'm expecting from my fragments will only be paid as the articles are published.

In addition I shall get money for the book from a publisher. My book isn't finished; I shall finish it at Honfleur, where I shall take all my notes.

I have written to a literary agent in Paris and asked him to negotiate for me the sale of four of my volumes: *Pauvre Belgique!* 1 vol.—*Paradis artificiels,* 1 vol.—*Mes Contemporains,* 2 vols.—and I have offered to give him a good percentage (what a percentage!) of the contract, if he obtains a good one.

If I find that matter taken care of on my return to Paris, then, but *only in that case,* I shall be able to give some money to my mother or to you.

From my trip to Belgium I shall have gained only the acquaintance of the most stupid people on earth (this at least is presumable), a very strange little book which will perhaps serve as bait for a publisher and induce him to buy others; and lastly the habit of a complete and prolonged chastity (laugh, if you will, at this vulgar detail), which *moreover is far from being a merit*, since the sight of the Belgian female repels any idea of pleasure.

Finally I have almost finished *Histoires grotesques et sérieuses* which is about to come out.—How bitterly I repent today having sold all my rights to my five volumes for 2,000 francs when I think that Michel Lévy will earn much more money by their continued sale!

That is my spiritual balance-sheet. Now I'm going to give you the material details which you asked me to give you with absolute frankness.

Imagine, my dear friend, what I'm enduring. Winter has come suddenly. Here one doesn't see any fire, since the fire is in a stove. I work yawning—when I work. Think what I am enduring, I who find Le Havre a black and American port, I who came to know the sea and the sky in Bordeaux, in Bourbon, in Mauritius, in Calcutta; think what I endure in a country where the trees are black and *where the flowers haven't any perfume*. As for the cooking, you will see I have devoted a few pages of my little book to it! As for conversation, the great, the sole pleasure of an intelligent person, you could travel through Belgium in every direction without finding a soul who *talks*. Many *gaping*, curious people have crowded around the author of *Les Fleurs du Mal*. The author of the *Fleurs* could only be a monstrous eccentric. All that rabble took me for a monster and when they saw I was cold, restrained and polite—and that I had a horror of free-thinkers, of progress, and of all modern foolishness—they decided (this is supposition on my part) that I was not *the author of my book*. . . . What a comic confusion between the author and the subject! That accursed book (*of which I am very proud*) must be very obscure, very unintelligible! I shall suffer a long time for having dared to paint evil with some talent.

Moreover, I must confess that for two or three months I have relaxed my hold on my temper, I have taken a special enjoyment in giving offence, in showing myself *impertinent*, a talent in which I excel when I wish. But here that doesn't suffice. One must be *coarse, to be understood*.

What a pack of scoundrels!—and I, who thought that France was an absolutely barbarous country, here I am forced to admit that there is a country more barbarous than France!

Whether I am obliged to stay here with debts or whether I escape to Honfleur, I shall finish this little book which, in short, has forced me to sharpen my claws. I shall use them later against France.—It is the first time that I have been constrained to write a book, absolutely humorous, both farcical and serious, where I have had to talk about everything. It is my separation from modern folly. Perhaps I'll finally be understood!

Yes, I need to return to Honfleur. I need my mother, my room, my collections. Moreover, my mother writes me gloomy letters and refrains from reproaching me with a moderation that pains me, as if she were afraid of abusing her authority in her last years for fear of leaving me bitter memories. It breaks my heart.—In Honfleur I shall complete this whole pile of unfinished things, *Le Spleen de Paris* (interrupted for so long), *Pauvre Belgique!* and *Mes Contemporains.*

.   .   .   .

Give my regards to Mme. Ancelle.

C. B.

Evidently Ancelle had encouraged his ward to apply for a loan, for in answer to his query Baudelaire ended his letter with a detailed account of all that he owed and a request for five hundred francs with which to pay his most urgent debts. His reply ten days later to Ancelle's assurance of payment shows how much good the promise of help had done him both physically and morally: 'As for my health, all my stomach ailments have disappeared. Only, I am never hungry and I have a fever every night. However, I can't blame Belgium entirely. I'm convinced I was already ill when I left Paris.

'I could add a number of moral reflections which would please you on my sincere desire to *remake my fortune* and to live the rest of my life in Honfleur.—You know that my *intentions* are always very good.'

Now that Baudelaire had money with which to pay his hotel bill in Brussels, he assured Ancelle that he would definitely come to Paris to take care of business matters and to talk about publishing his notes on Belgium, but once again he failed to keep his promise. To his guardian who had written demanding an explanation he answered:

At the last moment, the moment of leaving—in spite of my desire to see my mother again, in spite of the profound tedium of my life, a tedium greater than that caused by the stupidity of the French from which I suffered so greatly for so many years—a feeling of terror seized me, *the terror felt by a frightened dog*, the horror of seeing

my hell once more, of passing through Paris without any certainty
of being able to make payments large enough to assure me real peace
of mind in Honfleur. And so I wrote letters to newspapers and to
friends in Paris and to the person to whom I've entrusted the
business of selling my four volumes, the very ones I had come to
offer *so credulously* to Lacroix.

Baudelaire must have wondered while he wrote these words if the
time would ever come when he could return to Paris without fear of
facing his creditors. Since his arrival in Belgium he had published only
a single prose poem. Aside from the one hundred francs he had received
for his lectures, his only income was the money sent him by Ancelle
and his mother. His position had never been more grim. Yet with a
dogged determination he clung desperately to a final hope—that of
publishing his works through the efforts of a literary agent. With the
end of the year approaching he was oppressed by thoughts of the past
and tormented by anxieties for the future. Tired, ill and discouraged,
he no longer feared death itself, he feared only the thought that death
would rob him of a final chance to prove his merit and to give his
mother cause for pride.

To Madame Aupick

Sunday, January 1, 1865

My dear mother, I do not need the solemnity of this day, the saddest
day in all the year, to think of you, and to think of all my duties and of
all the responsibilities that I have accumulated for so many years. My
chief duty, my sole duty even, is to make you happy. I think about it
constantly. Will that ever be granted me?

I sometimes shudder to think that God may brusquely snatch that
possibility away from me. I promise you first that this year you will
not have to suffer any importunities from me. I blush when I think of
all the privations I have had to impose on you. This year I shall even
try to send you a little money. I promise you also that I shall not let
a single day elapse without working. In the end, surely some recompense must come.

My mind is full of gloomy thoughts. How difficult it is to do one's
duty *every day* without any break whatever! How difficult it is, not to
conceive a book, but to write it without growing tired—in short to
have courage every day!—I have calculated that all the things I have had
in my mind for a long time would have taken me only fifteen months
of work, had I worked assiduously. How many times I have said to

myself: 'In spite of my nerves, in spite of the bad weather, in spite of my fears, in spite of my creditors, in spite of the boredom of solitude, come, have courage! Perhaps something fruitful will result.' How many times God has already granted me an additional fifteen months! And yet I have often interrupted, too often interrupted until now, the execution of all my projects. Shall I have the time (supposing I have the courage) to retrieve all that I have to retrieve? If at least I were sure of having five or six years before me! But who can be sure of that? Nowadays I am obsessed by the thought of death, not accompanied by silly fears—I have suffered so much already and I have paid so fully that I believe I may be pardoned for many things—but hateful nevertheless because it would put an end to all my projects and because I have not yet accomplished a third of what I have to do in the world.

Doubtless you have guessed my fear of visiting Paris without money, of remaining in Paris, which is my hell, for even six or seven days without offering definite guarantees to some of my creditors. I do not wish to return to France unless it be *gloriously*. My exile has taught me to do without every kind of distraction. I lack the energy necessary for uninterrupted work. When I have it, I shall be proud and more tranquil.

I have good hopes. I have entrusted my literary affairs to someone in Paris—I think I shall be able to write you about that very soon.— I believe that my work is being given consideration.

You know all the things that I have to publish, alas! so many things that are behind schedule!

1.—*Histoires grotesques et sérieuses.*
(That will come out after the confusion of New Year's is over. Michel will send you a copy.)
2.—*Fleurs du Mal* (with additional poems).
3.—*Spleen de Paris.* [*Petits Poèmes en Prose.*]
(I have been working on that again, as you have seen in the *Revue de Paris* that I sent you.)
4.—*Paradis artificiels.*
5.—*Mes Contemporains.*
6.—*Pauvre Belgique.*
(I am impatiently waiting for replies from Paris about these last three works.)
As for a series of *short stories* and *Mon Coeur mis à nu*, I shall do

them when I am at home with you. Those will be happy days for you. May they not be days of premature old age!

Please tell me about your health *in detail*. What about your colds?—What is the weakness in your legs and back that you spoke about recently? Keep me informed about that. Apparently that is something new, since you have not mentioned it before.—Are you still satisfied with Aimée?

I embrace you tenderly, with all the affection of a child who loves only his mother.

I shall bring you two or three little things that will please you.

Charles

To Mme. Meurice, as well as to his mother, Baudelaire would sometimes show a side of his nature that he revealed only in rare moments to those he loved. Mme. Meurice had disliked Baudelaire on first meeting him, but as she learned to know him and to see through the saturnine pose that he adopted as a sort of protective shell, she came to be genuinely fond of him. Baudelaire's New Year's letter to her is plainly indicative of his sincere affection.

To Madame Paul Meurice

Tuesday, January 3, 1865

Dear Madame,

It would be very disagreeable for me, quite unwarranted even, to let a new year begin without wishing you happiness and good fortune. We all need such a wish and, for my part, I feel a kind of affection for those who graciously offer me their New Year's wishes.

Should I tell you how much I love you?

Should I tell you how much I wish you peace of mind, prosperity, and those quiet pleasures which even the most virile souls require?

Need I tell you also how often I have thought of you (every time that I have forced a Belgian to play a passage from Wagner, every time that I have had occasion to discuss French literature, every time that there has occurred another example of that Belgian stupidity of which you had spoken to me so often)?

Here I have been taken for a *police officer* (it serves me right), (thanks to that fine article I wrote about the Shakespearean banquet); for a *pederast* (I myself spread that rumour, and *they believed me!*); then I was taken for a *proofreader*, sent from Paris to correct the proofs of *obscene books. Exasperated at always being believed,* I spread the rumour that I had *killed* my father, and that *I had eaten him*; that moreover, if I had been allowed to escape from France, it was because of services I was performing for the French police, AND THEY BELIEVED ME! . . . *I am swimming in dishonour like a fish in water.*

Dear Madame, do not answer me; in spite of all your wit, you would be embarrassed to reply to such a letter. Forgive one who at times seeks those in whom he may confide and who has never stopped thinking of your kindness and goodness.

I pray that you may be happy (for I pray for all those whom I love), and I beg you not to forget me in your prayers, when you feel a sense of humility equal to your intelligence.

Give your husband my wishes for a good year.

Ch. Baudelaire

Recognizing the unhappiness and distress that lay behind Baudelaire's strange behaviour, Mme. Meurice wrote a warm and charming letter in which she urged him to return to his friends:

> I smiled at first on reading of your folly; on rereading your letter, I felt a sort of pity; don't be annoyed, there's nothing offensive about my pity—quite the contrary. If I'm not mistaken, it seems to me that something has hurt you and that you would have liked to tell me. But your diffidence, your pride have prevented you from doing so; with me, that is not right. You must know me well enough to realize that I don't always laugh and that I am your old friend.
>
> . . . .
>
> Do we have to have you fetched by the police or by an armed force? Once more, come back, we miss you. Manet, discouraged, tears up his best studies; *Bracquemond doesn't argue any more;* I wear out my piano, hoping that the sound *will reach you* and bring you back.

Much as Baudelaire must have longed to accept the invitation of his old friend, he continued to stay in Brussels, more in desperation than in hope. From France came nothing but bad news. Henry de la Madelène wrote that the *Revue de Paris* was in such serious financial straits that he was unable to send Baudelaire any money for the prose poems that had already been published. Ancelle, whom Baudelaire had asked to pay interest and renew time on things he had either stored or pawned, was strangely silent. Finally a letter came from his mother telling him of a recent illness and of her terrible loneliness in Honfleur.

Ashamed at the thought that he could do nothing to help her, Baudelaire wrote and tried to comfort her as best he could.

To Madame Aupick

Friday, February 3, 1865

My dear mother, I have had a frightful cold which made it impossible for me to think or to write for several days.

The letter which you wrote me at the beginning of January affected me strangely. To learn that you had escaped danger, can you imagine the effect that that must have had on me? To find out at the same time about your illness and your recovery! It seemed to me that I too had just escaped a very grave danger. I shall not hide from you a very shameful feeling, a very selfish feeling that I experienced. I was very happy that you had concealed your illness from me; I would have suffered too much.—But is that recovery really true, really certain? Tell me about it. You say that you have regained a health which you haven't enjoyed for a long time—that you are walking about and that you are eating well; that's enough to fill me with joy. But are you sure you are taking every precaution to avoid a relapse, to preserve your health?

Realizing that you were bored, but full of confidence in your patience and in your courage, I was sure that you were at least all right. And then suddenly the other letter arrived, the one in which you speak so alarmingly about your boredom, your loneliness and your discouragement, about Paris even! You made me feel very badly. But you did the right thing. I like to know everything you think, even when it is disagreeable. And then that letter made me ashamed. It is certainly my responsibility to comfort you and divert you. I have never been so unhappy at not being able to carry out my wishes immediately. If I could have left at that very moment, I would have done so. But what can I do? Even if I had plenty of money, I wouldn't leave. It is not only a matter of Brussels; it's a matter of Paris; it's a matter of business; it's a matter of literature.—This month I sincerely believe I shall have important news, and when I tell you of books that have been sold, you can say: he is ready to return to Paris—and when I write you from Paris, you can say: he is going to come back to me.

I well know from my own experience what a frightful torture boredom can be. Here I consider myself as in prison or doing penance. I long to get away from my penance. I assure you that the Belgian prison is harder for me than that of Honfleur is for you. You are in a pretty home and you see *no one*. I have no books, I am poorly lodged, I am without money and I see only people whom I hate, ill-mannered people who seem to have invented a special form of stupidity for themselves, and every morning, my heart pounding with excitement, I go to the concierge to see if there are any letters, if my friends are doing anything for me, if my articles are being published, if there is any money, if my books have been sold—and I find nothing, nothing. Ancelle, to whom I've entrusted three errands which I consider important, hasn't written me for a month (don't let this impel you to write him). I would give almost anything to have a drink in a tavern in Le Havre or in Honfleur with a sailor, a convict even, provided he were not Belgian. As for seeing again the gay little house where my mother lives, my books and my collections, it's a joy I don't dare dream about.

. . . .

What amazed me most in your heart-rending letter is the idea of seeing Paris again. That strange dream is proof of your good health. That's the only consoling thing I can find in it. But what utter madness!

In this season! in a deluge of water, of mud and of snow! Paris with its marvellous gardens is only beautiful in the sunshine. And after all, think a little about me and about my anxiety if I knew that, old and alone, you were in that chaos. Even I am always afraid there! Really, I wouldn't be able to sleep.

It's now five o'clock. It's better to write you a sketchy letter than to send you nothing at all. I embrace you with all my heart, and I shall try to write to you twice a week.

The *Revue de Paris* is collapsing. Still more money lost, not only the money for what it has of mine, but also for the little that has appeared.

Charles

When on March 16 Michel Lévy published the fifth and final volume of Baudelaire's translations of Poe, the poet waited in vain for the complimentary copies that had always been sent him in the post. Only by instructing Ancelle to ask Lévy in person for the copies did he succeed in seeing the book on which he had lavished so much care and attention. Having received an unusually kind and affectionate letter from Sainte-Beuve in which, however, no mention was made of his book, Baudelaire realized that the critic must not have received a copy and wrote to explain what had happened.

To Sainte-Beuve

March 30, 1865

My dear friend,

I thank you for your excellent letter; can you write other than excellent ones? When you call me: *My dear child*, I am touched and at the same time I have to laugh. In spite of my long white hair which makes me look like an academician (to foreigners), I have great need of someone who loves me enough to call me his child. . . .

I notice that in your letter there is no reference to the copy of *Histoires grotesques et sérieuses* which I asked Michel Lévy to send you. I have the right to conclude that that bookseller, belonging to a race which crucified Our Lord, very naturally managed to economize on one copy at your expense. I swear, moreover, that I haven't the slightest intention of coaxing you to write *anything whatsoever* about the book. Realizing how well you can distribute your time my only purpose was to furnish you an opportunity to enjoy once again an astonishing subtlety of logic and sentiment. There are people who will think that the fifth volume is inferior to the preceding ones, but that makes very little difference to me.

Malassis and I are not as much in the dumps as you think. We have learned *to do without everything* in a country where *there is nothing* and we have learned that certain pleasures (those of conversation, for example) increase as certain needs decrease.

In connection with Malassis, I will say that I marvel at his courage, at his activity and at his incorrigible gaiety. He has attained an amazing erudition in matters of books and prints. Everything amuses him and everything instructs him.—One of our great amusements is when he sets himself to play the rôle of the atheist and when I exercise my wits in playing the part of the Jesuit. You know that I am capable of becoming devout through contradiction (*especially here*) just as I could be made impious by coming in contact with a *filthy* priest (filthy in mind and body).—As for the publication of some *risqué* books which he has amused himself in correcting with the same devotion that he would have given to Bossuet or Loyola, I have even derived a small unexpected benefit—*that of a more clear understanding of the French Revolution*. When people amuse themselves in a certain way, it is a good diagnosis of revolution.

Alexandre Dumas has just left us. That good man came to show himself off with his usual ingenuousness. Even while forming a line to

218

shake his hand, the Belgians made fun of him. That is disgraceful. A man may be respected for his *vitality*. The vitality of a Negro, it is true. But I think that many others who like me are fond of the serious, have been carried away by *La Dame de Montsoreau* and by *Balsamo*.[99]

As I am very impatient to return to France, I have written to Julien Lemer and entrusted him with my small business matters. I would like to gather together in *three* or *four* volumes the best of my articles on *stimulants*, on *painters*, and *on poets*, adding to them a series of *Considérations sur la Belgique*. If in one of your infrequent strolls, you go along the Boulevard de Gand, stimulate his good will a bit and exaggerate your opinion of me.

I must admit that three important fragments are lacking—one on *la Peinture didactique* (Cornelius, Kaulbach, Chenavard, Alfred Réthel) —another, *Biographie des Fleurs du Mal*—and a final one: *Chateaubriand et sa famille*.[100] —You know that my passion for that old *dandy* is incorrigible. In short, not much work, ten days perhaps. I have a great many notes.

Forgive my indiscretion in asking a delicate question; my excuse lies in my wish to see you happy (always supposing that certain things would make you happy) and to see everyone do you justice. I hear a great many young people say: Well! Isn't Sainte-Beuve a senator yet? Many years ago, I said to E. Delacroix with whom I was completely outspoken, that many people would prefer to see him remain a pariah and a rebel (I was alluding to his insistence on presenting himself as a candidate to the Institute). He answered me: 'My dear Sir, if my right arm were suddenly paralysed, my position as a member of the Institute would give me the right to teach, and even supposing that I remain perfectly well, the Institute can help pay for my coffee and my cigars.' In short I believe that a certain accusation of ingratitude directed at the government of Napoleon is being formed, relative to you, in the minds of many other people besides me. You will pardon me, won't you, for violating the limits of discretion; you know how fond I am of you; moreover, I'm chattering like someone who rarely has occasion to talk.

. . . .

Very affectionately,
Charles Baudelaire

Without any transition, I will tell you that I have just found an admirable, melancholy ode by Shelley, composed at the gulf of Naples, which ends with these words: 'I am one whom men love not,—and yet regret!' Bravo! That's poetry.

Baudelaire's claim that he could compose his essays in a matter of ten days was a slight exaggeration. To his mother less than a month earlier (February 11) he had given a more accurate account of his abilities: 'I don't know how many times you have spoken to me of my *facility*. It is a commonly used term which applies only to superficial minds. Facility in conception or facility in expression? I have never had either one or the other, and it must be very obvious that the little I have done is the result of a very painful effort.'

Badly as Baudelaire needed the support of Sainte-Beuve at this moment, it is apparent from several letters to his mother that he was not guilty of insincerity in writing as he did. When Mme. Aupick suggested that he should take advantage of the critic's influence, he answered in shocked surprise (May 8):

What fantastic things you write me about Sainte-Beuve! Do you take me for a cad?—And can you really believe that I should be sly and prudent in order to curry favour with a man who, in spite of my relative youth, has always taken me for his equal? I have already quarrelled with him ten times; for, despite his age, he is more petulant than I. And so you imagine his new dignity increases his literary influence. What a strange mistake! I who know him thoroughly can assure you that, even if I offend all his opinions, he will always do for me anything I ask, if the thing is at all possible.

Sainte-Beuve was never to find it possible to do what Baudelaire most wanted. True to his custom he left unsaid the few words that might have done much to change the destiny of his loyal friend and admirer. If he bothered to read the 'admirable ode' by Shelley, he could hardly have failed to perceive why the French poet was so moved. In it are to be found all that Baudelaire must have thought and felt during his last months in Brussels.

*   *   *

Frequent references to Manet in Baudelaire's letters show the affection he felt for the young painter. Nor was the friendship any less sincere on Manet's side. His warm letters to Baudelaire, his many acts of kindness give ample evidence of his admiration and liking. Before the poet left Paris, it was to Manet he turned for financial assistance, and during his stay in Brussels it was Manet who often acted as his intermediary, whether it was to keep an eye on the activities of Baudelaire's literary agent Lemer, or to intercede with some editor on his behalf. Different though the two men were, their friendship involved certain artistic and personal affinities: their sense of colour, as Henri Peyre has noted, as well as their interest in dress.[101]

Deeply discouraged by his lack of success in the Salon of 1865, Manet turned to Baudelaire for advice and encouragement. The answer he received was prompt and bluntly severe.

To Edouard Manet

Thursday, May 11, 1865

My dear friend, thank you for the good letter that M. Chorner brought me this morning, as well as for the piece of music [The *Rhapsody* of Liszt requested by Baudelaire].

For some time I have been planning to make two brief visits to Paris, one on my way to Honfleur, one on my return; I have not confided in anyone except that crazy Rops, asking him to keep it secret, for I shall scarcely have enough time to greet two or three friends; but, according to M. Chorner, Rops has told several persons; hence naturally a lot of people think I am in Paris and consider me negligent and ungrateful.

If you see Rops, don't attach too much importance to some of his decidedly provincial ways. Rops likes you, Rops has understood the value of your intelligence, and has even confided to me certain observations that he has made about people who hate you, (for it seems that you have the honour to inspire hate). Rops is *the only true artist* (in the sense in which I, and perhaps I alone, understand the word *artist*), that I have found in Belgium.

I must talk to you once again about yourself. I must endeavour to prove to you your own worth. What you demand is really stupid. *People scoff at you, the gibes get on your nerves; you aren't properly appreciated*, etc., etc. . . . Do you think you are the first man to find yourself in such a situation? Have you more genius than Chateaubriand or Wagner? And yet they were certainly scoffed at. They didn't die from it. And so as not to inspire in you too much pride, I will tell you that these men are models, each in his own genre and in a world rich in genius, and that *you are only the best in a decadent period of art*. I hope you will not be angry with me for the *unceremonious* way in which I am treating you. You know my friendship for you.

I wanted to have M. Chorner's *personal* impression, if a Belgian may be considered a *person*. I must say that he has been kind and that what he told me is in accord with what I know of you and with what several intelligent people say of you: '*He has faults, weaknesses, a lack of assurance, but he has an irresistible charm.*' I know all that; I was among the first to understand it. He added that the picture of a nude, with the Negress and the cat [*Olympia*] (is it really a cat?), was much better than the religious picture [*Christ Scourged*].

Nothing new about Lemer.—I think that I shall go and shake up Lemer myself. As for finishing *Pauvre Belgique* I am unable to do so; I have lost my strength, I am dead. I have a considerable number of *poèmes en prose* to publish in two or three magazines. But I can't do any more. I am suffering from an illness which I do not have, just as I did when I was a boy and when I was living at the end of the world. And yet I am not a patriot.

C. B.

Baudelaire undoubtedly intended to give the artist a severe jolt, to goad him into defying a hostile and critical public, though having seen only the earlier works of Manet, he may well have had certain reservations about his abilities. Ten years later the artist himself admitted the beneficial effect of that 'good and terrible letter'.

Baudelaire's deep concern about Manet's lack of courage as well as his admiration for his talent are reaffirmed in a fragment that remains of a letter to Champfleury. Knowing that Baudelaire was "full of Daumier" and that he had admired him for twenty years, Champfleury had asked the poet to write some verses which were to accompany a portrait of the artist in his *Histoire de la Caricature*. It is of interest to note that what the author of *Les Fleurs du Mal* chooses to praise above all in his verses is the goodness and beauty of Daumier's heart.

To Champfleury

Thursday, May 25, 1865

. . . I meant that Daumier's satirical genius had nothing in common with satanic genius; it is worth saying in a period when the portraits of certain characters, that of Jesus Christ for instance, are falsified by self-seeking idiots. . . .

. . . Manet has great talent, a talent which will stand the test of time. But he has a weak character. He seems to me crushed and stunned by the shock. What strikes me also is the joy of all the imbeciles who believe he is done for. . . .

Verses for Honoré Daumier's Portrait

The man whose image this presents,
In art more subtle than the rest,

222

Teaches us sagely, as is best,
To chuckle at our own expense.

In mockery he stands apart.
His energy defies an equal
In painting Evil and its sequel—
Which proves the beauty of his heart—

Melmoth or Mephistopheles,
His mirth has naught akin to theirs.
The flambeau of Alecto flares
To singe them, while it makes us freeze.

Their merriment they come to rue
So steeped in treachery and guile,
While his frank radiating smile
Declares him to be good and true.[102]

Having learned from Manet that Baudelaire had asked about her, Mme. Meurice wrote one of her delightful letters in which she chided the poet for his delay in returning and complained to him of the monotony of her life: 'I get up, I come, I go, I dream, I get angry, I'm sorry, I don't know whether I love or detest humanity, vacillating between these two opinions twenty times an hour; I pray to my God who is quite different from yours . . .' [103]

In his response Baudelaire makes no effort to explain his own conception of God, though he is obviously aware that that of Mme. Meurice has been influenced by the democratic and humanitarian thinkers of the day. To Mme. Meurice he makes no further comment, but a few months later (October 28), in speaking of Victor Hugo and of his absurdly pretentious ambitions 'to save the human race', he confided to Manet: 'I don't give a hang about the human race, and he [Hugo] hasn't even noticed it. You understand, my dear Manet, that I am writing you *secretly* in regard to many things—so if you see Mme. Meurice, it is useless to disturb her convictions. That excellent woman, who at an earlier time would have found pleasure in living, has fallen, as you know, into democracy like a butterfly into gelatine.'

Had she read his comment to Manet, Mme. Meurice would probably not have taken Baudelaire too seriously, knowing his tendency to exaggerate whenever he was angry, exasperated, or even deeply moved. She would have doubtless realized that he was not necessarily rejecting the God of the humanitarians or the human race, as he claimed to Manet, but rather what he considered the false philosophy on which the humanitarians had based their ideas.

In his last years Baudelaire was still concerned with a wish and a need to believe, though not to the same extent as during the crisis that he experienced in 1861. His last reference to religion in his correspondence (September 3, 1865) is his request to his mother to pray for him: 'I love you, I love you very much; I am filled with sadness; I have great need of strength. Ask God to give me that strength. Perhaps that will help me to find it.'

To Madame Paul Meurice
Wednesday, May 24, 1865

You must, my dear Madame, be very coquettish at heart or else very sceptical about friendship to have welcomed illness in the hope that it would make you more interesting. You have, I assure you, no need of occasional ornaments and let me add that you must also be very credulous to imagine that illness attracts friendship. It may attract true friendship (that which is inspired by *my* God; for as regards your God, I don't know *who he is,* unless he be that of Messrs. Rogeard, Michelet, Benjamin Gastineau, Mario Proth, Garibaldi, and the Abbé Chatel). But it never attracts a frivolous and commonplace friendship. I remember that one day when I was in a very serious condition, I asked one of my friends [probably Banville] four times to come and see me. Finally his father replied in his place and asked me to excuse his son, since the latter had *an insurmountable fear of blood* and could not bring himself to come and see me. I recovered, I saw my friend again and I have never teased him about his cowardice regarding blood.

I am very glad that you suffer a little now and then.—Everyone profits from having passed through the fiery furnace; I shall not be so brutal as to tell you like that lout Veuillot that, *if you suffer, it is because you have sinned!*[104] I think that it is good for the innocent to suffer. I am not very gallant, am I? And I dare to write to a woman without seasoning my letter with pretty compliments and a lot of silly nonsense. How many times, finding you so friendly, so gracious, so kind, haven't I felt like throwing my arms around you and embracing you? But that wouldn't have been *proper*; you know my respect for the *proprieties*; and then, to confess everything, I said to myself: *She is a woman; hence she will not understand the meaning of my embrace. Ouf!* Now that I've told you that, I shall never mention it again.

224

When you see Manet, tell him what I tell you: that torment, raillery, insults, injustice are excellent things, and that he would be an ingrate if he didn't thank injustice. I know very well that he will have trouble in understanding my theory; painters always want immediate triumphs; but, really, Manet has such light and brilliant faculties that it would be unfortunate if he became discouraged. He will never overcome the lacunae in his temperament. But he has *a temperament*, that is the important thing; and he doesn't seem to suspect that the greater the injustice the more the situation will improve—provided he doesn't lose his head; (you will know how to say all this cheerily and without hurting him).

I was *obliged* some time ago to dine at the home of Mme. Hugo; her two sons preached me a regular sermon, but I acted like a good child, I who had been a republican before they were, and I thought to myself of a malicious engraving picturing Henry IV on all fours carrying his children on his back.—Mme. Hugo unfolded a majestic plan for *international education* (I think it is a new craze of that great party which has agreed to be responsible for the happiness of the human race). Not being able to speak easily at any hour, especially after dinner, especially when I feel like dreaming, I had all sorts of difficulty in explaining to her that there had been great men BEFORE *international education*; and that since children only care to eat sweets, drink liqueurs on the sly, and run after prostitutes, there wouldn't be any more great men AFTERWARDS.—Fortunately for me, I am considered mad and I am allowed a little indulgence.

Very seriously, very definitely, I shall come and call on you between the 1st and the 5th of June.—If my name should be mentioned in your conversations with your husband, give him my regards and explain to him that I have the right to consider myself an *honourable man*—even though I *don't have the same ideas as he.*

The famous man himself [Hugo] also preached me a two hour sermon (that is his idea of a conversation) at the end of which I simply said: *Sir, do you feel yourself strong enough to love a turd who doesn't agree with you?* That made the poor idiot gasp!

Your very devoted friend,
C. B.

Baudelaire's attitude toward Victor Hugo had always been somewhat ambivalent. Though he admired the picturesque and 'dazzling qualities' to be found in such works as *La Légende des Siècles*, he was repelled by Hugo's conception of himself as 'saviour of the human race', a second Christ who could presume to give advice even to God himself (*Conseils à Dieu*). His hostility was further increased by the injustice which had brought fame and fortune to Hugo, but only poverty and obscurity to himself. Even in his most bitter moments, however, Baudelaire seldom failed to acknowledge the genius of the great romantic poet. In a letter to Ancelle early in February he had written:

> One can be both a *wit* and a *boor*—just as one can possess *a special genius* and be a *fool* at the same time. Victor Hugo has indeed proved that to us.—By the way, the latter is coming to live in Brussels. He has bought a house in the Leopold quarter. It seems that he and the Ocean have quarrelled. Either he hasn't had the strength to endure the Ocean, or the Ocean *itself* has become bored with him.—It was hardly worth while to carefully fit out a palace on a rock! As for me, alone, forgotten by everyone, I shall sell my mother's little house only in the last extremity.—But I have even more pride than Victor Hugo, and I feel, I know that I shall never be as stupid as he.—One can be happy anywhere (provided one is well and has books and prints), *even in the presence of the Ocean.*

For a time Baudelaire refused to accept any invitations from the Hugos, but finally in May, as he wrote his mother and Mme. Meurice, he was obliged to dine at their home. His visit did not change his opinion, and for a long time he still remained firm in his dislike of the entire family. As late as November 3 he confided to his mother: 'Victor Hugo . . . who wants me to go and spend some time on his island [Guernsey], has tired me and bored me a great deal. I would accept neither his fame nor his fortune, if at the same time I had to *possess* his enormous fatuity. Mme. Hugo is half idiotic, and her two sons are complete fools.'

However, Baudelaire was soon to rescind his judgement of Mme. Hugo and to become very fond of the frail old woman. In December he wrote his mother that he had been a frequent guest in the Hugo home and a short time before he suffered the stroke from which he was never to recover he wrote (February 16): 'Mme. Hugo, who seemed only ridiculous to me at first, is decidedly a good woman. But she rather likes to mother all her friends. She has insisted that her doctor come to see me.'

On one occasion when illness had prevented Baudelaire from dining at her home, Mme. Hugo wrote a friendly note assuring him of her family's devotion and reminding him that a place was always laid for him at their table. And when Baudelaire was left gravely ill and helpless from his stroke, both Victor Hugo and his wife tried to obtain for him the best medical help and advice available.

* * *

In July news came from Poulet-Malassis that sent Baudelaire rushing to Paris in search of money. In desperate financial straits Malassis found himself obliged to sell the mortgage of five thousand francs which Baudelaire had given him in 1862 in lieu of paying a debt of two thousand francs. Had Malassis sold the mortgage, Baudelaire would have lost the rights to three volumes of his most saleable works and would have been faced with complete ruin.

On July 4 Baudelaire arrived in Paris late at night, tired, distraught and without baggage. The young poet Catulle Mendès tells how he met him coming out of the Gare du Nord and, sensing that he was without money, invited him to spend the night in his apartment. That night Mendès awoke in the dark and heard Baudelaire weeping in the next room, but fearing to embarrass his guest he pretended to be asleep. The next morning Baudelaire was gone, having left a note with only the word farewell.

In Paris Baudelaire could find no solution to his predicament and he went on to Honfleur with a feeling of hopelessness and dejection. There Mme. Aupick drew from him his story and, recognizing the dangers involved, insisted on borrowing money to settle the debt. Released from his torturing fears, Baudelaire returned to Belgium, hopeful that through Lemer's efforts he would obtain the money needed to pay his debts in Brussels and free him forever from his Belgian imprisonment.

Lemer had led Baudelaire to believe that the Garnier brothers were on the point of offering him a contract, but when the months passed with no further word, the poet grew more bitter and desperate. Too poor to afford a clock he had to strain to catch the distant sound of the bells as they struck the hour. What hurt him most was to see displayed in shop windows the cheap, worthless books of mediocre authors, while his own lay forgotten.

I see in the windows of all the bookshops all sorts of stupid, useless things, and I wonder what prevents me from selling five or six good volumes. At times I conclude *very seriously that I shall never have anything of mine printed again and that I shall never again see my mother or my friends*. Besides, I'm not working at all any more. Needless to say I don't see anyone (I even feel a shudder of hate when I see certain faces) and my only concern is to know each morning whether I shall be able to sleep the following night. I would like to sleep forever.[105]

When Christmas came and went with no word from Lemer, Baudelaire began to suspect his literary agent of duplicity or at least of indifference. Some time later his suspicions were strengthened by Ancelle's discovery that Lemer, contrary to his assertion, had not even seen Hippolyte Garnier. About the same time Lécrivain, a friend who was attempting to unravel the Lemer 'mystery', convinced Baudelaire that the agent had subtly and deliberately tried to discourage the Garniers, hoping to acquire the rights to the volumes as cheaply as possible for himself.

Even before Lécrivain questioned Lemer's integrity, however, Ancelle conceived the idea of taking matters into his own hands and of acting as Baudelaire's literary agent. He wrote to his ward that he himself had gone to see the Garniers, and Baudelaire, humbly grateful, but immensely worried about his guardian's lack of experience, replied with letter after letter filled with instructions and admonitions.

In the meantime Baudelaire's health, adversely affected by anxiety and disappointment, was steadily growing worse. About the middle of January he confided to Ancelle:

> I have been sick again, very sick. Dizziness and vomiting for three days. I had to stay on my back for three days, for even when I was sitting on the floor, I would fall headfirst. I think that I was poisoned by bile. The doctor recommends nothing but Vichy water; and I don't have a cent! . . . I can't smoke any more without feeling queasy. For a smoker that's really discouraging. Just now I was obliged to interrupt this letter and throw myself on my bed, and that's a very difficult thing, for I'm always afraid of dragging with me the furniture to which I'm clinging.

Realizing that his condition was becoming very serious, Baudelaire wrote to his mother asking her to seek advice from her doctor.

To Madame Aupick
Tuesday, February 6, 1866

My dear good mother, although I think of you constantly, I could even say at every moment, I scarcely give you any proof of it. But the fact is that it is very difficult for me to write. You have wisely told me that it is always wrong to frighten our friends. So I don't want you to become frightened. In the first place *I am not suffering at all, not at all*, except during an attack. But as I am not satisfied with my doctor, who seems very unsure of himself, I beg you to read this note to your friend, M. Lacroix, *provided you feel well enough to go to that trouble.* He may burst out laughing. My doctor likewise didn't take things too seriously until I had an attack under his very eyes. Besides, it is pretty ridiculous to spend one's life in bed and not be able to work any more. Now I am an *oyster.* Perhaps M. Lacroix knows this type of illness.

(My debts, my powerlessness to work, my guardianship, your health, the Garnier affair, all those things put my head in a turmoil, and my inactivity increases the turmoil.)

And then, before anything else, what about yourself?

What about your legs? your back and the turpentine?

Ancelle, as you know, rushed off somewhat impetuously to see the Garniers, without notes, without documents, knowing nothing about the practices of the firm. Scold him? I couldn't do that, since his intentions were good.—I have insisted that he go to Lemer to obtain documents. (He had seen only the wrong Garnier), and then I am directing him by letters (how exhausting!). Finally, one of my friends, (French) has gone to Paris and will instruct him a little about the publishing business.

I ask nothing better than to see your cousins. But when? Give them my best regards.

I assure you again that I am not suffering at all. But my powerlessness exasperates me. I feel that *it is nothing serious*, disagreeable as it may be. If I could walk a few miles around Paris in the sun, I should be cured, I think. But when?

I love you very much. Write me a few lines, if you can.

Charles

NOTE

In February, 1865, neuralgia (?) or throbbing rheumatism in my head (?)—no remedy. Diet.—There were periods of relief and renewed attacks. 10 days.

In December 1865, more neuralgia or rheumatism in the head (?) with intermittent attacks; it lasted a long time, 15 days perhaps (pills composed of quinine, digitalis, belladonna, and morphine).

Is there any correlation with that?

In January, and again now, without having eaten and without any apparent cause, suddenly a little haziness, apathy and stupor. And then, frightful headaches, dizziness. Even when I am seated, I can't help falling. Then cold sweats, vomiting bile or white froth. Rather pro-longed stupor.

(Treatment: valerian, ether, Vichy water, Pullna water (purgative).)
Better for a few days.
New attacks.
(Pills which are partly composed, as I remember, of valerian, zinc oxide, asafoetida, etc.; hence they are anti-spasmodics.)
Always apathy and stupor—heaviness in the head.
Marked awkwardness, clumsiness, weakness.
The doctor mentioned the word: hysteria. That means: I give up.

Alarmed at the symptoms which Baudelaire had detailed for the doctor, Mme. Aupick wrote and begged her son to return without further delay. Ancelle could perhaps raise the money, she suggested, or she herself could borrow money so that Baudelaire could pay his debts and leave Belgium. But Baudelaire remained adamant (February 10), still hopeful that a contract with the Garniers would soon be arranged.

> *I have done you a great wrong in telling you about my infirmity* and even about my neuralgia. Think of all the nervous upsets and all the migraine headaches you have suffered for so many years. Is it at all surprising if I take after you somewhat and if, with my bilious temperament and my sensitivity, I experience a few upsets?
> *I don't want you to write Ancelle. I don't want you to disturb him.* He knows I have been ill several times. He knows I have the greatest desire to return and to pay what I owe here. . . .
> *I absolutely refuse your help. I don't want any more money from you. I refuse to send from Brussels information about the amount I owe here. At most I would only dare to accept if my contracts were signed,* because I would then have some chance of repaying you the money. I have confidence in Ancelle; it is only a matter of directing him.— *I have a terrible dread of your imagination and I don't want you to be upset.*

. . . .

> You don't tell me about your health. *It is more serious for me than mine, since you are weaker than I.*
> *You must not write to Ancelle, promise me you won't.* That poor man has enough troubles finding his way around in business matters that are new to him.— *You mustn't be hurt by my refusal.* I am very ashamed of all the money that I have already extracted from you.

When it seemed to Baudelaire that nothing worse could happen, a letter arrived from Ancelle, a terrible letter which told of the Garniers'

refusal to publish his works and which put an end to the hopes that had
sustained him during those long months.

To Ancelle
Sunday, February 18, 1866

My dear friend, your terrible letter just arrived as mine was leaving.

I am very sorry that Lécrivain did not go to see you, or that you did
not wait for my letter. Lécrivain was convinced that an agreement
would be made with the Garniers:—there were, I can see, many misunderstandings in that conversation. Hippolyte G. had not seen Lemer
—*for a year!* What is the meaning then of the letter, or rather of the
two letters, from Lemer which I sent you, and of Garnier's visit to
Sainte-Beuve?—What difference does it make that I am in Brussels? I
have done a book here (the last) for Michel Lévy.—*Les Paradis* has
had a very great literary success; few books have received so many
reviews. Only the bankruptcy of Malassis prevented a wide circulation
and financial success.—*Les Contemporains* is *absolutely unknown.*
Several excerpts have appeared, but in *obscure* magazines, *completely
unknown.*—*Les Fleurs du Mal,* a forgotten book!

This is too stupid. It is *still* in demand. Perhaps it will begin to be
understood in a few years.

—*Hetzel!* why Hetzel had not even begun to carry out the arrangement. He had bought the *Spleen de Paris* and the *Fleurs* from me.[106]
But in Brussels, where we saw each other, since I told him that I
wanted to sell everything together, he released me from my promise,
because, like me, like Lemer, he thought those two volumes would
facilitate the sale of the complete works. There is nothing to settle
with Hetzel except a small matter of money.

And now, what shall I do? Divide up everything? I consider that
unwise and too long drawn out. Do you want to undertake another
negotiation, if only tentatively, until I get to Paris? Do you feel well
posted now?

But avoid any sudden move, any impulsive action, and calculate
every step that you take.

List of possible publishers.

—Lévy (Michel)

Two years ago I offered him *everything.* He wanted to *drag things
out,* so as to acquire my works *cheaply.* He found out that I was
negotiating with Hetzel. He became furious and told me that Hetzel

had taken the *pick of the basket*. If it is necessary to go back to Michel, you will have to tell him that I cancelled my contract with Hetzel *because of him* and that *Les Fleurs* and *Le Spleen* are back in my hands.

But a lie, and unpleasant relations (always unpleasant!) with Michel Lévy, how humiliating!!!

—*Maison Hachette* (today his sons-in-law).

A big and well-established firm. Deschanels [*sic*] offered to introduce me to them. Moreover, I am well known there. But imagine what horror my books must inspire in a firm made up of schoolmasters, professors, pedants, pedagogues, edifying hack writers, and other riff-raff!

—FAURE

A very good choice. But he came to Brussels, I dined with him, and if he had any interest in my books, he would have given me some indication. As for me, I offered him nothing.

—AMYOT

—Good, but a last resort.

—DIDIER

—Good, but a last resort.

—DENTU

Reread the last sentence of my letter to Dentu, sent you yesterday. You may find it will give you an opening. But if you think it feasible, merely broach the subject. In business, it is always important to arouse interest and not to appear to be at the mercy of anyone.—Enclosed is a note for Dentu, to be used only in the event that you speak to him of this matter, excluding *la Belgique déshabillée*.

By the way, you mention excisions that you are making in my notes. If you have made any in the plan of *la Belgique*, you must offer the original version to Dentu.

C. B.

And you were CHILDISH enough to go and listen to that numskull Deschanels [who had just given a reading of Baudelaire's poems in Paris], a professor for girls! a democrat who doesn't believe in miracles and believes ONLY IN GOOD SENSE (!), a perfect representative of second-rate literature, a petty popularizer of the commonplace, etc.!

Yesterday, Saturday the 17th, he was neatly dealt with in connection with that same lecture, in the *Chronique* of the *Temps*, signed *de la*

Madelène. He was taken to task in a manner that was really skilful and witty.

And you were CHILDISH enough to forget that *France* has a HORROR of poetry, of *real* poetry; that it admires only slovenly writers like Béranger and de Musset; that *anyone who concerns himself with spelling is considered heartless* (which is logical enough however, since passion always expresses itself badly); finally, that poetry which is profound, but complicated, bitter, coldly diabolical (in appearance), is less appropriate than any other for eternal frivolity!

Must I tell you, you who have not guessed it any more than the others, that in this *atrocious* book [*Les Fleurs du Mal*] I have put all *my heart*, all *my love*, all *my religion* (travestied), all *my hate*? It is true that I shall write the contrary, that I shall swear by all the gods that it is a book of *pure art*, of *mimicry*, of *virtuosity*; and I shall be a shameless liar.

And by the way, what is *fanciful* poetry? I shall never be able to guess. I defy Deschanels to explain it, as I defy any journalist or any professor *to explain the meaning of a single one of the words that he uses*. —There is then *fanciful* poetry and poetry *which is not fanciful*. What poetry is there which is not based on the fancy of the artist, of the poet, that is to say *on his way* of feeling?

Speaking of *feeling*, of the *heart* and other feminine trash, remember the profound saying of Leconte de Lisle: *All elegists are boors!*

Enough, don't you think? And forgive my diatribe. Don't deprive me of the only friend to whom I can speak my mind! [107] But is it really believable? to go to a lecture by Deschanels!

———

I have adopted and have been putting into practice for two months the hygienic regimen which you suggested to me.

I am utterly averse to accepting your offer to extricate me from Brussels, unless we have behind us the guarantee of literary contracts with specific dates for payment. I shall speak to you about that some other time.

What you said about that fine pedant sent me into a rage. You know that as a rule error causes me nervous crises, except when I deliberately cultivate stupidity in order to extract its quintessence, as I did for 20 years in *Le Siècle*.

Except for Chateaubriand, Balzac, Stendhal, Mérimée, de Vigny,

Flaubert, Banville, Gautier, Leconte de Lisle, all the modern rabble are obnoxious to me. Your academicians, obnoxious! Your liberals, obnoxious! Virtue, obnoxious! Vice, obnoxious! The flowing style, obnoxious! Progress, obnoxious! Never speak to me again about such fatuous fools!

Yours,
C. B.

Though Baudelaire was undoubtedly sincere in scolding Ancelle for attending Deschanel's lecture, he must have been secretly pleased at receiving even so slight a recognition. And though Deschanel had made himself absurd with his prim and deprecatory remarks, his reading of the poems had evoked murmurs of admiration in the audience, as la Madelène had reported in his review. To his mother Baudelaire scoffed (February 26): 'Deschanel, a professor doted on by women and girls, (you can picture the man from that) gave a *public lecture* on my poetry in France. . . . As I know Deschanel, I can imagine his lecture. Besides, the remarks of Ancelle, who knows as much about literature as elephants know about dancing a bolero, have confirmed my opinion.'

Of more importance must have been the news which Sainte-Beuve had written him about a month earlier. The critic had told him of an article published in *L'Art* (November 16, December 20 and 23, 1865) and written by an obscure young poet, Paul Verlaine, in enthusiastic praise of the author of *Les Fleurs du Mal*. Sainte-Beuve had concluded by saying: 'If you were here, you would become, whether you wished it or not, an authority, an oracle, a consulting poet.'

Knowing how much it would please his mother, Baudelaire sent her two of Verlaine's articles on March 5. 'There is talent among these young people; but how much nonsense! what exaggerations and what youthful infatuation! For some years I have been detecting here and there imitations and tendencies which alarmed me. I know nothing more compromising than imitators and I like nothing so much as to be alone. But that is not possible; and it seems that *the Baudelaire school* exists.'

Unable to bear the tension of waiting any longer and fearful that Ancelle would put him at the mercy of prospective publishers by revealing his desperate need, Baudelaire decided to go to Paris as Lécrivain had advised. As kindly as possible he explained his decision to his guardian and informed him of his plan to leave for Paris on March 15.

From March 5 until March 20 there was a strange silence. On March 20 Baudelaire sent a short note to his mother, the last he was ever to write with his own hand, telling her he was forcibly detained in Brussels, but offering no explanation for his delay. In an effort to reassure her he teased her gently about her spelling and offered to send her a copy of Hugo's latest novel.

To Madame Aupick

Tuesday, March 20

My dear mother, I am neither well nor ill. I work and I write with difficulty. I shall explain to you why. For I've been intending to write to you for a long time and I think that this evening or tomorrow morning I shall reply about everything that you have asked me. I am putting off my trip to Paris, because I must. But I shall go, for it is absolutely necessary.—Hereafter, I shall not wait so long to write you.

Poor dear little mother, it is my fault that you have been so *worried*! (*with two r's*).* Spelling has varied so often in France, however, that, like Napoleon and Lamartine, you can well afford a few small eccentricities.

If you don't receive the two letters at the same time, you will receive the second a day after this one.

I embrace you.

Charles

If you feel like reading *Travailleurs de la mer* [Hugo], I shall send it to you in a few days.

What Baudelaire failed to tell his mother was the reason why he had suddenly postponed his trip to Paris, the same reason, he might have added, that made writing and working so difficult for him. From the accounts of his friends, the events of those March days have been reconstructed.

Before leaving Brussels, Baudelaire and Poulet-Malassis had been invited by their good friend Rops to come to Namur. In Namur Baudelaire wished to see once more the lovely Jesuit church which with unforeseen appropriateness he had once called 'that terrible and delightful catafalque'. It was there, while he was admiring the carving of the confessionals, that he suddenly staggered and fell to the floor. To the friends who were accompanying him, Baudelaire pretended he had slipped, but Poulet-Malassis, observing the strangeness of his manner, soon became convinced that the poet was seriously ill.

---

* In original : *'inquiète avec un seul "t"' *.

On his return to Brussels Baudelaire felt too unsure of himself to go to Paris. One evening the photographer Neyt invited him to dinner. Baudelaire seemed strangely sad and quiet, as if preoccupied by some terrible anxiety. At times a bewildered look came into his eyes and with the greatest effort he forced himself to follow the conversation of his host. Suddenly he rose to take his departure and left the restaurant with uncertain steps. Neyt allowed him to leave, but later, remembering Baudelaire's strange behaviour and fearing he might be ill, he set out in search of his friend. He found him late at night at the Taverne Royale sitting, haggard and dazed, with a glass of brandy before him. Baudelaire allowed Neyt to help him home and to carry him up the stairs to his room, but when Neyt laid him on the bed and tried to undress him, he kept crying to him to go away until the photographer was finally obliged to leave. The next morning Neyt returned and found Baudelaire lying fully dressed on the bed, the lamp still burning on the table beside him. At Neyt's touch the poet opened his eyes, but was unable to speak. The doctor who was summoned gave a diagnosis of aphasia resulting from a stroke.

Three days later Baudelaire had recovered sufficiently to dictate two short notes for his mother.

To Madame Aupick
Brussels, Friday, March 23, 1866

My dear mother,

M. Ancelle hasn't answered me anything for a long time, for a very long time. I had intended to put off my trip to Paris until I had finished some work and received some money on account for the Hotel; but three days ago, since my last letter, a new attack occurred and here I am helpless.

Write and ask M. A., if you can, to send some money *at once* to Mme. Lepage, proprietress of my hotel—whatever he wants or is able to send. Above all, *no indiscretion nor too much zeal* on his part. Underline this in your letter.

The doctor, who is kind enough to write at my dictation, urges you not to get excited and tells me that in a few days I shall be ready to resume my work.

I embrace you.

Your son,
Charles

The desperate courage and stoic determination that Baudelaire had shown during those long months in Brussels did not leave him even when he lay helpless and paralysed. Unable to guide his pen he bravely continued to dictate letters to Poulet-Malassis or to others who were willing to serve as his amanuensis. To Catulle Mendès, who had sent him proofs of sixteen poems that were to appear in *Le Parnasse contemporain*, Baudelaire sent a note containing his usual meticulous corrections.[108] To Ernest Prarond, a friend of his early years, he sent a grateful acknowledgment of the volume of verse which had been given him by the author. And in his last letters to Ancelle and to his mother, he refused to admit defeat or even to give up his search for a publisher.

To Catulle Mendès

Brussels, March 29, 1866

My dear friend,

Thank you very cordially: everything that you tell me is fine and I am pleased with your title. Yesterday I received [proofs] from a printer named Toinon with shops in both St. Germain and Paris; yesterday evening I returned the proofs to the Paris office, corrected half by me, half by Millot, because, being very ill, I write in an illegible hand. You will receive this letter tomorrow morning, Friday; I shall be very grateful to you if you will check our corrections.

Yours,

Charles Baudelaire

per

G. Millot

P.S. It is MADRIGAL TRISTE and not LE MADRIGAL; it is ÉPIGRAPHE POUR UN LIVRE CONDAMNÉ and not ÉPIGRAPHE POUR UN LIVRE; A UNE MALABARAISE and not A UNE MALABRAISE.

The last line of the poem entitled BIEN LOIN D'ICI should be preceded by a dash (—), in order to give it a kind of isolation and separation from the rest.

LES PLAINTES D'UN ICARE instead of LES PLAINTES D'UN ICARRE.

Nouvelles Fleurs du Mal should be printed so that the title FLEURS DU MAL is distinguished from the word NOUVELLES.

C. B.

To Madame Aupick

Brussels, Friday, March 30, 1866

[Baudelaire's last letter]

My dear mother,

The answer sent Monday reached you Tuesday evening. Wednesday, Thursday and today, Friday, you could have written me about yourself; if you haven't done so, you evidently imagine I am concerned only about myself.

It is absolutely essential that you tell me about yourself.

I received a letter from Ancelle saying that he will come soon. It is useless, premature at least.

1. Because I am in no condition to move.

2. Because I have debts.

3. Because I have six cities to visit in two weeks. I do not wish to lose the fruit of a long period of work.

I believe he is determined above all to please and obey you; that's why I am writing you about it; moreover, I am inclined to return as quickly as possible.

Write me at length and in great detail about yourself.

I embrace you with all my heart.

Charles

As Baudelaire's condition became more serious, Ancelle, who had been summoned by Poulet-Malassis, hurried to Brussels where he had his ward placed in a Catholic nursing home. Though he partially recovered the use of his limbs, his speech grew steadily worse until he could remember only the two words 'sacré nom' which he would shout in impotent rage when exasperated by his inability to make himself understood. When Mme. Aupick was finally told of her son's illness, she started out for Brussels accompanied by her maid, hoping to be able to bring Charles back with her to Honfleur.

After a fortnight in the nursing home, Baudelaire was able to return to his hotel, much to the relief of the nuns and their patients who were appalled as much by his profanity as by his alleged satanism. For two and a half months he continued to convalesce in Brussels, apparently serene and happy in spite of his partial paralysis and his inability to speak. With his good friends Poulet-Malassis and Arthur Stevens the poet would take drives in the country or go out for dinner, occasionally showing his frustration at not being able to join in the conversation by looking upwards with an air of helpless resignation.[109]

On July 2, 1866, accompanied by his mother and Arthur Stevens, Baudelaire returned to Paris by train in a private compartment which had been hired for him by his friends. As he got off the train with his cane hanging from the button of his coat and leaning heavily on Stevens, he caught sight of Asselineau waiting to greet him. When he saw the tears in the eyes of his friend, Baudelaire broke into a long, sonorous laugh which chilled the heart of Asselineau and made him wonder if the poet were completely sane. They had not been together more than a quarter of an hour, however, before Asselineau realized that Baudelaire had never been 'more lucid or more keen'. To the conversation of the many friends who visited him daily he would listen avidly and he would struggle until he was exhausted to make himself understood in whatever way he could.

Two days after his arrival in Paris Baudelaire entered the clinic of Doctor Emile Duval. Soon afterwards, on the advice of the doctors who felt that her presence was irritating and worrying her son, Mme. Aupick returned to Honfleur. During his first months at the clinic Baudelaire appeared happy, even gay. He sang, seemed delighted to see his friends or to go out with them to dine, listened contentedly to the music from Tannhäuser which Mme. Meurice or Mme. Manet played for him. Soon, however, Baudelaire began to refuse the invitations which he had first accepted with such alacrity. Realizing that his excursions were over-exciting him and increasing his insomnia, he declined even to attend the weekly dinners with his old acquaintances which Nadar had arranged in his honour and to which he had looked forward wth such pathetic eagerness.

In his mind Baudelaire had set March 31 as the date by which he expected to have made his recovery and he had even made plans to go to Nice and to Honfleur in the happy days to come. To Michel Lévy who, persuaded by Asselineau, had offered to begin an immediate reprinting of *Les Fleurs du Mal*, Baudelaire showed a calendar on which he had marked the 31st with a heavy line. It was clear he expected that by that time he would be able to supervise the publication himself.

When March 31 arrived without any improvement in his condition, a great change came over the poet. He became depressed and resigned, without the will to struggle or the desire to live. Soon he no longer left his bed, and though he continued to welcome his friends, his eyes were shadowed by an expression of infinite sadness, unforgettable to those who knew and loved him. In July Asselineau sent for his mother. She took a room in a small hotel nearby and remained with her son through July and August. On August 31, 1867, about eleven o'clock in the morning Baudelaire died peacefully in her arms, aged forty-six years and four months.

Even in death Baudelaire was pursued by the ill luck which all his life had dogged his footsteps. Only a hundred persons attended the funeral and of these not more than sixty followed the procession to the grave. Neither Sainte-Beuve nor Gautier was present.[110] Nor did the *Société des Gens de Lettres* send a representative, in spite of Asselineau's request. Others failed to receive their invitations in time or had left Paris to escape the August heat.

At the grave Théodore de Banville, ill and deeply moved, pronounced the funeral oration in which he acclaimed *Les Fleurs du Mal* as the work of a genius which would take its place in the literature of its day as a work 'essentially French, essentially original, and essentially new'.

Banville was followed by Asselineau who, choked with emotion, strove vainly to dispel the legend which enveloped and hid the real Baudelaire and which was 'only the reflection of his scorn for stupidity and proud mediocrity'. With the rare perceptiveness of one to whom love has given understanding, he saw beneath the external mask which Baudelaire had so carefully created for himself: 'His sincere and delicate spirit possessed the modesty of his virtues, and through horror of affectation and hypocrisy, seized upon an ironic reserve which in his case was only a supreme form of dignity. I can only pity those who were deceived by it.'

But even as the faithful Asselineau spoke and commended the memory of the great poet to those who remained, the autumn rain which had been falling grew heavier, silencing the speaker and dispersing the crowd. In death as in life Baudelaire was left alone and forgotten:

> The dead, the poor dead have great sorrows,
> And when October's wind, stripping the old trees,
> Sounds its melancholy song among the marble tombs,
> Surely they must find the living cold and heartless . . .[111]

SELECTED BIBLIOGRAPHY

Asselineau, Charles. *Charles Baudelaire, sa vie et son oeuvre*. Paris, Lemerre, 1869. Reprinted in *Baudelaire et Asselineau*, Textes recueillis et commentés par Jacques Crépet et Claude Pichois. Paris, Nizet, 1953.

Bandy, W. T. *Baudelaire Judged by his Contemporaries* (1845–67). New York, Institute of French Studies, Columbia University, 1933.

Baudelaire, Charles. *Oeuvres complètes de Charles Baudelaire*, ed. Jacques Crépet (in collaboration with Claude Pichois for the three final volumes). 19 vols. Paris, Conard-Lambert, 1922–53. *Les Fleurs du Mal* (1 vol.). *Curiosités esthétiques* (1 vol.). *Petits Poèmes en Prose* (1 vol.). *Les Paradis artificiels* (1 vol.). *Oeuvres posthumes* (3 vols.). *Histoires extraordinaires* (1 vol.). *Nouvelles histoires extraordinaires* (1 vol.). *Aventures d'Arthur Gordon Pym* (1 vol.). *Eureka* (1 vol.). *Histoires grotesques et sérieuses* (1 vol.). *Correspondance générale* (6 vols.).

——. *Les Fleurs du Mal*. Edition critique établie par Jacques Crépet et Georges Blin. Paris, Corti, 1942. Reprinted with addenda in 1950.

——. *Journaux intimes, Fusées, Mon Coeur mis à nu, Carnet*. Edition critique établie par Jacques Crépet et Georges Blin. Paris, Corti, 1949.

Bennet, Joseph D. *Baudelaire, a Criticism*. Princeton, Princeton University Press, and London, Oxford University Press, 1944.

Billy, André. *La Présidente et ses amis*. Paris, Flammarion, 1945.

——. *Sainte-Beuve, sa vie et son temps*. 2 vols. Paris, Flammarion, 1952.

Blin, Georges. *Baudelaire*. Paris, Gallimard, 1939.

——. *Le Sadisme de Baudelaire*. Paris, Corti, 1948.

Crépet, Eugène. *Baudelaire*. Etude biographique. Revue et complétée par Jacques Crépet. Paris, Messein, 1907.

Feuillerat, Albert. *Baudelaire et la Belle aux cheveux d'or*. New Haven, Yale University Press, and Paris, Corti, 1941.

——. *Baudelaire et sa mère*. Montreal, Editions Variétés, 1944.

Gilman, Margaret. *Baudelaire the Critic*. New York, Columbia University Press, 1943.

Hyslop, Lois Boe and Francis E. *Baudelaire on Poe*. State College, Bald Eagle Press, 1952.

Jones, P. Mansell. *Baudelaire*. New Haven, Yale University Press, 1952.

Laforgue, Dr. René. *L'Echec de Baudelaire*. Paris, Denoël et Steele, 1931.

Lemonnier, Léon. *Edgar Poe et la critique française de 1845 à 1875*. Paris, Presses Universitaires, 1928.

Massin, Abbé Jean. *Baudelaire entre Dieu et Satan*. Paris, Juillard, 1946.

Mouquet, Jules, et Bandy, W. T. *Baudelaire en 1848*. Paris, Emile-Paul, 1946.

Nadar (Félix Tournachon). *Charles Baudelaire intime: Le Poète vierge*. Paris, Blaizot, 1911.

Peyre, Henri. *Connaissance de Baudelaire*. Paris, Corti, 1951.

Pia, Pascal. *Baudelaire par lui-même*. Paris, Editions du Seuil, 1952.

Pommier, Jean. *La Mystique de Baudelaire*. Paris, Les Belles Lettres, 1932.

——. *Dans les Chemins de Baudelaire*. Paris, Corti, 1945.

Porché, François. *La Vie douloureuse de Charles Baudelaire*. Paris, Plon, 1926.

——. *Baudelaire: Histoire d'une Ame*. Paris, Flammarion, 1945.

Prévost, Jean. *Baudelaire*. Essai sur l'inspiration et la création poétiques. Paris, Mercure de France, 1953.

Quennell, Peter. *Baudelaire and the Symbolists*. London, Chatto and Windus, 1929.

Rhodes, S. A. *The Cult of Beauty in Charles Baudelaire*. 2 vols. New York, Institute of French Studies, Columbia University, 1929.

Ruff, Marcel. *Baudelaire, l'homme et l'oeuvre*. Paris, Hatier-Boivin, 1955.

—— *L'Esprit du Mal et l'esthétique baudelairienne*. Paris, Colin, 1955.

Sartre, J. P. *Baudelaire*. Paris, Gallimard, 1947.

Shanks, Lewis P. *Baudelaire: Flesh and Spirit*. London, Douglas, 1930.

Starkie, Enid. *Baudelaire*. London, Gollancz, 1933.

Tabarant, Adolphe. *La Vie artistique au temps de Baudelaire*. Paris, Mercure de France, 1942.

Turnell, Martin. *Baudelaire*. A Study of his Poetry. London, Hamilton, 1953, and New York, New Directions, 1954.

Vandérem, Fernand. *Baudelaire et Sainte-Beuve*. Paris, Leclerc, 1917.

Vivier, Robert. *L'Originalité de Baudelaire*. New ed. Brussels, Académie Royale, 1953.

1. In later years Baudelaire made no effort to hide his disapproval of his mother's second marriage. According to Jules Buisson, who knew him as a young man at the Pension Bailly, he was 'inexhaustible on this subject, and his terrible logic was always summed up thus: "When one has a son like me" —like me was understood—"one doesn't remarry." ' See Eugène Crépet, *Baudelaire. Etude Biographique.* Revue par Jacques Crépet (Paris, 1907), p. 11.

2. *Ibid.*, p. 13.

3. *Ibid.*, p. 14.

4. The Oliviers had been close friends of M. and Mme. François Baudelaire at the time Charles was born. After Caroline's remarriage they became equally friendly with M. Aupick. The latter asked M. Olivier to be a member of the family council in 1841.

5. *Poems of Baudelaire*, trans. Roy Campbell (London and New York, 1952), p. 42.

6. Authors' translation.

7. Albert Feuillerat, 'Baudelaire est-il allé dans l'Inde?' *The French Review*, XVII, 5 (March, 1944), 249–54. See also Marcel Ruff, *L'Esprit du mal et l'esthétique baudelairienne*, pp. 171 and 464–6.

8. E. Crépet, Letter to Aupick published in the Appendix of *Baudelaire*, pp. 221–6.

9. As a direct result of an incident on shipboard, Baudelaire wrote the famous sonnet, *L'Albatros*, which he published only in the second edition of *Les Fleurs du Mal. A une Malabaraise* and *Bien loin d'ici*, written at a later date, were obviously inspired by haunting memories of his voyage, as was also true of his prose poem, *La belle Dorothée.*

Baudelaire himself indirectly admits the value of this exotic experience in an article which he wrote in 1855 on the exhibition of art being shown at the *Exposition Universelle.* In speaking of the sympathy which a distant country can inspire in an intelligent man, he maintains that this sympathy 'will sooner or later be so keen, so penetrating that it will create in him a new world of ideas, a world which will become an integral part of him and will accompany him in the form of his memories until his death'. Quoted from *Curiosités esthétiques*, p. 221. Unless otherwise specified, references are to Jacques Crépet's edition of the works and correspondence of Baudelaire, *Oeuvres Complètes de Charles Baudelaire*, Paris, 1922–53.

10. Translated by Roy Campbell, p. 84.

11. Claude Pichois has discovered that Jeanne called herself Berthe as early as 1838–9, and concludes that *Les Yeux de Berthe* was certainly written

for her. See his article, 'A Propos d'un Poème de Baudelaire: du Nouveau sur Jeanne Duval', *Revue de l'histoire littéraire de la France* (Avril-Juin 1955), 191–205.

12. The article in question is unknown.

13. Probably either *De la Peinture* or *De la Caricature*.

14. A reference to the court jester in Hugo's *Le Roi s'amuse*.

15. A reference to Diderot's novel, *La Religieuse*.

16. A reference to Chateaubriand's famous Romantic hero, René.

17. Authors' translation.

18. In the *Salon de 1845* Baudelaire boldly affirmed that Delacroix, Ingres, and Daumier were the three greatest draughtsmen of the period; he rose to the defence of the middle class; he hailed Delacroix as the most original painter of both past and present.

19. On May 25 Baudelaire published *A une Créole* in *L'Artiste*.

20. Letter to Mme. Aupick, January 20, 1858.

21. E. Crépet, p. 61.

22. *Oeuvres posthumes*, ed. J. Crépet, I, 492.

23. W. T. Bandy, 'La vérité sur *le Jeune Enchanteur*. Baudelaire et Croly', *Mercure de France* (Février 1950), 233–47.

24. A reference to the Byronic hero of a play by Dumas père.

25. *One Hundred Poems from Les Fleurs du Mal*, trans. C. F. MacIntyre (Berkeley and Los Angeles, 1947), p. 329.

26. *Oeuvres posthumes*, I, 246.

27. *L'Art romantique*, pp. 275–6.

28. The *Salon de 1846* is less a systematic account of an exhibition than a group of essays about different aspects of painting. Many of the ideas were borrowed, sometimes too freely, from Delacroix, Diderot, and especially Stendhal; others were the result of Baudelaire's own experience and temperament. More theoretical and more provocative than its sister publication of 1845, the *Salon de 1846* reveals the same intense admiration for Delacroix and stresses in even greater degree the changing, variable nature of beauty and the need for the modern artist to do in painting what Balzac had already accomplished in literature.

29. *L'Impénitente*, later known as *Don Juan aux Enfers*, was published September 6 in *L'Artiste*, and *A une Indienne*, which later became *A une Malabaraise*, was published in the same magazine on December 13.

30. On August 14, 1855, Baudelaire wrote George Sand asking her aid in obtaining a rôle in her play *Maître Favilla* for Marie Daubrun. For his private opinion of George Sand, see *Oeuvres posthumes*, ed. J. Crépet and C. Pichois, II, 96–8.

31. Albert Feuillerat, *Baudelaire et la Belle aux cheveux d'or* (New Haven and Paris, 1941), p. 76.

32. E. Crépet, p. 79.

33. *Oeuvres posthumes* (*Pauvre Belgique*), III, 215–16.

34. Théophile Thoré, liberal journalist and art critic, whose pen name was William Bürger. See Baudelaire's letter to him (June 1864). Pierre-Joseph Proudhon, French socialist, author of *De la Justice dans la Révolution et dans l'Eglise*. Pierre Dupont, poet and song writer, was exiled in 1851 because of his revolutionary activity. Jules Fleury-Husson, journalist, realistic novelist and art critic, whose pen name was Champfleury. Charles Toubin, a medical student when he met Baudelaire, later published *Dictionnaire étymologique de la langue française*.

35. Baudelaire's journalistic venture as editor-in-chief of *Le Représentant de l'Indre* abruptly ended after the publication of his first and only issue. With his usual superb disregard for tact and diplomacy he shocked his associates and fellow-townsmen in every possible way. At a banquet given in his honour he disconcerted the guests by maintaining a grim silence, explaining that he had come only to be the servant of their minds; in the office he startled an old woman who served as typesetter by inquiring about the brandy provided for the editor. What was even worse, word had spread that the young editor was living with a mistress. In answer to the accusation of a notary who was a member of the board of directors, Baudelaire ironically replied that a poet's mistress could sometimes be as good as a notary's wife. The answer only made a difficult situation worse. After hardly more than a week in Châteauroux, the poet was dismissed and on his way back to Paris.

36. A few months after Napoleon's *coup d'état* in December 1851, Baudelaire wrote to Ancelle: 'You did not see me at the polls; that is a decision I have taken. DECEMBER 2 *physically depoliticized me. There aren't any general ideas any more*. It is a fact that *all of Paris* is *Orleanist*, but that doesn't concern me. If I had voted, I could only have voted for myself. Does the future perhaps belong to *classless* men?' (Letter of March 5, 1852.)

36a. Marcel Ruff believes that this letter was written to Madame Aupick. See his book *L'Esprit du mal et l'esthétique baudelairienne*, p. 437, note 67.

37. E. Crépet, p. 266.

38. The brochure to which Baudelaire refers at the beginning of his letter was undoubtedly his article about Pierre Dupont. In his laudatory article he expresses for the last time his sympathy for the political views of liberal thinkers. He speaks of the songs and poems of Dupont as revealing a 'love of humanity', 'popular hopes and convictions' and 'an infinite preference for the Republic'.

39. *Les Paradis artificiels* (*La Fanfarlo*), p. 250.

40. De Maistre, author of the *Soirées de Saint-Petersbourg*, had a powerful

influence on almost every aspect of Baudelaire's thought, particularly on his theological, political and social ideas. It is to be seen in both his poetry and prose, perhaps nowhere more clearly than in *Mon Coeur mis à nu*.

41. The story in question was 'Joseph, fils de Jacob', an Arab legend translated by Dr. Perron in the *Salmis de Nouvelles* (Librairie nouvelle, 1853).

42. W. T. Bandy, 'New Light on Baudelaire and Poe', *Yale French Studies* (1952), 68.

43. *Ibid.*, p. 69.

44. E. Crépet, p. 115.

45. Because of its combination of sensuality and sadism *A Celle qui est trop gaie* was one of six poems to be condemned by the court in 1857 and ordered to be removed from the first edition of *Les Fleurs du Mal*.

46. *The Flowers of Evil*, trans. William Aggeler (Fresno, California, 1954), pp. 151–3.

47. Of the plans which Baudelaire mentions to his mother nothing is known, except that the director of the Opera, M. Roqueplan, had asked the poet to write a libretto for *La Fin de don Juan*.

48. Mme. Aupick herself was to consider *Le Reniement de Saint Pierre* blasphemous. Many years later she requested Asselineau to omit the poem from the posthumous edition of 1868, assuring him that in the last years of his life her son had shown what she called 'religious inclinations'.

49. *The Flowers of Evil*, ed. Marthiel and Jackson Mathews (New York, 1955), p. 56 (trans. F. P. Sturm).

50. *Ibid.*, pp. 57–9 (trans. Lois Saunders).

51. Enid Starkie, *Baudelaire* (London, 1933), p. 200.

52. In a letter to Godefroy (November 12, 1856) concerning the second volume of his translations of Poe, Baudelaire admits that he composed with the greatest effort: 'I am busy writing the preface and, as I create only after severe labour pains, it may take quite some time.' Nowhere is his tendency to repeat himself more obvious than in the very essay to which he is referring. Baudelaire also admits his lack of facility in a letter to his mother, dated February 11, 1865.

53. Campbell, p. 56.

54. Mathews, p. 59 (trans. Sir John Squire).

55. Campbell, p. 55.

56. *Ibid.*, p. 196.

57. In an introductory essay concerning the *Exposition Universelle*, published in *Le Pays* on May 26, Baudelaire presented a number of general ideas, among them, some reasons for taking a broad, sympathetic and 'cosmopolitan' view of the strange, exotic arts of different civilizations. He further attempted to distinguish between material and artistic progress, and

in a manner strongly reminiscent of Poe, to explain the place of the *bizarre* in the beautiful. Another chapter published on June 3 in *Le Pays* and devoted to a perceptive and enthusiastic appreciation of a group of pictures by Delacroix, brought a cordial letter of thanks from the grateful and somewhat discouraged artist.

An additional chapter of Baudelaire's study, appearing in *Le Portefeuille* on August 12, gave a just, though cool appraisal of Ingres, an artist to whom the critic was fundamentally unsympathetic. 'Old Ingres gave me a devil of a time,' he confessed to his friend Dutacq in a letter dated June 9.

58. René Huyghe, *Courbet. L'Atelier* (Paris, 1944), p. 7.

59. Margaret Gilman, *Baudelaire the Critic* (New York, 1943), p. 80.

60. *Correspondance générale*, ed. J. Crèpet, I, 357, note 1.

61. *Les Paradis artificiels (La Fanfarlo)*, pp. 274 and 276.

62. Described by Asselineau as one of the men who reformed the art of typography in France in the nineteenth century, Poulet-Malassis succeeded in producing editions which even today are much sought after by discriminating bibliophiles.

After the death of his father from whom he inherited a press at Alençon, Malassis returned to his home town where he worked in partnership first with his mother and later with his brother-in-law, de Broise. Bored by the routine nature of his work, he began to print small literary pamphlets of exquisite workmanship, including several by Asselineau and a fragment of Poe translated by Baudelaire. So highly prized was his work that he later came to print the books of some of the finest French authors of the nineteenth century, among others, Banville, Gautier, Sainte-Beuve, and Leconte de Lisle.

63. *Correspondance générale*, II, 55, note 3.

64. *The Poémes nocturnes*, designed as a pendant for *Les Fleurs du Mal* and later entitled *Petits Poèmes en Prose*, began to appear in August 1857. Two had already been published in 1855 and others were to follow in the 1860's. *Le Mangeur d'opium*, a translation and adaptation of *Confessions of an English Opium Eater*, was issued in serial form in 1858 and 1859 and was eventually to be known as *Les Paradis artificiels* when it appeared as a book in 1860.

65. At the request of Baudelaire, Sainte-Beuve prepared a line of argument known as the *Petits moyens de défense*. Baudelaire's lawyer was to plead first that the poet had no other choice of subject, all other themes having been pre-empted in the realm of poetry, and second that other writers, notably Musset and Béranger, had written with impunity poems of a highly suggestive nature. Though Baudelaire and his lawyer did not follow the first suggestion of the critic, they did use his advice, and that of Flaubert as well, in citing scurrilous passages from the writings of Béranger, Musset and Gautier.

66. ⌐ :udelaire's article on *Madame Bovary* appeared in *L'Artiste* on October 18, 1857, and was highly praised by Flaubert in a letter to the critic dated October 21: 'Your article gave me the greatest pleasure. You entered into the arcana of the work, as if my mind were yours. It is thoroughly felt and understood.'

67. E. Crépet, p. 124.

68. *Les Fleurs du Mal*, p. 358.

69. *Correspondance générale*, II, 128, note 2.

70. The 'stoic's book' to which Baudelaire refers is *De la Justice dans la Révolution et dans l'Eglise* by Proudhon.

71. Baudelaire's claim that he was 'an incorrigible Catholic' has been subject to much debate among scholars and critics. So much contradictory testimony is to be found both in his letters and his works that it is extremely difficult to arrive at any definite conclusion in the matter.

72. The *Salon de 1859* is considered the most important and famous of his salons. It is here that Baudelaire develops at length the concept of imagination which he had first briefly indicated in his letter to Toussenel, in *Notes Nouvelles sur Edgar Poe*, and in the *Poème du haschisch*. As 'queen of faculties', imagination represents more than analysis, synthesis and sensibility. It is the creator of analogy and metaphor. It teaches man the meaning of the visible world and, by 'decomposing all creation', creates a new world and produces the sensation of the new.

73. Constantin Guys, an extremely modest and humble artist, was to become the subject of one of Baudelaire's most famous critical essays, *Le Peintre de la vie moderne*.

74. In the *Salon de 1846* (*Curiosités esthétiques*, p. 87) Baudelaire had written: 'Thus a sonnet or an elegy can be the best commentary on a picture.' In his poem *Les Phares* he showed his extraordinary skill in evoking the sense of a painting or of an artist's style.

75. Baudelaire's letter is really the germ of the article on Wagner which he published a year later.

76. *L'Art romantique*, p. 511.

77. Baudelaire's ideas on the superiority of the short poem over the long poem echo what he had already said in his third essay on Poe, much of which, in turn, was drawn from Poe's *The Poetic Principle*.

78. Among the Americans living in Paris, Baudelaire must have consulted Mr. W. W. Mann, the American correspondent, from whom he obtained copies of the *Southern Literary Messenger*.

79. The dedication of *Les Paradis artificiels* to J. G. F. has been the subject of much interesting speculation, perhaps because the author deliberately intended it to be unintelligible. The claim has been made that the initials stand for Mme. Juliette Gex-Fagon, who was a warm and admiring friend of

the poet. Since no proof has been offered to support the claim, it seems more reasonable to believe that Baudelaire actually intended the dedication for Jeanne, for 'one who, though ill, is always active and living in me . . .'

The fact that the poem *L'Héautontimorouménos*, so unmistakably inspired by Jeanne, was likewise dedicated to J. G. F. and that Baudelaire at this time felt deeply concerned and almost morally responsible for her condition lend credence to this belief.

80. Flaubert, *Correspondance*, 1854–61 (Paris, 1927), pp. 407 and 408.

81. On several occasions Baudelaire affirms his belief in the Devil. Cf. *Au Lecteur* 'The Devil holds the strings that move us!' Cf. also *Journaux intimes:* 'There is in every man and at all times two simultaneous impulses, the one toward God, the other toward Satan.'

82. The play *Le Marquis du 1ᵉʳ Houzards* with which Baudelaire hoped to make 50,000 francs was to have been based on a story by Paul de Molènes. Unfortunately, even after two years of struggle, he proved no more successful in adapting the story for the stage than he had been in writing another play, *L'Ivrogne*, in 1854.

83. The biography to which Baudelaire refers had been planned by the critic Edmond Duranty, but was never written. The poet's determination to 'strike a proper pose' for Duranty is quite consistent with his lifelong desire to be a 'perfect actor', which was an important aspect of his Dandyism. In his *Journaux intimes* he confesses that even as a child he wanted to be either an actor or a military pope.

84. Baudelaire's claim that his article on Wagner had been composed at the printer's in a period of three days was something of an exaggeration. In reality he had been working intermittently on the essay for more than a year. Most of it, in fact, had been written before the first full performance of *Tannhäuser* given at the Opera in Paris on March 13, 1861. Perhaps what he had 'improvised' under the eye of the printer were the concluding paragraphs in which he tried to dismiss the failure of *Tannhäuser*: 'In what history has one ever read that great causes were lost in a single battle?'

The essay finally appeared on April 1, 1861, in the *Revue européenne* and was subsequently published with the addition of *Encore Quelques Mots* in pamphlet form by Dentu in May of that same year under the title *Richard Wagner et Tannhäuser à Paris*. Baudelaire promptly dispatched a copy of his article to Wagner who graciously thanked him in a warm and cordial letter.

85. Baudelaire's reference to *Mon Coeur mis à nu* is the first to be found in his correspondence. A collection of miscellaneous notes begun in 1859 and continued until the time of his last illness, it offers important documentary evidence relating to the psychology of its author. The poignant notations

made by the poet in his desperate struggle with himself and his circumstances help to reveal the greater spiritual maturity which he achieved during the last lonely and solitary years of his life.

86. Baudelaire himself was puzzled by the fact that vulgar women attracted him. In the *Journaux intimes* he writes: 'Why does a man of intelligence prefer prostitutes to society women in spite of the fact that they are equally stupid?' *Oeuvres posthumes*, II, 100.

87. The public attack on M. Villemain to which Baudelaire refers in a number of letters never materialized. In a later letter to his mother he mentions having written an article, *L'Esprit et le style de M. Villemain*, but only extensive notes for such an article were found among his papers after his death.

88. E. Crépet, p. 267.

88*a*. The tomb of Pâris refers to the tomb of a Jansenist deacon where the Jansenist convulsionaries were said to have performed a number of miracles.

89. True to his own aesthetic beliefs Baudelaire insists that perfection in photography is impossible. He was never to repudiate the opinion expressed in his *Salon de 1859* that photography could never rival painting and that its true function was 'to be the servant of the sciences and arts'.

90. Algernon Charles Swinburne, *A Pilgrimage of Pleasure*, ed. R. G. Badger (Boston, 1913), pp. 37, 42–43.

91. When Swinburne heard the false rumour of Baudelaire's death in 1866, he wrote *Ave Atque Vale*, which he dedicated to the French poet.

92. It is thought that Whistler must have met Baudelaire some time after his first visit to France in 1855, possibly through a mutual friend, the painter Fantin-Latour. What is certain is that the French poet was a great admirer of the American artist, that he owned a number of his etchings, and that he was one of the first to praise his work (*L'Eau-forte est à la mode* and *Peintres et aquafortistes*).

93. A letter which Nadar was to have delivered to Whistler met with the same fate as that addressed to Swinburne. The famous photographer and balloonist could hardly be blamed for his oversight, carried away as he was by enthusiasm for his own mission in England. As Baudelaire indicates in his letter, Nadar may be considered a precursor in the field of aeronautics, having already foreseen the possibility of modern aircraft. At the age of eighty-eight he followed with passionate interest the experiments being made by Santos-Dumont and Wilbur Wright.

94. The poet's decision to go to Brussels was not a sudden impulse on his part. Asselineau tells how Baudelaire was inspired by the success of writers such as Dickens, Thackeray, and Poe who recouped their fortunes by giving lectures and readings at home or abroad. As early as July he had mentioned to Michel Lévy his plan of going to Brussels; in August he announced his

imminent departure to Poulet-Malassis who, nevertheless, preceded him in Belgium by seven months; and two days later he informed his mother that he intended to spend October with her in Honfleur before leaving for Brussels in November.

95. *L'Art romantique*, p. 92.

96. Before leaving France, Baudelaire had written a letter published in *Le Figaro* in which he suggested that the approaching celebration of Shakespeare's birthday was being used as a pretext to advertise Hugo's forthcoming book on the English dramatist. There seems to have been some truth in his accusation, but his letter was hardly calculated to win Hugo's support with the publisher Lacroix.

97. E. Crépet, pp. 250–3.

98. Thoré acceded to Baudelaire's request and in a second article, devoted to the Salon and published on June 26, admitted the possibility of 'mysterious coincidences'. He quoted what Baudelaire had written to him of his kinship with Poe and concluded by affirming that Manet was a 'real painter, worth more than the whole group of Rome prize winners put together'.

99. Baudelaire was much less enthusiastic about Dumas fils whose utilitarian concept of art was the antithesis of his own. In a letter to Ancelle (January 2, 1865) he wrote: 'I am glad that Dumas fils is getting married. I hope that the torments of marriage will punish him for his execrable books.'

100. Of the three essays mentioned Baudelaire only succeeded in writing a fragmentary article about Chenavard, which was published after his death. See J. C. Sloane, 'Baudelaire, Chenavard, and "Philosophic Art"', *The Journal of Aesthetics and Art Criticism* (March 1955), pp. 285–99.

101. Henri Peyre, *Connaissance de Baudelaire* (Paris, 1951), p. 118. For the relations of Baudelaire and Manet see George H. Hamilton, *Manet and his Critics* (New Haven and London, 1954), pp. 20–37.

102. Campbell, p. 200.

103. *Correspondance générale*, V, 99, note 2.

104. The journalist Louis Veuillot had enraged Baudelaire by writing that the poet had made himself offensive by 'the boring spectacle of his wounds [and] the repulsive spectacle of his pleasures'. Baudelaire's incomplete projects for a preface for *Les Fleurs du Mal* were aimed at Veuillot. See *Les Fleurs du Mal*, pp. 378–9.

105. *Correspondance générale*, V, 174.

106. On January 13, 1863, Baudelaire had sold to the publisher Hetzel the exclusive rights (for five years) to *Les Fleurs du Mal* and *Le Spleen de Paris*, a volume of prose poems. As advance payment he received the sum of 600 francs for each volume. Although Baudelaire had originally planned to write forty or fifty prose poems, he later decided to do one hundred with the idea of selecting the best for publication. In the meantime Hetzel was kept

waiting. Baudelaire never succeeded in completing the volume and at the time of his death the prose poems numbered only fifty.

107. Ancelle's affection for his ward was noted by Asselineau in a letter to Poulet-Malassis written during Baudelaire's illness in Brussels. After attending a dinner at the home of Ancelle where Mme. Claude Baudelaire had also been a guest, he wrote: 'The only person there who really loved Charles is good old Ancelle; he is a worthy man. He is often badly mistaken about our friend, but after all he loves him. He speaks of him every day with warm affection.'

That Baudelaire had some justification for his impatience with Ancelle's dilatory methods is indirectly corroborated by Asselineau in a letter to Poulet-Malassis written after Baudelaire's death. While arranging for the posthumous publication of the poet's works he wrote: 'M. Ancelle is a man impossible to find, unreliable, always late, and the difficulty in meeting him doesn't expedite matters.' See J. Crépet and C. Pichois, *Baudelaire et Asselineau* (Paris, 1953), pp. 223–4, 243.

108. The scrupulous corrections that Baudelaire dictated for the benefit of Mendès make it clear that even in the most catastrophic circumstances of his life his devotion to literature did not fail. On an earlier occasion (October 23, 1864) he had written to Ancelle: 'literature comes before everything, before my stomach, before pleasure, before my mother'. Whatever the poet's failings may have been, it must be granted that he fulfilled his youthful determination to be a man of letters.

109. Arthur Stevens was a Belgian journalist whose brothers, Alfred and Joseph, were painters.

110. In a letter to Poulet-Malassis describing the funeral of Baudelaire (E. Crépet, p. 273), Asselineau mentions that Sainte-Beuve was too ill to attend and that Gautier 'could not be counted on when it came to funerals'. He adds that it was also Gautier's day to compose his feuilleton. According to Adolphe Tabarant, however, Gautier had been in Geneva for three weeks at the time of the funeral. See his book, *La Vie artistique au temps de Baudelaire* (Paris, 1942), p. 500.

111. Authors' translation.

INDEX